SEND A RANGER

My Life Serving the National Parks

TOM HABECKER

FALCON

ESSEX, CONNECTICUT

An imprint of Globe Pequot, the trade division of
The Rowman & Littlefield Publishing Group, Inc.
4501 Forbes Blvd., Ste. 200
Lanham, MD 20706
www.rowman.com

Falcon and FalconGuides are registered trademarks and Make Adventure Your Story is a
trademark of The Rowman & Littlefield Publishing Group, Inc.

Distributed by NATIONAL BOOK NETWORK

British Library Cataloguing in Publication Information available

Library of Congress Cataloging-in-Publication Data

Names: Habecker, Tom, 1948– author.
Title: Send a ranger : my life serving the National Parks / Tom Habecker.
Description: Essex, Connecticut : Falcon Guides, [2023] | Includes bibliographical references.
    | Summary: "Send a Ranger: My Life Serving the National Parks is the story of one park
    ranger's journey from Gettysburg to Denali and back, raising a family, contending with bears,
    and rescuing hikers, in four national parks, for more than 30 years. Interspersed with real-
    time journal entries, these reflective, engaging, stories illustrate the real life of a national park
    ranger"—Provided by publisher.
Identifiers: LCCN 2022027569 (print) | LCCN 2022027570 (ebook) | ISBN
    9781493066803 (paperback) | ISBN 9781493066810 (epub)
Subjects: LCSH: Habecker, Tom, 1948– | Park rangers—United States—Biography. | United
    States. National Park Service—Officials and employees—Biography. | National parks and
    reserves—United States—History—20th century. | Denali National Park and Preserve (Alaska)
    | Glacier National Park (Mont.) | Yosemite National Park (Calif.) | Gettysburg National
    Military Park (Pa.)
Classification: LCC SB481.6.H33 A3 2023 (print) | LCC SB481.6.H33 (ebook)
    | DDC 363.6/8092 [B]—dc23/eng/20220610
LC record available at https://lccn.loc.gov/2022027569
LC ebook record available at https://lccn.loc.gov/2022027570

Though small in number, their influence is large. Many and long are the duties heaped upon their shoulders. If a trail is to be blazed, it is "send a ranger." If an animal is floundering in the snow, a ranger is sent to pull him out; if a bear is in the hotel, if a fire threatens a forest, if someone is to be saved, it is "send a ranger." If a Dude wants to know the why of Nature's ways, if a Sagebrusher is puzzled about a road, his first thought is, "ask a ranger." Everything the ranger knows, he will tell you, except about himself.

—Stephen T. Mather,
first director of the Park Service, circa 1928

Contents

INTRODUCTION

"Send a ranger." It's as true today as it was when Stephen Mather, the first director of the National Park Service, wrote those words in 1928. Rangers are the guardians of the parks. They enforce the law, manage disasters, fight fires, provide medical care, and rescue those in distress. When the emergency phone rings in the middle of the night, it's the ranger who answers, and it's never good news. On call 24/7, rangers are the first to respond to emergencies, whether it be a car wreck, fire, lost child, or heart attack at the lodge. They are given the tough jobs: recovering a body from a river, notifying a parent that their son or daughter has died in an accident, or dispatching a rogue bear. When the chips are down, it's "send a ranger" to handle the job. This is the profession I chose, and it's what this book is all about.

National parks are unique places—treasures that preserve our nation's history, conserve outstanding scenery, provide sanctuary for wildlife, and safeguard natural, historic, and cultural resources. They are the nation's playgrounds, places to find oneself and to rediscover who we are and where we came from. National park sites remind us of the birth of our country, the struggles to preserve it, and even the darker side of our history. The parks offer a glimpse into our nation's past and preserve vestiges of much earlier civilizations and cultures. They exist, in all their well-preserved glory, because of the tireless and often unsung work of advocates, volunteers, and dedicated employees such as park rangers.

Unlike many books about the parks, this book will take you behind the scenes of what it takes to run a major national park and what really happens in our parks. You will get a glimpse of a ranger's daily life—the sights, sounds, and emotions of the job. You will see the evolution of the ranger profession as it has changed with the times. You will also learn about the challenges and rewards of raising a family in remote areas under trying conditions.

On January 1, 1975, I began jotting down my daily life in a Sierra Club engagement calendar my wife gave me as a Christmas present. I continue to do it to this day, and the chronicles of my 32 years as a park ranger form the basis of this book. Besides the diaries, I've used case incident and other reports, news articles, my personal recollections, and discussions with colleagues. Some diary entries have been edited for brevity and clarity, are not always grammatically correct, and use many acronyms. Twenty-four-hour time is used throughout. Narratives following the entries complete the story. I have intentionally included mundane information because that is the reality of the job; it's not always lights and sirens—we also cleaned toilets. The most common entry in the diaries is "worked on paperwork."

The following stories represent the broad spectrum of my career. While everything you read actually happened, sometimes memories fail and stories get clouded. I've tried to accurately reconstruct events, interactions, and conversations as they actually occurred—my apologies for any discrepancies or misrepresentations.

A few days before I retired, I was walking, in uniform, through a crowded lobby at a Denali hotel. As I was weaving my way through the crowd, a mother with her young boy, perhaps five years old, stopped in his tracks, came to attention, saluted, and said, "Hello, sir." Dumbfounded, I stopped, stooped over, shook his hand, and said hello. That little incident remains with me to this day. It reminds me of who I was as a ranger, what I represented to that young lad. Perhaps he will become a park ranger one day.

Prologue

"Seven hundred, two zero one."

"Two zero one."

"Good morning, I'm in service." Each day, I began my tour of duty with those words. However, September 11, 1986, was my day off, or "lieu day" in government parlance. I was completing my first full year as the Lake McDonald Sub-District ranger in Glacier National Park. I was responsible for all law enforcement, fee collection, backcountry, bear management, and emergency services for the "headquarters district" on the west side of the park.

It had been a busy year: learning a new job and meeting new employees. Winter was filled with ski patrols, avalanche training, and getting ready for the busy summer. And what a summer it was: a suicide, climbing fatality, numerous medical calls, a car going over the wall on the Going-to-the-Sun Road, and a fatality on a concessioner-led horse ride. It was much like the mayhem I experienced in Yosemite, just different scenery. I was looking forward to a quiet day off.

I was relaxing at home when the park emergency phone rang. It was dispatcher Gerry Nelson. "Habecker, get your medical shit together. There's been a mauling at Granite Park. The helicopter will pick you up in a few minutes." It was "send a ranger" time.

I grabbed my emergency pack and donned a flight suit. The home phone rang, and I answered it. Incredibly, it was a reporter from the local paper, the *Hungry Horse News*, asking me what I knew about a bear mauling in the park. He had heard park radio traffic on his office scanner. I said, "Brian, I'm really busy right now. Got to go. Talk to you later."

Dan O'Brien, a very accomplished ranger who had been in Glacier many years and knew how to deal with bears, had already arrived at the helispot. He was the perfect guy to have on this thing. We each grabbed shotguns from our vehicles, loaded up our gear, and waited for the helicopter to arrive. I'd never gone to a medical with a shotgun before. Welcome to grizzly country.

The Kalispell Regional Hospital medical helicopter, ALERT, picked us up. The helo had already made one flight in and dropped off a flight nurse and medic to work on the victims. On the 30-minute trip to the chalet, Dan and I discussed a plan of action. We had few details, just that at least one person had been severely mauled by a bear in the vicinity of the chalet and that the bear might still be in the area.

We asked the pilot to fly in via the Highline Trail, which goes from Logan Pass to Granite Park, to see how many people were still hiking toward the danger zone, unaware that something terrible had happened. We needed to stop those people and keep the scene from getting worse. The trail was mostly clear, with only a few folks hiking toward Granite. We decided to proceed and deal with them later.

Granite Park Chalet, a historic lodge located high up in the tundra and alpine forest beneath the prominent geologic feature called the Garden Wall, was a place where hikers could obtain meals and spend the night in spartan sleeping areas. It was a popular venue that afforded a safe place to observe the grizzly bears that frequented the grassy meadows below. A small ranger patrol cabin was located nearby. It was periodically staffed by one of my bear management rangers who kept a close watch on bear activities and educated visitors on proper behavior in bear country. On this day, ranger Brian Kuhn was on duty.

Landing near the chalet, we went in to assist the medic who was treating one of the victims, Patty Duff, age 23. She was shaking and incoherent but still breathing. Patty's clothes were shredded, and she had numerous puncture wounds, bite marks, and a chunk of flesh torn from her leg. I could see her pulsing exposed femoral artery. She could have bled to death in minutes had it been nicked. She'd had the presence of mind to apply a bandana as a tourniquet to control the bleeding. The medic had started an IV and applied MAST (Military Anti-Shock Trousers) to boost her blood pressure. After getting her stabilized, we loaded her into the helicopter and evacuated to the hospital.

We asked several park employees who were there what had happened. They pointed us in the direction of the patrol cabin, where the second victim was receiving first aid. No one knew if the bear was still around. We assumed it was.

Dan and I proceeded downhill to the patrol cabin. I asked Dan to secure the area and look for a place to land the helicopter. When I got inside, there was controlled chaos. Brian was doing the best he could to help Jeff Brown, 26, the second victim. Jeff's clothing was in shreds, and he had multiple puncture wounds, bite marks, and two broken arms. His face was bloody, with claw and bite marks on his arms and head. It was dark in the cabin with only a Coleman lantern and some headlamps for light. As a parkmedic, I was trained in advanced life support and assisted the flight nurse with an IV to keep Jeff's blood pressure from crashing and bandaged major wounds.

Jeff was sitting up and was remarkably coherent and responsive. While waiting for the helicopter to return, he told me what had happened. Jeff related that he and Patty had been hiking in the area and stopped at the chalet, where they met ranger Kuhn, who talked to them about hiking in bear country and pointed out a large bear that was grazing in the valley below. This was *not* the bear that later attacked them. They ate their lunch on the picnic table, and Brian returned to his cabin downhill from the chalet. Jeff and Patty proceeded down the trail about half a mile past the patrol cabin, entering an area of subalpine fir and open tundra.

As they crossed an open area, they heard a growl behind them and turned to see a grizzly bear about 100 feet away in full charge. Patty immediately attempted to climb a small tree next to the trail, but the bear grabbed her by the boot and pulled her to the ground. Jeff yelled, dropped his pack, and hit the bear with his fist at least two times on its snout. At this, the bear began biting him. Jeff rolled into a ball and placed his hands on his neck to protect his head and face. Patty, meanwhile, took off her pack and threw it at the bear, which then turned on her. Jeff was still yelling, and the bear returned to him. It continued back and forth this way until Patty threw a rock, hitting the bear on the head. Patty rolled into a ball, covered her neck with her hands, and played dead. The bear then grabbed Jeff by the leg and pulled him approximately 50 yards off the trail, dragging him over rocks and a stump. The bear cached him behind a log, chewing on his arms and legs. Jeff said he tried to slow his breathing down and play dead, a very difficult thing to do. After about 10 minutes, the bear went off into the brush, where Jeff heard it huffing and growling.

After what felt like an eternity, things got quiet, and Jeff began crawling, finally getting upright and walking. He called to Patty, who was on her hands and knees and seemed to be in better shape, and told her to go for help. Patty staggered back uphill to the chalet, where she knew there were people. Yelling for help, she met National Park Service carpenter Jed Bryers and told him that she and her friend had been attacked by a bear and that her friend was still down there somewhere.

A big man at six foot four and 210 pounds, Jed had been a medic in Vietnam, and he performed quick first aid for Patty. He then grabbed a Stokes litter and the biggest clawhammer he could find and went down the hill to try to find Jeff. It was a courageous act, knowing there was a rogue bear in the area and having only a hammer to defend himself.

Jeff told me that he made it back to the trail and looked at his injuries. He had a deep wound in his thigh but was not bleeding too much. He made his way back up to the trail junction that goes to either the chalet or the patrol cabin. Not knowing which way Patty had gone, Jeff decided to go left to the patrol cabin and had the presence of mind to tear off a piece of bloodstained clothing and put it on the trail to indicate which way he had gone.

Brian Kuhn, unaware of the attack, said he was sitting in his cabin when there was a knock at the door. He was startled to see Jeff, who said in a calm voice, "We've been mauled by a grizzly bear down the trail." Jeff was bleeding from multiple wounds, his clothing in tatters. Bryers radioed Kuhn, unaware that Jeff had made it to the patrol cabin. Brian told him to return to the chalet to help Patty.

As Jeff finished his story, I heard the *throp, throp, throp* of the helicopter getting louder as it landed nearby. I was glad to hear it. It was "load and go" for Jeff, and he was on his way to advanced care in a matter of minutes. He received more than 60 sutures to close his wounds.

Bring your shotgun. The author at the Granite Park bear mauling.

After the evacuation, we brought more rangers in to help with the investigation and to locate the bear. There was no question we would kill it if we could find it. Ranger Brian Kenner, a member of the bear team and a good hand, flew in to assist. By this time, it was getting on toward dusk, and the clouds were lowering. Visibility for flying and ground searching was deteriorating. We had to work fast if we were going to find this bear.

We marked the area of the attack, took some quick photographs, and evacuated the remaining hikers but really concentrated on locating the bear. We moved down into the trees from where Jeff had been cached. The ground cover was duff, poor tracking conditions. Fog began to drift in, making it difficult to see for any safe distance. It was getting dark and, quite frankly, spooky. We didn't have a good description of the animal, and there were several grizzlies in the general area. We did our best, but the time came to call the search off for safety reasons.

In subsequent days, we continued to search, assembled evidence, interviewed Jeff and Patty in the hospital, and reconstructed the sequence of events. Jeff and Patty were hospitalized for several weeks. They had serious wounds, the risk of infection a real concern. They were eventually released and proceeded on their way, with memories that, I'm sure, will haunt them for a long time.

We never found the bear.

PART I

Gettysburg

The Journey Begins

Now we are engaged in a great civil war.

—From Lincoln's Gettysburg Address

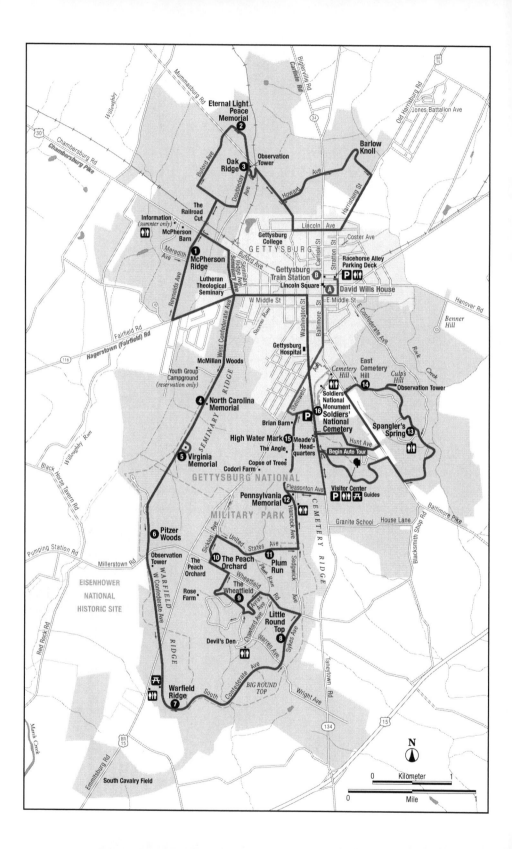

Starting Out

June 15, 1969. I walked into chief ranger Bill Birdsell's office, dressed in my fresh-out-of-the-box uniform, complete with a Smokey Bear flat hat. Bill shook my hand and immediately pulled my new white crew-neck T-shirt with his finger. "No T-shirt showing." It hadn't taken but a minute, and I'd already screwed up. My education as a national park ranger had begun.

I grew up in a small town in southeastern Pennsylvania—played in the creek, lived on a bike, and went to a one-room school in first grade. When I was 11, we moved to a house my parents built on the edge of my grandfather's farm. There I roamed the fields and forests and learned to hunt and fish with my father. I found the Boy Scouts and worked my way up to the rank of Eagle.

In 1963, I got the opportunity to go to Philmont Scout ranch in New Mexico's Sangre de Christo Mountains with a group of scouts. I'd never been west before and was enthralled by the vast open spaces, rugged mountains, and spectacular scenery. Philmont is a paradise of alpine meadows, trout streams, wildlife, and rugged trails. During our 10 days in the backcountry, I met a cadre of young men in their late teens or early twenties known as "rangers." Living in the backcountry, these rangers taught skills classes, helped scout groups with problems, and patrolled the wilderness. They were certified in advanced first aid, had rescue skills, and could handle any emergency. I knew then that I wanted to live out West and be some kind of "ranger."

Fast-forward to the spring of 1969. I was in my senior year at Penn State University, earning a degree in park administration. The National Park Service, in response to increasing needs for urban parks, announced a new recruitment program for recreation and parks majors. These "urban intake trainees," hired as permanent employees, would receive priority training to staff and eventually manage the new urban parks. Selectees committed to two-year assignments in an urban park. I applied, took the federal entrance exam, and waited.

I received a call from Bob Mullan, administrative officer for the Northeast Region, who offered me a summer position at Gettysburg. I was stunned—I was one of 40 students selected for the program. I immediately accepted and was hired as a Career-Conditional Student Trainee, GS-4, at $2.65 per hour. After deductions, my net pay was a princely $171.24 for a two-week pay period.

I lived alone in a government-owned 11-room house on the edge of the battlefield, a cannon in my front yard. In July 1863, 97,000 Union soldiers had camped at my doorstep. I used only three rooms, and at $19 per pay period, it was a sweet deal.

That first week at Gettysburg was a blur. There were two other student trainees. Joe Smith, a student at North Carolina State, married, and an air force veteran, also wanted to be a ranger. Alice Allen, a student at Texas A&M, sought a career in interpretation. Gettysburg took the training program seriously and provided learning opportunities not available to seasonal staff. During the summer, we each spent time with the various division chiefs and the superintendent to see what it really takes to run a major national park. I was particularly impressed with the maintenance division. Often underappreciated, they work tirelessly behind the scenes to make things work. With nearly 7 million visitors per year, keeping the park looking historically accurate and functioning is a huge job. My time with the maintenance division instilled an appreciation that I carried with me for the rest of my career. I've always tried to make their job a little easier when I could.

We met Colonel Jacob "Met" Sheads, a longtime seasonal interpreter and Civil War expert whose ancestors were living in Gettysburg during the battle. Colonel Sheads knew the events of July 1863 better than anyone and made sure we knew our facts. He coined the phrase "The Union was born in Philadelphia in 1776, but it was preserved at Gettysburg in 1863." He died in the Gettysburg house he was born in at the age of 91.

After our week of orientation, it was time to get to work. Joe and I were given a copy of Title 36, Code of Federal Regulations, and we were told to absorb it; 36 CFR is the bible all rangers use to enforce park rules and regulations. At the local shooting range, we shot a few boxes of shells at some paper targets and were deemed "qualified." I wasn't even 21 yet. Each patrol car, Park Service mint green with a "bubblegum machine" light on the roof, had a .38-caliber Colt Chiefs Special locked in the glove box. It was there in case we had to dispatch an injured deer. We

State-of-the-art patrol car circa 1969.

were issued a citation book and briefcase with all the necessary forms and handcuffs. There was no training on how to use them. We carried no personal defensive equipment.

I began doing ride-along shifts with permanent and experienced seasonal rangers, learning all the nooks and crannies of the 6,000-acre battlefield and all the procedures for day and night shifts.

There were a lot of duties: raise and lower several flags, unlock buildings, check comfort stations and interpretive audio stations, open and close the gates to the national cemetery, check traffic counters, and provide accurate information to visitors. One night, I was standing near the magnificent statue of General Lee on his horse Traveler. It was quiet, crickets chirping, no one around. Suddenly, a booming voice said, "During the three-day battle . . ." The audio station had somehow kicked on, scaring me out of my wits.

The battlefield was legally closed at 10 p.m. each evening. There were no gates, just posted signs. The closure reduced vandalism by 90 percent. All the locals knew this but sometimes took shortcuts and received a ticket. It was strange driving around the field in the dark after all the hordes had gone. Sometimes, I went against the one-way loop hoping to surprise violators. I got a surprise the first time I did it when I rounded a dark curve and was startled to see a rifle pointed right at me—it was one of the beautiful soldier monuments.

The Peace Light Memorial, located on a hill overlooking the battlefield, was a favorite place for the local high school kids to make out. They weren't supposed to be there after 10, and you never knew what you would find when you shined your flashlight into the car. I'll leave that to your imagination.

After two weeks of ride-alongs, Joe and I rotated into regular shifts. We were part of the team now, learning as we went. I enjoyed working nights—it was cooler, there were no crowds, and I had the battlefield to myself. I never tired seeing the beautiful monuments and historic farms, thinking about the men who fought there and the hardships they endured. It's an emotional place to work.

Chief ranger Bill Birdsell, our mentor, took a personal interest in our career development with weekly sit-downs, offering advice and counsel. An impressive man at over six feet and 200 pounds, Birdsell was soft spoken but drew a lot of respect. His uniform was immaculate, setting an example for all. Bill arranged for the three trainees to travel to the regional office in Philadelphia and the Washington office. We met key staff and learned how these offices interface with the parks. On a behind-the-scenes tour of Ford's Theater, I got to stand in the very balcony box where President Lincoln sat that fateful April night in 1865. It was a very moving experience to be that close to history.

The first three days of July were very significant at Gettysburg. On those days in 1863, it was a place of carnage. It's estimated there were between 46,000 and 51,000 killed, wounded, or missing over those three days. Just take a moment and let that sink in. We had a special opportunity to impress on visitors the history that was made right there on those very days in 1863. I took some time to walk out to the Bloody Angle, the apex of Pickett's Charge, hallowed ground. This was a place of death on a massive scale in 1863. A wave of brave men rushed headlong into a fiery wall of shot and shell, a clash of arms, Americans all, each believing their cause was just. I could almost smell the acrid smoke of the cannonade, hear the Rebel yell, and see the bodies lying in the hot sun. The men who lived and died here deserve our unending respect and admiration for what they endured. Gettysburg affected me in a personal way and remains a very special place for me.

One evening, I gave a campfire talk to a group of scouts. They were very interested in how I got my job and asked lots of questions about being a park ranger. It dawned on me that I had become a role model for them just as the rangers at Philmont had been for me. It was the first time that I realized that people looked at me in my uniform in a different way. I wasn't just some guy, I was a park ranger!

The long, hot, humid Pennsylvania summer wore on. Sometimes, the crowds and traffic were overwhelming. There were minor car wrecks and disabled vehicles, people got injured climbing on rocks and falling off of cannons, and a teenage beer party occurred one night in the national cemetery. I wrote a ticket to an elderly man who was using a metal detector, looking for artifacts. He honestly didn't know it was illegal to use such equipment and pled his case to the chief ranger. In those days, a chief ranger could settle some misdemeanor cases on the spot. The man paid his fine, and his equipment was returned.

Summer passed swiftly, and I was having a ball. There were after-hours potlucks and volleyball games, a time to socialize and blow off some steam. I was doing things I'd only dreamed about and couldn't wait to go to work each day, eager to wear my uniform. I was thrilled when Bill Birdsell called me "ranger" one day. In late August, my college adviser, Charlie Hartsoe, paid me a visit. This was my student practicum, and I was receiving credit for this course. Besides weekly progress reports, I had to produce a final comprehensive report to complete the class successfully. Mr. Birdsell praised my work and said that the park was very pleased to be associated with the university and the intake trainee program.

It was time to go back to school and finish my degree. Part of me felt it was a waste of time: after all, I already had a permanent job waiting for me. But I had to graduate to complete the intake program. I reluctantly said good-bye to new friends and the job I loved and returned to school.

Out West Again

On December 6, 1969, I graduated with a degree in park administration. On December 20, I married my high school sweetheart, who I had known since the eighth grade. Donna is the best thing that ever happened to me, and she is still with me on this incredible journey.

After graduation, I was back on the rolls as a career-conditional employee. I received "orders" to attend the next Introduction to Park Operations class at the Albright Training Center located in Grand Canyon National Park.

Since Donna had to complete her student teaching at Lock Haven State University, we said good-bye, and I drove out to Arizona. It was good to be back in the West again.

On January 12, 1970, I found myself seated in the classroom at Albright. The eight-week course was designed for new employees who were just getting started in their careers. There were 38 students representing a wide variety of job classifications, ranging from secretaries to maintenance workers, interpreters, rangers, and even a boat operator. Some had years of experience and were just now getting the chance to attend. As a new employee, it was perfect for me.

The class was a comprehensive overview of the history, mission, and philosophy of the National Park Service. We learned the history of the uniform and how to wear it properly—no T-shirt showing! We studied how parks were established and the environmental and political struggles that ensued. There were notable guest speakers and many skills classes: how to saddle a horse and pack a mule, how to set up anchors and rappel off the canyon rim, and how to raise a patient up in a litter. Classes ranged from basic firefighting techniques to how to troubleshoot a balky film projector.

Each student was required to develop and present an interpretive talk. I gave a demonstration of the loading and firing of a Civil War musket using a prop at the training center. After describing the rifle's range and effectiveness, we went outside to fire it. However, no one told the local rangers, and the loud *boom* brought them racing with lights and sirens. Oops!

Rescue training, Introduction to Park Operations course, Grand Canyon National Park.

After her graduation, Donna joined me at the Grand Canyon a few weeks later. While I attended class, she and some of the other wives explored the area. A small group of adventurous women did some exciting hikes into remote areas of the canyon and saw ancient Native American ruins. She got to see much more of the park than I did.

On a free weekend, Donna and I hiked to the bottom of the canyon and stayed in the ranger patrol cabin near Phantom Ranch. It rained hard overnight. The next day, as we began our long climb back to the rim, we began encountering snow. Being from the East, we hadn't considered the effect of elevation on the weather. As we climbed thousands of feet higher, the snow got deeper. Water cascaded over nearby cliffs, and we could hear boulders rolling in the usually dry streams. It was hard to see the trail in the nearly hip-deep wet snow. Gaining the rim, we were wet, exhausted, dehydrated, and nearly hypothermic. It was only then that we learned that the staff had been concerned about us and were preparing to send out a search party. This was the first of several "thank you for not dying when . . ." experiences that Donna and I would share in coming years.

WELCOME TO WASHINGTON

After eight weeks at Grand Canyon, it was time to move to my next assignment. In keeping with the goals of the intake program, I was to report for duty at National Capital Parks, Washington, D.C., where a variety of training opportunities in an urban setting awaited. I had been promoted to Park Ranger, GS-05.

We packed up and drove back East, reluctantly leaving the West behind. I was concerned that I would get stuck working in the eastern parks and would never get back. But my biggest worry was the military draft. I was part of the 1969 draft lottery, and I won—my birthday was drawn number 24. It was inevitable that I would be drafted. I had received several induction physical notices, but I was moving around so much that the paperwork never quite caught up with me.

We arrived in Washington and found an apartment near Andrews Air Force Base, and I prepared to work all over the metro area.

I first worked at the Rock Creek Nature Center in Rock Creek Park. It was a busy place with hundreds of school kids coming to see live animals, learn about interrelationships in nature, and attend a program at the planetarium. Growing up in the country, I took nature for granted. I had an intimate knowledge of the outdoors, so it was a shock to me when I spoke with children who had never seen a live chicken, turtle, or garter snake. Living in the city, many had never actually seen the stars! How could this be? It was then I realized just how important the nature center and parks in general were to urban residents.

One of my jobs was to take the "animal van" out to schools and give programs. The wildly painted van was equipped with cages so that we could take turtles, snakes, frogs, and other critters to show the kids. Well before the invention of GPS, the staff helped plan my route through the city using paper maps. I was not excited about driving around in traffic with a bunch of live animals, but somehow, I managed.

Presenting programs to school kids was a hoot. They were very enthusiastic and excited to see real animals. Creepy the garter snake always caused the most turmoil. The kids were fascinated but were fearful. Most thought snakes were slimy creatures, but once they got up the nerve to touch Creepy, they discovered he was harmless and a pretty cool guy. I had a lot of fun doing these programs and learned as much about urban kids as they did about nature.

Rock Creek Park was located on the opposite side of Washington from where we were living, and I had to commute on the Beltway each day. As an "urban ranger," this was a new experience for me, and I learned to navigate the maze of freeways and streets. I quickly learned to take an extra uniform shirt to work each day, as the humidity was brutal, and I was sweat soaked by noon.

After my time at the nature center, I was assigned duty at Fort Washington, a Civil War–era fort located on the Potomac River directly across from Mount Vernon. It was more rural, and I enjoyed being away from the city for a time. Summer in the Parks was a day-camp program designed to get inner-city kids out into the parks. We got busloads of kids, gave tours and environmental education programs, did minor maintenance, and patrolled the grounds. One evening after the fort closed for the day, we had a staff party on the grounds. I'm told that a beer can fits perfectly down the tube of a cannon and can be launched over the river at Washington's home—but I can't prove it.

In the spring, Donna got a position as a physical education teacher in a local school. That summer, she worked at the Oxen Hill Children's Farm, a Park Service historic working farm set in the nineteenth century. Dressed in period costume, she maintained a large garden, fed the chickens and livestock, and gave interpretive talks to visitors about farm life at the turn of the century. The farm was a popular stop for Summer in the Parks kids.

This was our first experience in city living. Washington has much to offer, and we took advantage of the Smithsonian, art galleries, and outdoor concerts. For a city, this wasn't an awful place to be, and we began to embrace it.

SEMPER PARATUS

After living four months in one place, the military draft paperwork caught up with me. I had been talking with recruiters from the various branches of the military about my options. Since I had a degree, they wanted me to attend Officer Candidate School and become an officer. The Vietnam War was escalating, and I just wanted to do my service and get out alive.

I received an induction notice and took an army draft physical. The next day, I enlisted in the U.S. Coast Guard. It was a four-year active-duty hitch, but I figured I would survive and maybe even learn something. Besides, the coast guard's mission was mainly humanitarian and service oriented, which appealed to me. I didn't want to leave my budding career, but the choice was not mine. I was officially placed on military furlough with the Park Service.

I spent the next four years at a small search-and-rescue station in Rockland, Maine. I stood radio watches, was on a boat crew for rescues and patrols, and worked in the base office. I was the only guy there with a degree, and the commanding officer took advantage of it. He kept me from being transferred several times. I became a storekeeper, in charge of all supplies and accounting, and managed the base exchange. Donna quickly found a job teaching physical education at the local middle school and high school. We settled in, became members of the community, and enjoyed the coast and rugged interior of Maine. It was a great place to do my military time.

Four years passed. About midway through my hitch, I received notice from the Park Service that I had been promoted to Park Ranger GS-7. They hadn't forgotten about me. Nearing my discharge, I sent a letter to their personnel office, notifying them of my intention to return to my career. There was no response, and I was discharged on August 16, 1974, not knowing what would happen next.

We moved back to Pennsylvania and stayed with my parents, uncertain of how long we might be there or where we might be assigned.

Fortunately, this uncertainty didn't last long. About a week after moving home, I received one of those phone calls that again changed the course of our lives. It was chief ranger Bill Wendt and Mather District ranger Herb Ewing calling from Yosemite. Bill had been an instructor at Albright when I attended the Introduction to Park Operations class. My name was on a list of reinstatement-eligible employees who had been furloughed for military service. Bill said, "Tom, how would you like to come and work at Yosemite?" I was shocked, bewildered, couldn't believe what I was hearing. It was like a dream. I said yes of course, and he told me that travel orders would be in the mail. Donna and I were about to begin the next chapter of our lives.

I didn't know it at the time, but the skills and experiences gained in the crucible that was Yosemite would set a firm foundation for the rest of my career.

Part II

Yosemite

The Range of Light

The mountains are calling and I must go.

—John Muir

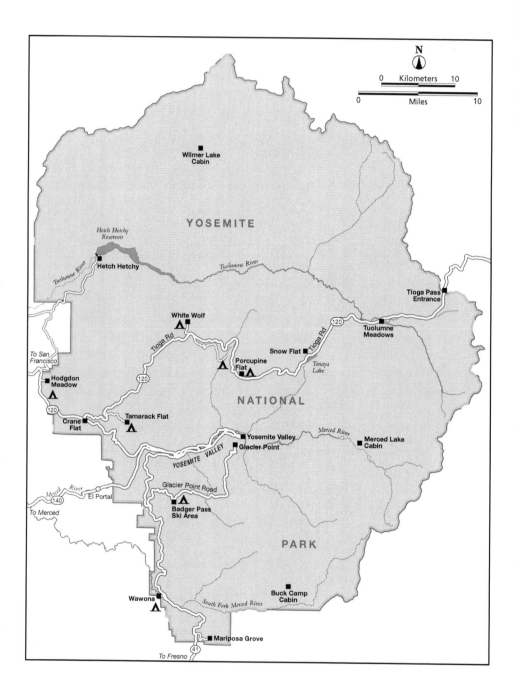

Almost Home

Our little red Land Rover creeped up the steep grade, the temperature gauge climbing toward red. Tioga Pass, nearly 10,000 feet in elevation, the eastern portal to Yosemite National Park, was just ahead. We left Pennsylvania on Labor Day 1974 and headed west. It had been a long, hot week, driving at 60 miles per hour with no air conditioning, the black interior like a bake oven. We drank gallons of water and iced tea to stay hydrated. The long journey was nearly over; we were almost home.

At the entrance station, a dark-complexioned little guy wearing a large Smokey Bear hat greeted us. He was full of enthusiasm and obviously loved his work. He tried to charge us the $3 entrance fee, but I explained that I was the new ranger reporting for duty. He immediately brightened and got on the radio to announce that the "new ranger" was here. It was our first experience with Ferdinand Castillo, "Mr. Tioga." He was the first person we met, and he was the last person we said good-bye to 11 years later.

The sharp granite peaks of the Kuna Crest framed a large alpine meadow of fading wildflowers as we descended west. Emerging from lodgepole forest, Tuolumne (too-AH-lum-nee) Meadows, one of the largest in the Sierra, came into view. Framed by the spires of Cathedral Peak and acres of glacially carved granite domes, this was a bustling place. There was a large campground, a ranger station complex, a lodge, concession stables, a store, and a visitor center. The Tuolumne River, birthed in the high mountains to the east, wound its way through the meadows. The Pacific Crest and John Muir trails skirted the meadow. I was smitten and wondered if I would ever get to work up here.

Tenaya Lake was next, a sapphire-blue gemstone set in granite. At Olmsted Point, we got our first glimpse of iconic Half Dome. Descending through forests of red fir and lodgepole pine, we unknowingly passed by our house at Crane Flat. Turning left at the junction, we continued on toward Yosemite Valley (hereafter the Valley), where I was to check in.

The narrow, twisty road tantalized us with glimpses of a deep void far below. Suddenly, breaking out of the forest, there it was: the incomparable Valley. Even Ansel Adams's dramatic photographs couldn't capture its grandeur. To the right was Bridalveil Fall, flinging a white spray of water out into space; the massive granite monolith of El Capitan loomed over the valley floor to the left and, centered in the distance, iconic Half Dome. The Merced River wound its way through deep pine forests and hidden meadows far below. It was a view I'd often seen in pictures that somehow didn't seem real. And then it struck us: we were going to live here!

At park headquarters, Bill Wendt greeted us warmly. It was good to see him again after four years. Our house wasn't ready yet, so, still on travel status, we got a room at Yosemite Lodge. After a few days, we moved into our house at Crane Flat.

Our moving van hadn't arrived, so we slept on army cots and made do with some basic government furniture. That first evening foreshadowed things to come. An ambulance with lights and siren went by the house on its way to the Valley. Later, the phone rang. It was park dispatch—they already knew I was there. The dispatcher asked if I would run up to the fire lookout to check out a report of someone walking around shining a flashlight. I didn't even know there was a lookout nearby, let alone where it was. I found it and met Al Hines, the fire lookout for many years. Together, we found a visitor who was just walking around with a flashlight, looking at the stars. I escorted him out. Welcome to Yosemite.

Our new life began. There was the traditional welcoming potluck to meet our coworkers and neighbors. I met my new boss, Jack Bixby, the Big Oak Flat Sub-District ranger. Bob Johnson was the assistant. He taught me the ropes, showed me all the nooks and crannies of the district. After college, Bob left his father's ranch in Texas and became interested in a career in the Park Service after working seasonally in Yellowstone. He got a permanent job in Yosemite in 1971 and worked his way up to Mather District and Valley District ranger positions and retired as special park uses officer in 2002. Bob and I spent countless hours together over the years, and we remain good friends.

It was autumn in the Sierra, warm days and chilly nights. Leaves were turning gold and red on the oaks and dogwood. Grasses turned brown, and flowers in the meadow disappeared with the first frost. It was all so beautiful. We explored our surroundings, took some amazing hikes. Sonora, 60 miles distant, was "town" for us—groceries, doctor, and dentist. It was all new, this California. We settled in, waiting for the first snow to arrive.

"PIG SCHOOL"

One of the first things Jack Bixby said to me was, "Have you been to 'Pig School' yet?" When I replied that I hadn't, Jack responded with, "Aw shit." Jack knew that I would be leaving for an extended period to attend the mandatory Basic Police School at the Consolidated Federal Law Enforcement Training Center in Washington, D.C. All permanent law enforcement park rangers, indeed all permanent federal officers, must attend this or a similar agency-specific basic law enforcement academy. It was a job requirement; there was no getting around it. Although I had just arrived, I would be leaving again soon.

Donna and I packed up and flew back East. On January 6, 1975, I began the 14-week Basic Police course. Donna spent time with our families in Pennsylvania. My fellow students—all 46 of us—lived in an apartment building leased by the government. We walked to class, a converted office building three blocks away. My roommate, Larry Trombello, a ranger at Shenandoah National Park, took charge of kitchen cleanup as I did all the cooking. It was kind of like being back in the dorms in college.

A comprehensive course, a few of the main topics included ethics and conduct, constitutional law, detention and arrest, search and seizure, court testimony, criminalistics, crime scene investigation, rules of evidence, interviewing, crowd control, bombs and explosives, narcotics investigations, and traffic accident investigation.

Physical defense tactics training was conducted in the makeshift gym several times a week. We learned takedowns, come-alongs, handcuffing, baton strikes, and other defensive physical maneuvers. Jim Hannah, my partner, was a big guy—about six feet four and 240 pounds, solid as a rock. He threw me around pretty good, and it was a challenge for me to do likewise to him. I had to work extra hard to control him, and he didn't make it easy. We became good friends, and I got to see him again in Alaska, where Jim was the ranger/pilot at Wrangell St. Elias National Park. At our annual law enforcement refresher training in Anchorage, Jim was my partner—it was like old times.

Proficiency with firearms is a crucial skill in law enforcement. We spent a great deal of time at various shooting ranges, doing combat shooting, shotgun qualifications, and special weapons familiarization with weekly qualifications courses. One of the best training opportunities was "shoot/don't shoot" drills. Realistic scenarios required us to make split-second decisions, to instantly determine whether to shoot the bad guy or not shoot an innocent person. It's purposely very stressful and needs to be, for it's often this way in the real world of law enforcement.

Defensive and pursuit driving training took place at an abandoned airport near Beltsville, Maryland. We received instruction on high-speed driving, escape maneuvers, and precision driving through a cone course. On the skid pan, a large area coated with oil and water, we learned to regain control and recover from a violent skid. It was good training for all the snow and ice I drove on for the rest of my career.

Weekly written exams compelled us to study to maintain the required minimum score. Flunk two exams, and you were sent home. No one wanted to fail, and the pressure was on. It was a long winter in Washington, and I was glad when April came and it was time to go home. We said our good-byes, promised to keep in touch, and wished each other well. You really bond with people when you spend so much time and share hardships together.

Donna and I flew back to California on April 12 and found our house literally buried with eight feet of snow on the ground. Springtime in the Sierra! Our good neighbors and friends had shoveled out our sidewalk so we could get into the house, and we were glad to be home and finally get back to work.

CRANE FLAT—THERE'S NO PLACE LIKE (THIS) HOME

We settled into our new home. But we weren't the first residents. Grind holes in granite slabs in the meadow and obsidian chips are evidence that Native Americans pounded acorns into flour, fashioned tools, and found this a good place to live long before white men arrived.

At 6,200 feet in elevation, Crane Flat is a hidden gem, offering respite from the hustle and bustle of the Valley and a chance to get away from the crowds. About 30 acres in size, the meadows are ringed by open forests of mixed conifer: sugar pine, red fir, lodgepole pine, Jeffrey pine, and incense cedar. Some of the trees are massive, estimated at more than 300 years old and approaching 200 feet high. A grove of giant sequoias was just down the road. In summer, the meadows erupt in a carpet of wildflowers: blue camas, pink shooting stars, purple lupine, corn lily, and bright yellow coneflowers. Crane Creek originates here, meandering through the meadows before plunging toward the Merced River far below. Spring peepers announce the arrival of the season when the snow melts in May. Fall brings golden oaks, crimson red dogwood, and faded wildflowers. Snow lies deep in winter, offering a chance to experience total quiet, skiing across the meadow in the moonlight, a million stars wheeling overhead in the cold, clear sky. It's home to deer, black bears, coyotes, and a pair of great gray owls. It was also our home for the next 11 years.

Our house was built in 1940 by the Civilian Conservation Corps, replacing the first patrol cabin built in 1915. The duplex provides living quarters for two families. There are also a four-bay garage, storage sheds,

Our house at Crane Flat.

and a generator house. Except for the nearby Yosemite Institute campus, we were the only residents, our nearest neighbors eight miles away.

The marginally insulated frame house was never intended for year-round occupancy. During our time there, a metal roof replaced the shake roof, and some minimal insulation was added. There was an entryway into the kitchen, a small bathroom, two small bedrooms, and a large living room that featured a 14-foot cathedral ceiling and large granite fireplace. A large picture window filled one end of the room.

Propane was expensive, so a beautiful wood-fired U.S. Army Cavalry–era cookstove became our primary source of heat. The inefficient fireplace, used only in the evening, took the chill off that part of the house. There was a gas range with an oven, but Donna learned to use the woodstove because it was always "on." The woodstove was handy to dry laundry during snowstorms or when the outdoor clothesline got buried.

Since wood was our primary source of heat, we spent a great deal of time finding, cutting, hauling, splitting, and stacking. An annual ritual was to fill one garage bay with stove-sized wood, shared with the

Donna tackles the never-ending chore of splitting wood.

neighbors. Donna spent hundreds of hours splitting wood. I worked at it after hours and on days off. Sometimes, the forestry crew dumped a load of lodgepole logs in our dooryard. We got a permit to cut wood on the adjoining national forest and hoarded the oak we found. We burned about six cords of wood annually.

An aging Witte four-kilowatt diesel generator provided our power. At first, the *tunk, tunk, tunk* sound of the "one lunger" was very evident. After a few days, however, it just became part of our background noise, and we never heard it—until it stopped and became dead quiet—which occurred more frequently as the years went on.

Living with an old diesel generator presented some challenges. We quickly learned not to use multiple heating-type appliances at the same time. For example, Donna had to unplug the space heater in the bathroom before she could use the toaster. We bought a dryer, only to discover we couldn't use it at all because it overloaded the generator. Our washing machine had to be modified so it didn't blow a fuse during the spin cycle. Brownouts were common. I quickly learned how to troubleshoot the beast, adding coolant when it overheated and keeping the oil topped off. A maintenance person came once a week or so to service the generator.

As a law enforcement ranger, I was subject to "required occupancy." This meant that I was required to live in the park to respond to emergencies. For the next 31 years, we lived in government housing. And, yes, we paid rent—there was no free ride.

Due to its location and because we were generous folks, our home became the place to stop for a cup of coffee and, if you were lucky, a piece of Donna's shoofly pie. People came in and out with just a quick knock on the door and made themselves at home—to get warm and dry out, use the phone, or just to say hi. The coffeepot was always on.

Our backyard was the perfect place for the bear techs to work up a captured bear. It was quiet and shady and had water available. It wasn't unusual to come home and find them tagging, measuring, and weighing a bear in our garage. We ran a "bear hotel" where bears in culvert traps spent the night for relocation the next day. It was routine to see bear traps, horse trailers, snowmobiles, and patrol cars in our backyard.

Life wasn't easy in winter. An average of 250 inches of snow fell at this elevation annually. Getting stuck in the driveway, lugging groceries into the house, and tunneling our way into the back door became routine. When the snow got really deep, we had to shovel the roof to avoid collapse. I'm sure Donna and I shoveled tons of snow over the years.

This was our home. Surrounded by massive trees, a meadow with a gurgling brook, wandering bears, and a beehive of activity, we settled in to work and play in this wonderful place.

LAW ENFORCEMENT—CRIMINALS TAKE VACATIONS TOO

Park rangers perform a wide variety of duties. Often, one event involves multiple disciplines, such as law enforcement, emergency medicine, and technical rescue. As the following examples demonstrate, a ranger must possess a diversity of skills to successfully accomplish the job in today's parks.

Law enforcement is one of the primary duties a ranger performs. In fact, it must comprise at least 51 percent of the job to qualify for enhanced annuity and mandatory retirement at age 57. But how did we get here? A quick look back at the history of law enforcement in the parks is in order.

A man named Harry Yount is widely recognized as being the first real park ranger. He worked as a "gamekeeper" in Yellowstone shortly after it was established in 1872. Harry was the sole person responsible for keeping law and order in the entire 2-million-acre park. As the first ranger, Harry is a hero to us all. An early photo shows him in his buffalo coat and mountain man hat, and he looks like a tough old bird. Harry felt overwhelmed by his responsibilities and resigned after one year.

As parks evolved, it became apparent that they needed protection. Park rangers, jacks-of-all-trades, were hired to do the job. They fought fires, rescued people in trouble, did game management, collected entrance fees, maintained law and order, and performed myriad other jobs. Over time, their job became more specialized and increasingly complex, requiring more technical training and equipment as more people visited the parks.

I was fortunate enough to begin my career at a time and place where some of the "old-time ranger" skills were still required. It was still a time when rangers wore many hats. We did law enforcement, fought wildland and structural fires, performed technical rescue work, provided emergency medical care, and made extended backcountry patrols with horses and mules. Trapping and relocating problem bears was part of the job. In winter, we traveled into the backcountry to do snow surveys and learned survival skills.

Today, things have become more specialized and require specific education and certification. In some parks, rangers focus only on law enforcement and emergency services. Some parks have turned over structural fire and emergency medical services (EMS) responsibilities to neighboring agencies. Many rangers do not get the opportunity to do resource management or routinely get out into the backcountry. Computerization and an increasing requirement for documentation have moved the job away from the days when you could just saddle a horse and go out on patrol for the day.

My personal experience might serve as a thumbnail of how law enforcement has evolved in my generation. When I started at Gettysburg, I received cursory on-the-job training doing ride-alongs with experienced staff—there was no academy back then. The .38-caliber revolver was locked in the glove box, and I had no defensive equipment or defensive tactics training. There were no fitness standards.

By the time I got to Yosemite, things had changed. On July 4, 1970, a large group of young people gathered in Stoneman Meadow in the Valley and began to party. They ignored requests to disperse, and things quickly got out of hand: injuries, arrests, and park lockdown ensued. This incident, known as the "Yosemite Riot," served as a wake-up call throughout the Park Service—the job needed to evolve.

As a result of this event, all permanent rangers were required to attend 14 weeks of law enforcement training at the Federal Law Enforcement Training Center in Glynco, Georgia. Today, every new ranger starts out with six months of law enforcement training, and it never stops. Annual 40-hour refreshers, quarterly firearms qualifications with reduced light, and special weapons qualification are part of a ranger's continuing education and skills maintenance.

By the time I retired, I was carrying a Sig Sauer semiautomatic pistol. A shotgun and an AR-15 semiautomatic rifle were mounted in my patrol car. I wore body armor, and on my duty belt, I carried a portable radio, pepper spray, handcuffs, a collapsible baton, extra ammunition, and a small flashlight. Today, rangers are trained to use and carry Taser immobilization devices. All permanent law enforcement rangers are issued credentials just like FBI agents. We also wear a badge that distinguishes us from other employees. Periodic extensive background checks, annual physical exams, and physical performance assessments are mandatory. Like all federal officers, park rangers have to retire at age 57. Things have come a long way since my time in Gettysburg!

Each officer approaches the job with a unique mind-set. My personal philosophy, which evolved over the years, was one of education—explaining why actions were illegal, harmful, or just plain stupid. I tried to be firm but fair and not jump to conclusions before I acted. I always came down hard on resource violations. I figured that's what I was there for. Err on the side of the resource—it can't protect itself.

Most visitors don't think about crime while on vacation in a park. The environment seems to lull them into a false sense of security. They let their guard down and do things they wouldn't do at home. They leave their cars unlocked with valuables in plain view, stop in the middle of traffic to take a photo, and ignore common sense safety precautions. An inside joke is that visitors check their brains in at the entrance station.

However, there is indeed crime in national parks. In 1980, across the entire national park system, there were 16 homicides, 69 rapes, 294 robberies, 643 assaults, 1,552 burglaries, 6,200 larcenies, and 250 vehicle thefts.[1] These were record numbers in a record year with 300 million visitors across the system. Crime follows people, and bad guys take vacations too. Everything that happens in a city also happens in national parks.

As a law enforcement ranger, you learn to deal with a seemingly never-ending series of events. I was deputized as a coroner and performed those duties at fatalities. Yosemite has a six-cell detention center, or "jail," and a full-time booker-jailer. There is a paddy wagon to transport prisoners. A full-time federal magistrate holds court five days per week. It mimics a small city.

What follows are sketches of just a few of the hundreds of law enforcement incidents with which I was personally involved. Most were minor offenses: traffic violations, underage drinking, possession of marijuana, resource violations, campground disturbances, or illegal camping. More serious incidents include driving under the influence (DUI), auto burglary, theft, or possession of stolen property. The highest level of offenses include rape, homicide, assault with a deadly weapon, armed robbery, and vehicle theft. Add to that the special events and just plain crazy incidents you can't explain. In Yosemite, you are exposed to it all.

It's important to note that almost every incident cited generated a paper report: case incident and supplemental, search-and-rescue (SAR) report, EMS run sheet, motor vehicle accident (MVA) report and diagram, and patrol report. Today, much of this is computerized, but it still takes an undue amount of a ranger's workday. And woe to anyone who has an accident with a government vehicle—there are reams of paper associated with that one!

SPRING ARRIVES—THE CHAOS BEGINS

After a long winter, people were ready to travel. Yosemite, with its world-class scenery and spectacular waterfalls, was a prime destination for many. Each Friday night saw a steady stream of vehicles entering the Big Oak Flat and Arch Rock entrances from the San Francisco Bay Area (hereaf-

A busy spring day at Big Oak Flat Entrance.

ter the Bay Area). With the high country under snow, the availability of campgrounds and other areas was limited. All park campgrounds filled to capacity by early evening. Despite a prohibition against "overflow" camping, people camped anywhere they could find a convenient spot. Late evening patrols contacted potential out-of-bounds (OB) campers and tried to accommodate them or suggest alternative destinations. After we went off shift, it was a free-for-all.

Saturday mornings found the turnouts full of RV campers, even tents. People drove into the forest or meadows unprotected by barriers. Some tried to conceal their camps; others did not. Of course, we knew all the nooks and crannies where people would camp, and I was amused at how surprised they were when we found them in their "secret" spot. We moved people continually to discourage this behavior because, over time, it damaged the resource. There were fire rings, litter, trees cut, human waste, tire tracks across fragile vegetation, and other issues. It was a frustrating, constant battle, and I dreaded going to work on Saturday mornings. The following journal entries capture the chaos.

> *May 10, 1975—Called out at 1100 to assist Jim Tucker with bikers—reckless, refused to stop, etc. Stopped them at the gate, arrested six, impounded bikes; checked out bear report—saw him later in the dumpster; all park CGs (campgrounds) are full [Saturday]; moved a snow slide on trip home, 2115.*

> *May 14, 1976—What a day; worked gate 08-1000; went to MVA (motor vehicle accident) at Crane Flat, trailer overturned, driver had a crowbar hitch welded to his bumper; all park campgrounds full at 1500; thousands more coming in with no place to go. Everyone asking the same question: "where can we camp?"; Moved several OBs (out-of-bounds campers) on the way home, ignored many more; beautiful moon.*

> *May 15, 1976—It's hard to believe all the masses; people are trying to camp everywhere; moved a token few this morning; office and gate duty in a.m.; Bob and I on road patrol afternoon; he, Terry and I*

arrested a guy at CF (Crane Flat) for DUI; wrote a ticket for bald
tires on a car at Hodgdon; people are still coming in—I don't know—
we just try to cope.

The long Memorial Day weekend kicked off the summer. Some of our seasonal staff were hired for the weekend to help handle the crowds, but we were simply overwhelmed, and calls for assistance had to be prioritized. There were car wrecks, sometimes with multiple and significant injuries, and many DUI arrests and intoxicated-persons incidents. Park ambulances were constantly on calls. People fell into the river, got stranded on cliffs, or slipped to their deaths over a waterfall. Long lines of vehicles stacked up at the entrance stations, only to learn that there was no place to stay. Eventually, it got so bad that rangers closed access to the Valley because there were no parking spaces available. Frustration grew and tempers flared as visitors drove around endlessly trying to find a spot.

Happy Campers

We spent a lot of time in the district's eight campgrounds, cruising through several times a shift to check on such things as proper food storage, unattended campfires, fee compliance, sanitation, and quiet hours. Nightly bear announcements were part of the routine. Things were usually quiet during the day as visitors were out hiking or touring other areas of the park. The fun started at night.

June 5, 1975—Called out at 0745 to WWCG (White Wolf Camp-
ground) to settle campground dispute; alleged simple assault, talked
them out of going to court; cleared at 1115; on way home assisted Jack
Fry, Lowell Lease and Bob Johnson with five arrests for intox, open
container, underage, theft; also cited a passerby for open container—
what a beginning and ending of the day! CF (Crane Flat) gas station
burglar alarm went off at 0215, back at 0300.

A great deal of our time was spent dealing with alcohol—DUIs, open container violations, and underage drinking. Teenage kids came to the park to party, bringing copious amounts of beer. We always tried to approach a "party camp" without being seen, not hard to do in dense trees in the dark. It was easy to find the offending campsite: just listen for the loud music and look for the large bonfire. It was very amusing to hear what these kids were talking about. One time, we heard a kid yell, "Bring on the f***ing rangers." The look on their face when we stepped out of the woods was priceless.

We always made the culprits pour out their own beer. We didn't want to get beer all over our uniforms, and it made them feel all the worse. There were a lot of drunken stump holes in our campgrounds.

THEY COME AT NIGHT—USUALLY

August 14, 1975—To work 0900 after being out until 0400 with kids throwing fireworks and drinking beer; checked CFCG, (Crane Flat Campground), pulled motorists over for slow-moving; investigated four car clouts at Ten Lakes trailhead (TH), all VWs with wing windows broken; looks like our "pro ring" has hit as other reports come in; picked Ron Bryan up at 1500; cited driver for unsafe riding—little girl sitting out the rear window.

All too frequently, we had to contend with "car clouts," also known as auto burglaries. Sometimes, vehicles are broken into by amateurs as opportunity permits. These are usually "smash and grab" jobs, with entry made by smashing a window with a rock. People often leave valuables in plain sight, just begging to be stolen. I've cruised parking lots and seen cameras, binoculars, audio and video equipment, and expensive sunglasses—all lying in plain view and easy pickings.

Several professional auto burglary rings make a living breaking into vehicles in national parks. They routinely travel from park to park, break into dozens of cars in a night or two, and leave. They pick door locks, use slim-jim tools, or punch out trunk locks, leaving little evidence, and are in and out in a matter of minutes. They hit places where vehicles are left unattended, such as trailheads and parking lots.

The Huddleston gang was a professional ring that plagued Yosemite and parks throughout the West in the 1970s and early 1980s. They were arrested many times in multiple jurisdictions. Yosemite investigators interviewed Mark Huddleston while he was incarcerated in California. He revealed many of their secrets and modus operandi. For example, they worked in teams, parked outside a park, and entered with another vehicle. They usually worked at night and especially favored dark, rainy nights because rangers "don't like to get out of their cars and get wet." Sometimes, they walked around campgrounds in socks to be extra quiet. They knew which cars were easily broken into and where to look for entry points. Their first moves were to pop the glove box and reach under the seats.

We knew we had been hit when folks started coming into the ranger station to report that they had been burglarized. We checked parking lots and trailheads and sometimes found broken glass or other signs of the crime. Purses were often dumped into nearby trash cans. We spent a lot of time on these cases, and it was frustrating to always be one step behind.

Badger Pass ski area had been plagued with many car clouts in the parking lot. During an undercover operation, rangers dressed in ski clothes walked around looking for anyone attempting to break into vehicles. I was assigned surveillance and sat on a small hill in the snow much of the day with a telescope, looking for suspicious activity. Only the rangers in plain clothes looked suspicious!

Auto burglaries have declined with the advent of electronic car alarms and other devices. People use credit cards and carry less cash. But it's still important to take proper precautions in these situations. Secure your valuables, preferably in a trunk or hidden storage compartment. Placing them under a seat or in the glove box isn't enough. Better still, take them with you. Don't leave cameras, purses, binoculars, audio equipment, and other valuables out in plain sight. Avoid parking in remote areas if possible. Trailheads are preferred targets for car thieves. If you are victimized, report it promptly to authorities.

It's Such a Pretty Spot—Let's Drive in It

I've never understood why visitors like to drive across fragile subalpine meadows or through creeks and forest. Is it because they have a four-wheel-drive vehicle that can go anywhere? Is it the need to go where no one else has gone? Or is it a place so different from where they live that it invites them to do something stupid? Whatever the reason, I was often frustrated to find evidence of such behavior after the fact: wheel tracks, smashed vegetation, streambed destruction, fire rings, and litter. It really made me angry, and I came down hard on any violator I found in the act. In November 1979, after five years of frustration, I cited to court the driver of a four-wheel-drive truck who drove out into the middle of Crane Flat meadow right near my house.

July 8, 1980—Got Youth Conservation Corps (YCC) working in a.m.; also, put a person who was working off a fine in the corral, shoveling manure, etc. While getting ready to ride—got a call that a truck was out in the meadow. 4WD Toyota almost in the river, 1600' from the road. Spent all day getting a court date set up for this idiot. Vehicle remains in the meadow.

It's tough to hide a Toyota in the middle of an alpine meadow in broad daylight. It caused considerable damage to the meadow and almost

It's so beautiful—let's drive out there.

ended up in the Tuolumne River. It was one of my "no excuse" offenses. I arranged to have planks laid across the fragile alpine vegetation to lessen the damage of removal. A tow truck removed the vehicle. It cost him $185 and a fine of $300.

This entry also references a person working off a fine. We occasionally got people who wanted to work off their fine and put them to work doing things we didn't have time for. Corrals always needed cleaning, and there never was time to wax a patrol car. Most folks took it in good spirit, and they got to see that rangers were real people just like them (well, almost).

"RESPOND TO AN MVA WITH INJURIES . . ."

How many times have I heard those words from park dispatch? MVAs were almost a daily occurrence in summer. Winter presented even more challenges. While many accidents were minor, such as driving off the roadway or hitting a deer, many more were major with multiple serious injuries and even fatalities. Take a visitor unaccustomed to driving on narrow mountain roads and add excessive speed, inattention, or alcohol—"Honest, officer, I only had a couple of beers"—and you have the recipe for a car wreck.

Throughout the years, I've investigated hundreds of MVAs. I've seen vehicles on fire, cars hundreds of feet down an embankment, vehicles flipped over on their roofs, and even a few cars in a lake! The worst were motorcycle wrecks, which usually ended with major injuries or death. We used traffic radar to enforce speed limits, and you could write tickets all day if you wanted to.

An accident requires a team effort. Someone must manage the incident and investigate what happened. Others must attend to the injured and transport to advanced medical care. Then there is traffic control and clearing the road while the tow truck guy does his job. Most MVAs take hours to clear followed by hours of paperwork. A few examples will suffice.

On Memorial Day 1976, I responded to a report of a car on fire near Gin Flat. It looked like a scene right out of the movies. The car caught fire and exploded, melting the pavement and sending flames into the brush on both sides of the road. The park helicopter and fire crew arrived on

Rangers work as a team providing emergency medical care and investigating a motor vehicle accident.

scene, caught the fire, and saved the day. The incident took four hours to clear, and traffic was backed up for miles. I cited the driver for an expired license and possession of marijuana. Lunch had to wait until 1600.

September 3, 1977—Back to road patrol, my backcountry detail is over. Worked 16-0100; bad accidents at 2100 above Crane Flat: drunk kids hit a tree, one may die; also, a Porsche flew off a curve near the first accident, one injury; I investigated this one. Jack and I went to Tamarack to quiet down a biker party, poured out a lot of booze. Welcome back to the "real world!"

February 12, 1978—What a day—snowed hard all day; a foreign national driver crashed into snowplow; another driver was involved in two accidents within ten minutes of each other. Waited for a tow truck for two hours! Road getting narrow, chains mandatory. I was the only one on duty today. Many reports to write.

I actually witnessed the February accident while helping the plow operator with a stuck vehicle. A car came barreling around the curve, lost control, and slammed into the blade of the plow. I jumped out of the way and would have broken both my legs if I hadn't leaped up onto the step of the plow. Thankfully, no one was hurt.

A car stop or accident investigation sometimes led to an arrest. There were many people driving around with outstanding arrest warrants or failure to appear in court. All drivers were identified and licenses checked electronically. A "hit" often resulted in an arrest and transport to jail in the Valley. This took hours and lots of paperwork.

March 24, 1977—Fair, warm. Investigated an accident at the tunnel on the way home: a car crashed into granite divider. Then stopped a car with a wobbly wheel and no brake lights. The guy had four FTAs (failure to appear), marijuana, a loaded .45 Colt auto. "Arrested of course." Home at 2100 after leaving for home at 1630.

On the morning of June 13, 1981, I responded to Tenaya Lake, where a motorcyclist, traveling at high speed, left a sharp curve and hit a tree, dying instantly. Ranger Tom Smith, on his way to report for summer duty, stopped to assist. It would be a busy summer. After completing my investigation, I transported the body to the morgue in the Valley.

June 21, 1981—Cleaned the restrooms at Tioga—it's not all cops and robbers! Called to an MVA below May Lake: Corvette hit a tree at high speed and exploded into pieces, female with airway problem, C-5 fracture. Flew her to the Valley, suctioning her airway, she's paralyzed, couldn't move at the scene. Got a ride back to Tuolumne, home to Crane Flat 2230.

A week later, another bad one. When I arrived at the scene, there was complete chaos. The car had been traveling at high speed while passing two other vehicles, overcorrected, left the road, and hit a large red fir tree. The fiberglass Corvette disintegrated into hundreds of pieces, the engine block lying against a large tree. The female passenger was ejected, lying in a boulder field, experiencing breathing difficulty with multiple injuries. Naturalist Jim Sano and I applied a cervical collar, immobilized the cervical spine, started an IV, and maintained the airway. The park helicopter landed on the road nearby. I supported her airway on the flight to the clinic, where she was intubated and evacuated by air to the hospital in Modesto. To my knowledge, she remains a quadriplegic. The driver had minor injuries.

This accident resulted in a major lawsuit that went on for years. The insurance company tried to sue the government for improper maintenance of the road, arguing that the road edge was not flush with the shoulder. Investigating ranger Ron Bryan testified at the trial, where the government prevailed and was not held liable. I was relieved to learn there was no issue with medical care, and it was stated that we saved the woman's life.

IT'S NO FUN TO DRAW YOUR GUN

In my 32 years in law enforcement, I had to draw my weapon or shotgun only a handful of times in the line of duty. It's a serious matter and necessitates a report to the chief ranger.

I was involved in several felony or high-risk car stops or takedowns of wanted individuals. We trained for this, but it was never easy and was always stressful. Pointing a firearm at a person is a serious matter and gets your heart rate going. The incident stays with you long after it is over. Here are a couple of incidents with a twist.

August 26, 1977—Cited a visitor who drove his motor home across lower Dana Meadows. A kid had a BB gun and I drew my weapon when I saw a rifle barrel go back into the door. Guy was very belligerent.

As I approached the RV, I saw a rifle barrel disappear as the door slammed shut. I immediately drew my sidearm and cautiously approached, ordering the occupants to come out. On further investigation, it turned out the kid had a BB gun—of course, it looked real to me. The father went ballistic as I tried to explain my cautious reaction. He went to the chief ranger and complained about my actions. I was called in and gave my version of the story. Chief ranger Bill Wendt totally supported my decision and said I would have been wrong *not* to have drawn my weapon.

August 4, 1975—Went into WW (White Wolf) and discovered the lodge was burglarized. Investigated, called LEO (Law Enforcement Office), dusted for prints, collected evidence, trailed tracks; home at 0615, slept until 1530.

While on a nighttime bear hunt, I discovered that the lodge had been forcibly entered. I needed to search the building, not knowing if anyone was inside. I had my sidearm out, expecting the worst. I crept from room to room, just like in the movies—it was almost surreal. However, no one was inside.

I am thankful that I never had to shoot anyone. It would be a terrible thing to live with, but it's part of the job.

THE COMMANDER PAYS A VISIT

July 20, 1979—Took lengthy offense report of auto burg involving government property: two six-watt radios, fire packs, etc. Lifted latent prints, took photos. Called out 1830 to a person with a gun— arrested a 19 y/o with an AR-15 with bayonet. Also checked for a rape suspect. "Commander Brady" was here, a 51-50, he said "Secret" was killing him with the radar.

The Commander Brady story lives on in Tuolumne Meadows ranger lore. A group of us were BS-ing in the ranger station one day when a man in his late sixties popped in and said, "I'm Commander Brady. Just wanted you boys to know I'm in the area." We all looked at each other, thanked the man, and he left. A few days later, we got reports of a man fitting Mr. Brady's description who was totally disheveled and kept jumping into the river. Finally, someone brought him into the ranger station for help. Commander Brady told us that someone named

"Secret" in Nevada was boring holes in his head with radar, trying to kill him.

It was clear that Mr. Brady needed psychological help, and we needed to get him to the Valley for further evaluation. After some discussion, we convinced the commander that he would be safer in the Valley because the thicker air at lower elevations would block the beams. Someone fashioned a sort of hat out of aluminum foil to put over the top of his head—we told him this would deflect the radar beams. It always worked for me.

We put the commander in the patrol car and transported him to the law enforcement office in the Valley. Investigators there discovered that Mr. Brady had wandered from his home in the Bay Area and that his sister was looking for him. She was contacted and came to pick him up. We learned that the commander was a brilliant nuclear physicist and had gradually become mentally disturbed. If you ask anyone who was working in Tuolumne in those years, they will remember the story of Commander Brady.

What? Watt!

Dignitary protection is part of a ranger's job. Presidents, queens, department secretaries, members of Congress, and other "important people" visit national parks too. A dignitary visit usually triggers a high level of planning and preparation. Rangers work closely with the Secret Service, the Executive Protection Service, and state and local officials to ensure the protectee has a safe visit. Here are a few examples.

On October 30, 1981, controversial Secretary of the Interior James Watt was scheduled to visit the park, and Superintendent Bob Binnewies drove to the local airport to meet him. Watt, however, grew impatient and ordered a helicopter to bring him to the park. A group of rangers scrambled to greet him and Regional Director Howard Chapman at the Crane Flat heliport. We hurriedly changed into Class A dress uniforms and raced to the heliport. Since Watt had been threatened several times, he was afforded Secret Service protection. We hadn't anticipated being on a security detail and had no part in the preparation for the visit. I put additional rifles and shotguns into the trunk of my car. It was a seat-of-the-pants operation on our part.

Five of us were standing at attention in a line as Watt exited the helicopter. We were wearing our flat Smokey Bear hats, of course. Watt, dressed in blue jeans and down vest, walked over to us, shook our hands, and said, "Are you guys rangers?"

"Yes sir," we replied, stunned at his lack of recognition of who we were.

Watt wanted to get going, and he and the regional director piled into my car with the Secret Service agent in the front. Without any planning or discussion, I became the chauffeur and drove to the Valley. The conversation going on in the backseat was fascinating, and I was all ears. "Well, Howard, what are we going to do about commercial rafting in the Grand Canyon?" They began discussing commercial rafting and other juicy tidbits. The agent wanted to talk about bears, so I obliged him. It was an interesting trip.

That evening, Watt attended a dinner at the Yosemite Institute at Crane Flat. After all the planning and scrambling to make things go smoothly, a group of us ended up standing outside in the dark and snow, providing security. Someone thought to send out steak dinners for us, so it wasn't a total bust.

Elizabeth *Regina*

In late 1982, we learned that Queen Elizabeth II and Prince Phillip would spend the weekend in the park after meeting with President Ronald Reagan and the First Lady Nancy in San Francisco. The visit was scheduled for March 1983, and planning began immediately with Secret Service and Dignitary Protection Service staff. However, like all good plans, things quickly went awry.

Security was tight in the days leading up to the visit. There were plans for every contingency. Climbers were placed on emergency hire to provide additional surveillance on the cliffs near the Awahnee Hotel, where the queen and her entourage would be staying. Agents were assigned at entrance stations to monitor suspicious persons entering the park. A guy came into our entrance and made a wisecrack about the Irish Republican Army and found himself in handcuffs, instantly whisked away for interrogation—there was no fooling around. Seasonal rangers were brought on for the weekend to help cover the three shifts each day.

Our district was not involved in much of the security plan, as the queen was supposed to enter and exit the Valley via the Arch Rock entrance on Highway 140. Torrential rains caused a rockslide on that road, forcing a last-minute change in itinerary. On March 4, we were told the motorcade would enter the park through the Big Oak Flat entrance station the next day.

March 5, 1983—One of the most hectic days of my life! Preparing for the Queen's visit, three secret service agents were killed in a head-on collision outside of the park. Plans were changed and I got to drive the "tail car" in the motorcade. Went to press conference at the Awahnee. Rest of the day was quiet, but I was exhausted.

Agents and local law enforcement scrambled to secure the new travel corridor. Local roads in this area are two lane, very narrow, and tortuous. Tragedy struck when a car with three Secret Service agents collided

The Queen visits Yosemite, March 5, 1983.

head-on with a sheriff's deputy, killing all three agents instantly. Both parties thought they were the only ones on the road and were traveling at high speed. The agents were driving ahead of the motorcade to the hotel to get some sleep before taking the night shift. The royal motorcade and a van of photographers passed by the scene 30 minutes after it happened.

At the last minute, I was told I would be driving the last car in the motorcade. A Secret Service agent climbed into the front seat, and we joined up with the entourage as it passed through the entrance station. The agent told me to stay a few car lengths behind the motorcade and hug the center of the road. I asked why. He said, "If anyone tries to pass us, we'll kill them." And he wasn't kidding!

All access roads in our area were blocked. It wasn't much of an issue since there were few visitors in March. Local residents were permitted to stand at the road junctions to see the queen as she passed. Donna and the girls, the only residents at Crane Flat, were thrilled when the queen gave them her famous wave as the motorcade passed by.

A WALK THAT ENDED BADLY

Most people are shocked to learn that serious crimes happen in our national parks. They are on vacation and don't think about such things amidst all the beauty. I always told victims of a crime that despite the beautiful scenery, the same things that happen in cities happen in parks. There were several homicides while I was in Yosemite. This is one in which I was directly involved.

March 17, 1985—Called to help on the homicide investigation. Went with scent and tracking dogs all over the talus at Washington Column. All day on OT.

Eighteen-year-old Danish citizen Helle Olsbro went for a walk behind the Awahnee Hotel, where she was staying. Minutes later, a passerby heard a shriek and came upon the girl, who was stumbling and covered in blood. She had been stabbed repeatedly. Her unseen attacker apparently slipped away into the woods. There was a massive search and intense effort to solve this case; the FBI was brought in, and more than 150 persons were interviewed. Divers searched nearby lakes, and bloodhounds were brought in to search the surrounding area. There was national media coverage. Park visitors and residents were rattled—things like this just don't happen in paradise.

I was detailed to work horse patrol in the Valley for several days. I spent eight hours per day on horseback, riding area trails, questioning visitors, and looking for anything and anyone suspicious. Everything that could have been done was done. I don't think this case was ever solved.

THE REST OF THE STORY

My diaries are filled with numerous minor incidents, some of them humorous and perplexing. One July day, I was following a car on the Tioga Road with my partner Bob Cole. I noticed the occupants in the car passing something between them and smelled the distinct odor of marijuana wafting from the open window. I said to Bob, "Those guys are smoking dope." "Get out of here," he replied. "You can't smell that from this distance." I assured him I could and pulled the vehicle over. Sure enough, I seized a small quantity of marijuana and wrote the pair a ticket. I was known as "The Nose" for a while after that.

September 15, 1983—Called out at 1815, to back up Roger for a DUI arrest. Transport to Siesta Lake; subject blew a 0.26 (blood alcohol level) four hours later!

Seasonal ranger Roger Dittberner had a sixth sense when it came to detecting DUIs. Roger loved to work nights, and we could almost count on his making a "deuce" arrest, especially on a Saturday night. An arrest consumes a lot of time. Besides the paperwork, there was the transport to jail in the Valley. If you were lucky, the paddy wagon met you half-way. Roger began his career with the Park Service in 1978, working as a jailer in the Valley. He eventually became a full-time deputy for the Tuolumne County Sheriff's Department and served on the SWAT team and as coroner commander. He retired as a lieutenant in 2008. Roger was always ready to go the extra mile and was an excellent law enforcement ranger.

August 12, 1982—A hectic day: Worked all day on an auto-burg with Fred, and we arrested two persons at Tenaya for possession of stolen goods. Had an ambulance run, a woman fell off a horse at the stables.

Fred Koegler's name appears quite often in my diary. Fred has been a fixture in Tuolumne for many years, beginning as a seasonal ranger in 1965. He continues to serve as a mounted patrol ranger as of this writing. Fred, his wife Debbie, and two now-grown sons were always there to support the Tuolumne community. His wealth of knowledge and historical perspective continues to prove invaluable to today's rangers.

Campground disputes were never fun. People clashed over campsites, noise, pets, firewood—you name it. We couldn't always resolve the conflict and sometimes had to separate the parties or ask them to leave. Ranger Jack Fry tried to calm a man and his wife who got into an argument about his drinking. She was a Mormon, and Jack had little success.

Jack Fry was a long-term seasonal who traveled with his family each summer once his college teaching duties ended. A consummate professional, Jack worked to resolve difficult issues to the satisfaction of all. He was one of the finest seasonals I've worked with.

July 20, 1980—Rode up Lyell Canyon, got a hiker with a dog, moved five OB campers and confiscated a bong.

It wasn't always riding around in vehicles. Horses allowed us to quickly get into the first few miles of the heavily used trail system. We checked for proper wilderness permits, broke up illegal fire rings, picked up trash, checked food storage compliance, and often found more significant violations. Dogs in the backcountry were a particular pet peeve of mine.

Walking in a campground in plain clothes was often very productive. People often put stolen booty out in plain sight. It was easy to find drug paraphernalia, alcohol, firearms, axes sticking into trees, pets off leash—you get the idea. A bouquet of wildflowers on the table was an opportunity to educate folks about conserving natural resources for others to enjoy. Folks had no idea who we were, and the "gotcha" factor was high.

To sum it all up, law enforcement was the primary focus of my job. It was often frustrating, but I tried to do my best, protect the resource and the public, and, I hoped, make a difference.

SAR: Get Lost—We'll Find You (Usually)

Search and rescue occupied a significant portion of my time during my Tuolumne years. The area's granite peaks and domes attract hundreds of climbers who sometimes require technical rescue or advanced medical skills. Thousands of hikers and backpackers access the backcountry on the hundreds of miles of trails. Sometimes, they get into trouble crossing or falling into raging rivers, tumbling off cliffs, or getting lost. Injuries and medical emergencies requiring evacuation kept us busy.

Park rangers are usually the first to respond to emergencies. From a big-wall rescue on El Capitan to a carryout of an injured hiker or search for a lost person, rangers are tasked with managing the incident. When someone is in trouble, send a ranger.

With more than 4 million visitors annually, Yosemite has one of the busiest SAR loads in the entire park system. During my 11 years, there were an average of 138 SAR incidents annually. More recent figures for 2015 indicate 216 SARs at the cost of more than $463,665 for 275 individuals and 15 deaths.[2] *Big Walls, Swift Waters* by Charles R. "Butch" Farabee is the definitive text on the history and evolution of SAR in Yosemite. It is an excellent book, and I highly recommend it to anyone who wants to learn more about this complex subject.

Sometimes, the lines between what is SAR and a medical or a law enforcement incident overlap. Often, there are elements of each. A few examples of the dozens of incidents my colleagues and I experienced illustrate the many challenges in SAR.

Heli-Tales

I did a lot of flying in helicopters in Yosemite. Many incidents occurred in remote backcountry locations or required quick response to transport injured persons. My young daughters got so accustomed to seeing me in my bright orange flight suit that they began saying, "Dad's in his copter jammies" when I suited up for a mission. I'm sure I spent hundreds of hours over the course of my career flying in helicopters and fixed-wing aircraft, all in rugged mountain terrain. It's risky business, and we received special hazardous-duty pay for flying. Here are a few examples.

July 6, 1975—What a day. Took off on my first helo rescue up Tuolumne River Canyon near Ten Lakes; airlifted an injured hiker out; landed on a postage stamp-sized piece of green in one of the most rugged areas of the park. I then hiked out from Ten Lakes and got into another rescue at Yose. Creek—carry out of a girl who fell off a cliff. Dead tired, up at 0500, called out at 2100 to arrest a drunk at the entrance station—took to jail, in bed by midnight!

The Ten Lakes rescue was my first experience flying in a small helicopter. It was a Hiller, a small machine with the large "bubble" canopy. Although I wrote "landed" in the diary, we actually hovered, tail rotor sticking out over the edge of a cliff as pilot Gordon Seibel gently touched a toe of the skid onto the rocky ledge and I stepped off. The steep cliff and small waterfall prevented a landing, and it was the only way to get to the patient. I hadn't been trained to do this, and I'm sure my heart was beating a mile a minute. I got the injured hiker down to a place where Gordon could land and put him in the helicopter. I later received an "attaboy" letter from the hiker's partner who witnessed the rescue. I didn't know it at the time, but this was the first of many helicopter flights, most not as hazardous as this one.

August 12, 1979—Up at 0500 with three hours restless sleep and flew to Sawtooth Ridge at 0600 in park helo. Had to exit in a hover, couldn't land. Got victim stabilized and to a helispot Paul Cowan and I constructed. Flew to Bridgeport hospital. Took the "scenic" flight home. Arranged another rescue in Lyell Canyon via horseback, sprained foot. Loaded wood and got to CF at 1730—very tired!

We performed lots of rescues out of Tuolumne, and this was not an atypical day. Sawtooth Ridge is located on the park's eastern boundary, a remote, rugged area of serrated "sawtooth" granite peaks and talus where few people venture. Because of the steep, rocky terrain, we couldn't land close to the victim, so Paul and I exited the helicopter at a hover, then climbed up to him. The hiker had fallen down a steep scree slope at the base of a climb called "Doo Dad," sustaining multiple lacerations and a broken nose. We climbed up about 100 yards with medical packs and a Stokes litter, got him stabilized, and packaged for flight, then worked to improve a small helispot nearby. We got him down to the "improved" helispot in the Stokes. With minimal rotor clearance, Bill the pilot was able to land in the tight space and get us out of there. It's always "exciting" working under the hurricane of whirling rotor blades of a helicopter, dust and debris flying, the smell of Jet-A fuel, the turbine engine screaming near your helmeted head. Hypervigilance is called for—*never* go near the tail rotor. The small hospital in Bridgeport was much closer than the Valley, so we elected to take the patient there. After the excitement and distress of managing a patient, it's always nice to sit back and enjoy the scenery on the trip home.

A Stokes litter is a body-shaped wire basket that's used to carry an injured person. It can be disassembled and transported on a pack frame or attached to a wheel assembly to aid in carrying over a trail. A Stokes is one of the most frequently used tools in SAR.

October 4, 1978—Pulled out of class in the afternoon to go on a rescue on El Cap. Flew to the top and helped to operate a "Z" rig to raise climber with broken foot, 800'. Flew off in the dark at 1915, a wild ride down! Had a few beers with the team then went home.

I had been attending a boring supervision class in the Valley and gladly went on this rescue. It was my first time on top of El Capitan. The experts had assembled a complex raising system: a spiderweb of ropes, pulleys, carabiners, and other gear—I was impressed. I was just a "grunt," there to pull on the ropes that raised the litter. When the team leader yelled "pull," we marched upslope like mules, pulling the main haul line. Pull, reset the haul system, and pull again. It was slow going, but eventually we got the injured climber to the top. But the most memorable part was the ride home in the helicopter. It was almost dark, and I was with one of the last groups to fly off. We lifted off, and the helo immediately plunged 3,000 feet down the wall of El Cap, my stomach in my throat, the meadow below getting larger by the second—it was like dropping the height of two and a half Empire State Buildings in an elevator—but it was a blast.

September 17, 1984—Did paperwork. Flew to Booth Lake to medevac a patient who fell out of a tree and fractured their wrist and pelvic contusion.

On the flight home after this medevac, Bill, the pilot, said to me, "Look for a place to land immediately." A statement like that gets your attention! A "chip light" indicating a problem had illuminated on the instrument panel. We quickly spotted a small meadow and set down. Bill contacted his mechanic via radio, and it was decided we could continue our flight.

I never felt uncomfortable in a helicopter, even in risky situations. Our pilots were experienced mountain pilots with many hours of flight time. The helicopters were well maintained and had to meet stiff government certifications. I definitely accumulated my frequent-flyer miles!

GOD BLESS ANGEL ONE

April 13, 1977—Took remit (entrance fee remittance) to Valley and some more SAR training; went to Big Meadow and got to fly in Angel One—about 20 minutes—what a ride!

Based out of Naval Air Station Lemoore, Kings County, California, Angel One, a UH-1N "Huey," was an integral part of numerous rescues in Yosemite. The pilots proudly displayed the Yosemite employee sticker we gave them on the aircraft's windshield. We trained with them regularly, and on this day, I got to ride in the aircraft with the crew.

November 30, 1981—Had helo training with NAS Lemoore. I got flown around in a Stokes litter dangling from the ship with a crewman. Also got hoisted in a "horse-collar." Fair and warm.

"If something goes wrong we're both dead." A thrill ride with Angel One. Author in Stokes litter.

Another one of those unforgettable moments. On a training mission, I volunteered to be a "victim" and was secured into a Stokes litter that was then hoisted under the hovering Huey helicopter. A crewman in harness was clipped into the litter above me in a sitting position. We flew around the Valley for about 20 minutes, skirting the sheer granite walls, admiring the scenery from that unique vantage point. As we flew gently swaying in the breeze, the crewman said to me, "You do realize that if anything goes wrong with the ship, they'll cut us loose and we're both dead." Very few people ever get to experience something like this, and I had quite a story to tell Donna that evening.

LITTLE BOY LOST—THE ORIN SAMPLE SEARCH

June 14, 1977—Rode out from Vernon Lake after breakfast; stopped at trail crew camp far end of lake; got to Hetchy 1230; helped Bob on search for seven y/o at Porcupine Flat CG; got things organized, phoned Scott Air Force Base (AFB), Illinois, for dogs; to bed 0145.

June 15, 1977—Up at 0500; Erskine and I flew to Porcupine at 0630, began air search; boy was found safe and sound by dogs at 0730; came home and went to bed at noon, up at 1800; what a screwed-up day!

Searches for lost children are always gut wrenching. No effort is spared to find a missing child. This was my first large search, with many more in my future. I was working as a backcountry ranger that summer and came out from a patrol for days off and got involved in the search.

Seven-year-old Orin Sample was camping with his family at Porcupine Flat campground along the Tioga Road. Sometime during the early evening, he told his sister that he was going to look for pinecones. She advised against it, but Orin was determined to find some neat pinecones and wandered away from camp. His parents and other campers began calling and looking for him and called the rangers for assistance at about 7:30 p.m.

Ranger Bob Johnson became the incident commander and got an incident command organization together. Additional resources were ordered as the search expanded. Ground teams conducted a hasty search, establishing containment perimeters to keep the search area from expanding. The park helicopter did a quick aerial search until it became too dark to fly. Bob asked me to join the overhead team. I called Scott Air Force Base, which serves as the national Rescue Coordination Center, to arrange for search dogs and additional resources. The Coordination

Center is "one-stop shopping" for all emergency resources and the clearinghouse to get things going quickly. Two dog teams would be coming from the Bay Area, and other resources were placed on standby.

Ground crews searched but could not locate the boy. Before midnight, Bob wisely decided to pull all searchers out of the field and let all human scent "cool down." This would help any dog team find only Orin's scent.

The next morning, ranger Doug Erskine and I flew an aerial search in the park's helicopter. This was my first experience at actually searching for someone from the air, and I thought it would be easy—it wasn't. Even in the relatively open forest, at low altitude and speed, it's tough to see a person, let alone a small boy. I soon discovered that, unless a person is out in the open and actively waving, they probably won't be seen.

Sandy Bryson, a founding member of an organization called Wilderness Finders (WOOF), had been hired as a seasonal ranger that summer. She and her German shepherd, Hobo, became an important resource in the park for several seasons. Sandy and Hobo engaged in many searches, conducted avalanche training, and even quieted down rowdy campers.[3]

At first light on July 15, Sandy and Hobo began working to locate Orin. A scent article was provided by the family, so Hobo knew what to look for. I was flying overhead in the helicopter looking down through the trees. It didn't take long for Hobo to pick up the scent, and he homed in on Orin, who was sitting quietly under a tree, about two miles uphill from the campground. Typically, lost children travel downhill. Orin was brought back into camp and reunited with his family. We were elated, and it's always gratifying when things turn out okay. I later learned that they don't always end this way.

Where's Stacey?

Late in the evening of July 17, 1981, ranger Valerie Cohen called to tell me that the manager of the Sunrise High Sierra Camp had notified park dispatch that a 14-year-old girl had gone for a walk that evening and had not returned to camp.

Stacey Arras and her father, George, were clients on the guided horse trip into the Sunrise High Sierra Camp earlier in the day. Sunrise is approximately eight miles from Tuolumne Meadows at an elevation of 9,600 feet. According to the manager, Stacey had gone for a walk at about 1530 hours toward nearby Sunrise Lakes. She was supposed to return to camp for supper. Dressed in a light blouse, windbreaker, and shorts, she had no food, water, or survival gear. A wrangler last saw her standing on a rock above the corral. He said she turned and walked away. She was never seen again.

I didn't know it at the time, but this would be the largest, most complex incident that I would manage in my entire career. The search grew exponentially, and at its height, 161 people were involved, including ground searchers and support staff. For many years, it was the largest, most expensive search effort ever conducted in Yosemite.

Diary entries offer only a sketch of what really happened. The final report and supporting documentation are almost two inches thick. The memories of those exhausting days still haunt me, and I will always wonder, "Where's Stacey?"

The vast majority of searches for lost people end in a few hours. Many simply wander out to civilization on their own. Frequently, a hasty search beginning at the "point last seen" produces quick results: the person is located within a short distance of where they were last seen. Rangers typically do not immediately begin an extensive search for a reported overdue person unless it is a child or an impaired person, when things can escalate rapidly. Also, we usually do not commit resources to the field at night—it is simply too dangerous for searchers unless there are extenuating circumstances.

Ranger Butch Farabee always advised to "wait a bit" and let things work themselves out rather than immediately go to a full "firehouse" response. Search statistics support this course of action, and usually the person shows up on their own. This didn't happen with Stacey.

Early the following morning, rangers Tom Smith and Don Pimental rode horses up the two trails from Tuolumne Meadows and Tenaya Lake hoping to intercept Stacey, while ranger Kerry Maxwell rode from Merced Lake to Sunrise. Mr. Arras provided a physical description and more details. The Sunrise camp manager marked the point last seen, ground zero for where to start looking.

Shortly after noon, naturalist Jim Sano and I flew the first of many aerial recons in the park's helicopter. I always envisioned finding the person on the first try, but it usually doesn't happen. Even flying low and slow, the terrain whizzes by, trees and vegetation obscure the ground, and tight places just cannot be observed. I always envisioned the person standing out in the open, waving their arms—but it never happened for me.

As that first day wore on, I ordered more resources; four containment teams were flown in to establish camps at key trail junctions, looking for signs and interviewing hikers. There were no positive results.

July 19, 1981—This is becoming a full-blown search. Dog teams are here, trackers, field searchers. Lemoore Naval Air Angel 4 doing aerial recons. Climbers sent to check Tenaya Canyon and Clouds Rest. I am the Incident Commander with an overhead team. Planning session goes to 0100.

This incident was escalating, and I needed to get some control before it really became overwhelming. I established an Incident Command System with myself as incident commander. My staff filled the other positions of plans, operations, logistics, and finance, adding an air officer, tactical adviser, communications, and others as the search grew larger. The Incident Command System is a proven method of managing all sizes and types of events. In my career, I used it many times to bring order from chaos. It works!

Mr. Arras provided articles of Stacey's clothing to use as scent objects for the search dogs. Professional trackers, the Mountain Rescue Association, and other volunteer groups joined the search. These people volunteer their time to respond to all kinds of emergencies nationwide. They work tirelessly for no pay and are true professionals.

Each day began with a morning briefing to distribute maps and the plan of operation for the day. We worked late into the night planning the next day's action, copying maps, ordering resources, and arranging for food for teams in the field, helicopter fuel, and myriad other things. All this was done manually, using typewriters, pencil and paper, and

Briefing bulletin board with photo of Stacey taken the morning of her trip.

crude copy machines. As time passed, our small staff grew exhausted and needed help. On the second day, SAR officer Mike Durr and SAR guru John Dill and others arrived to lend their assistance. Their expertise proved invaluable in the days to come.

As the search escalated, the press took notice. I was shocked one day to see a TV satellite truck parked in front of the ranger station. Three TV stations and several radio stations were broadcasting the story. I was far too busy to speak with them, so a public information officer was assigned to manage the press. I appreciated the park superintendent's visit and his offering his support and encouragement. Personally, I was under extreme stress and felt the weight of responsibility for finding this girl and the safety of all the people working so diligently.

A person claiming to be a psychic called to offer her assistance. I'm not a believer in such things, but psychics have, in fact, located people and missing objects. It's unexplained, kind of like dowsing for water, but it has happened. This lady told me she had a vision that Stacey was "lying in a groove between some rocks, under some manzanita bushes." She said there was an "88" above her head. I thanked her and said we would look into it. I conferred with my team, feeling somewhat foolish, but at this point, I was willing to try anything. We looked at the map and discovered a place near Sunrise where the 8,800-foot contour line intersected a rocky area. I sent a team in to investigate. They reported back that they found a place that was eerily similar to what the psychic had described: a slot in the rocks with bushes in it. My guys said they had chills when they saw it and warily entered the slot. But alas, no sign of Stacey.

We tried everything, thinking out of the box. Trained search dogs arrived; teams of technical climbers scoured the cliffs and inaccessible escarpments. Snorkel and dive teams searched the nearby shallow lakes. A team using a high-power telescope scanned distant terrain looking for clues. Color photos of Stacey taken on the day of her trip were distributed throughout the park and surrounding communities. We got a court order to secure the records of area pay phones in case she made a call. More than 100 hikers who had wilderness permits for that time period were interviewed. All physical clues found—a comb, a lens cap, and articles of clothing—were brought into the search base and discounted by Stacey's parents.

Mr. Arras was brought into the search base, and ranger Tom Smith was assigned to be with him at all times. They were about the same age, lived near each other, and were of similar temperaments. "Smitty" kept Mr. Arras apprised of what we were doing and offered moral support. When Mrs. Arras arrived in camp, she was upset that we could not find her daughter. It seemed a simple matter to her. I got the idea to do an overflight with the parents to show them firsthand what we were facing. Flying over the primary search area, I had the pilot gain some altitude to get the big picture of the terrain. There were hundreds of square miles of forests, meadows, cliffs, granite outcroppings, brush, and lakes. Once they saw this, Mr. and Mrs. Arras began to understand the immensity of the task at hand. I arranged a horseback trip into the scene for them so that both of them could experience what we were facing on the ground. They asked no further questions about what we should or should not be doing.

Along with the formal search, there was a parallel criminal investigation. Although there was no evidence of foul play, we could not discount it. Did Stacey run away? What about her friends and boyfriend? Would she hitchhike? Was she abducted? These and many more questions were asked and answered. Ranger-investigator Paul Ducasse traveled to Stacey's hometown to interview the rest of the family, friends, and classmates. Leads on hitchhikers and "suspicious" hikers were tracked down. All persons at Sunrise High Sierra Camp and trip participants were thoroughly interviewed.

Meanwhile, routine park business continued: fees collected, roads patrolled, and emergencies resolved. My diary notes responding to a heart attack in the campground after two hours of sleep. On July 25, we performed a night backcountry carryout evacuation of a climber with a fractured skull, doing a rare nighttime helicopter evacuation. On July 26, I did my first field IV on a stroke patient at White Wolf. The stress was relentless.

The tenth and final day of intense searching arrived. The remaining teams were tasked with searching areas of high probability and point last seen one more time. There comes a time in any comprehensive search when you have to make the tough decision whether to continue or cease operations. After analyzing all the data, evaluating the probabilities of detection, examining all the maps showing terrain covered, debriefing team leaders, and consulting with the parents, I made the decision to end the operation. I didn't want to give up but had to face the facts—we'd done everything in our power to find Stacey but were unsuccessful. The final teams came out and were debriefed, fed, thanked, and sent on their way. The search continued with limited resources on an informal basis until it snowed. It was over. I entered Stacey Arras into the National Crime Information Center database as a "missing person" along with her dental records in the event her body might someday be discovered.

I was responsible for a full accounting of what had occurred. We expended more than 8,000 hours of regular, overtime, emergency hire, and volunteer time. Flight time totaled 57 hours. Food, equipment, and other items cost more than $16,000. The total cost was more than

$177,000, equivalent to more than $464,000 in today's dollars. We had searched approximately 40 square miles of wilderness.

I was so proud of my staff. Most were seasonal employees who performed far beyond expectations. I've never seen such a diverse group of people come together and work as a cohesive team as these folks did. I also owe a huge debt of gratitude to the other divisions—interpretation and maintenance—for all their hard work and support. They adjusted their schedules and work routines and put in many hours of overtime to directly participate and support the search. Although we hadn't found Stacey, we formed a bond that lasted for years to come.

> *August 8, 1981—Did paperwork all morning. Boxed up Stacey's personal items we had for the search and the deceased girl's effects from yesterday's recovery. Went riding to Dog Lake in the afternoon, need to get out of here. First time in four weeks I've been on a horse.*

It was a horrible summer. On August 7, I helped recover the body of a girl who had fallen 300 feet to her death near Tenaya Lake. Going riding was a way for me to clear my head and relieve some stress. I needed to get away from people, phones, and demands on my time. They say the outside of a horse is good for the inside of a man.

I kept in contact with Mr. Arras over the years. He stopped to see me in Tuolumne a few times. His family was having a difficult time adjusting. We were all at a loss in different ways.

So what happened to Stacey? Did she run away? Was she abducted? Was she murdered? Did she have some sort of accident and crawl into a place we couldn't find? Perhaps she was kidnapped by aliens. Without all the details and facts, it's difficult to judge. No trace of her has ever been found. Where's Stacey? You decide. As for me, I think . . .

TRAGEDY ON FALLS CREEK

> *July 5, 1982—Spent all day on a search and body recovery on Falls Creek, above Vernon Lake. Charlie Peterson and I got flown in, searched sets of cascades and the river. I found the 23 y/o male at*

*1440, hung up on a log, his head was split open. Helped retrieve the
body, did coroner's duties and flew out. Home to Tuolumne at 2100
and watched the lunar eclipse.*

Twenty-three-year-old Vincent L'Heureux and his friend were hiking in the Falls Creek area near Vernon Lake, a few miles north of Hetch
Hetchy reservoir. After camping the first night at the lake, they decided
to go cross-country to nearby Branigan Lake. To reach Branigan, they
needed to cross Falls Creek. The creek in this area flows through a vast
expanse of sloping polished granite and glacial erratics. Stream flow was
unusually high, cold, and swift due to the heavy winter runoff.

The pair searched for a safe place to cross, finally deciding on a spot
where five boulders spaced several feet apart might provide a route. After
shuttling equipment from boulder to boulder, they set up a crude safety
line, wedging a carabiner into a crack in the rocks.

L'Heureux's partner crossed first, using the rope. All went well until
the last jump. Leaping across the five-foot gap, the man severely sprained
his ankle. They passed more equipment across, and then it was L'Heureux's turn.

L'Heureux held on to the line, jumped, and landed on his hands and
knees. The rope pulled tight, and the carabiner jerked loose. L'Heureux
lost his grip and was swept away. Visibly struggling for 100 feet, he
slipped over a ledge into the raging current and, in an instant, was gone.

The partner ran downstream as best he could with his injured ankle
but couldn't find his friend. After searching for several hours, he decided
to go for help. He left L'Heureux's backpack at the spot where he had
gone in, then worked his way upstream, where he found some other
campers. It was dark by then, and he camped with the group.

The next day, the friend slowly made his way to the Hetch Hetchy
Ranger Station, where he reported the incident to ranger Mike Murray.
Murray got the necessary information and called for assistance. Ranger
Tim Dallas was flown in, and he and Mike did an extensive aerial
search until dark, then stayed in the Vernon Lake patrol cabin for the
night. Mike called for additional resources the next day. That's where I
came in.

The next morning, rangers Charlie Peterson, Joe Cowell, and Paul Ducasse and I were flown to the scene. The helo dropped Charlie and me off on the north side of the creek while the others searched the south side.

Charlie and I went to the point last seen and evaluated the water. It was later found to be 41°F and moving six miles per hour at 400 cubic feet per second. There was a set of violent rapids just below the entry point. After some preliminary searching, we realized that we were looking for a body. Studying the current, I had the idea to throw chunks of driftwood in to see where they went. We did this several times, watching the current take them swiftly downstream. The wood kept going toward a bend in the creek near a tree. Approaching this spot, I saw a blue and white tennis shoe and part of a leg exposed above the water line. The body, tangled in tree roots, was barely visible. It was on the opposite side from us, and I called for the others to try to retrieve the body. Wearing life vests, Tim, Joe, and Paul roped up and struggled to recover the body. I examined the body as coroner and found a massive head wound and

Recovering the body of Vincent L'Heureux.

58

multiple skull fractures; his clothes were completely shredded. I believe death came quickly.

A BAD PLACE TO DIE: THE DAN HOWARD SEARCH

June 27, 1985—Caught up on paperwork in the morning. Went to WW (White Wolf) to trailer Maynard and horse to search for 18 y/o Dan Howard in the Ten Lakes basin. Search gearing up. Bob wants me to co-IC with Charlie Peterson. Got home 2000.

The Sierra has been called the "gentle wilderness." While that may be true, it also can kill you in an instant. Inattention, a poor decision, or lack of preparation can all lead to tragedy. It happened to 18-year-old Dan Howard.

Dan and three friends from the Bay Area drove all night to get to Yosemite, where they planned to hike and camp in the Ten Lakes basin. After obtaining a wilderness permit and supplies, the group set out from White Wolf campground on the trail toward Ten Lakes. After hiking five miles, they made camp. According to his friends, Dan seemed very tired and had trouble carrying his pack. Dan went to bed early and slept for 15 hours.

After a late lunch near Half Moon Meadow, they continued on toward their goal. Dan continued to lag behind and was last seen on a "plateau" near the Ten Lakes/Yosemite Creek trail junction. One member of the party continued on to Ten Lakes, dropped his pack, and returned to help Dan and his friends, where he learned that Dan was missing, having wandered away from the group. They split up to look for Dan but couldn't find him and decided to camp at Ten Lakes, thinking Dan would show up at the intended destination eventually. He did not.

On June 26, two of Dan's friends continued to search for him while one hiked 10 miles back to White Wolf to report his friend missing. This began a five-day search involving more than 120 persons, dog teams, trackers, horse patrols, climbers, and aerial support.

On June 27, Bob Johnson asked me to assist Charlie Peterson on the overhead team. I worked on plans and logistics and did hours of aerial searching via helicopter. There were many natural hazards: creeks and waterfalls, slick granite, and steep cliffs leading into the treacherous Grand Canyon of the Tuolumne River. It was a place no one ever goes and an awful place to be lost or injured.

On Sunday, June 30, Mead Hargis and I were flying on an aerial recon when we spotted a small plume of smoke in Pate Valley near the head of Hetch Hetchy reservoir. We landed and found a smoldering log near a campfire ring. No one was around. The fire was the size of a kitchen table and could have quickly been extinguished, but we had no tools or water. It was in dry grass and had potential, but we had to get back to the search. We reported it to fire dispatch and took off.

By early afternoon, a column of smoke grew in the west. The fire was now estimated at 200 acres and expanding rapidly. The helo was diverted from the search to move a crew into the fire. Winds increased, and the fire blew up the canyon into the search area. Surrounded by flames, a team of four searchers escaped to a rocky ledge where they were trapped and called for help. The incident commander called for assistance from Lemoore Naval Air Station, and Angel Three responded to pluck the stranded searchers from the ledge. As the fire advanced, an observation team abandoned their post and escaped by jumping into a small lake. Later, a "search within a search" was launched for two members of a team who got lost in rugged terrain when they fled the fire. They found their way to Glen Aulin High Sierra Camp, one with a sprained ankle. The fire grew to more than 1,000 acres.

Meanwhile, Mead and I did an aerial grid search of one of the four main drainages below the point last seen. We flew up and down the canyon, visibility changing with the fading light. Hovering over the plunge pool near the base of a waterfall, the lighting changed. I spotted what looked like a body bobbing in the water, obscured by air bubbles and turbulence. We got lower: it was definitely a body. We had found Dan. It was getting dark, and we returned to base to plan the recovery.

The next day, July 1, Mead, Bob Johnson, and I flew to the scene and began an investigation. The helo set us out on a small level spot, far above the pool. It was a horrible place to work: a steep incline of polished granite, rushing water, brush, and vicious mosquitos. We found

Dan's pack in a small clump of trees at the top of a long algae-slick waterfall chute. We found a shoe—apparently, below the place where Dan fell into the water. He had slid more than 100 yards down the granite chute, lost a shoe, gone over the falls, and lodged in the plunge pool. It was over in a few seconds. We'll never know why Dan wandered away from a marked trail and ended up in this dangerous place. Evidently, he got too close to the water and slipped on the slick algae and polished granite.

We worked our way down to the body, mindful that we too could slip on the smooth granite. After struggling to get the body into a body bag, we called the helicopter for a sling load, as there was no safe place to land nearby.

It was several hours before the helo returned to pick up the body. We waited in the broiling sun, swatting mosquitoes by the rushing cascade in this hellhole. Finally, the helo returned, and under the noise and violent rotor wash, we got the bag into the cargo net and attached the eye of the net harness into the dangling sling hook, and it was gone. Silence returned to the canyon as we made our way back up to the small helispot for extraction. It was a nasty place, and I was glad to get out of there. So this is what I had signed up for as a young college kid.

Work Worth Doing

SAR work is often intense, exciting, and very rewarding. It's a satisfying feeling to be able to help someone out of a jam or maybe even save a life. I was fortunate to work in a place with almost limitless opportunities to perform these duties. The stories highlighted above represent only a few of the more than 100 incidents I participated in. Many were more mundane: a midnight hike to find two girls who were lost and sought refuge in an outhouse and flying out people with sprained ankles and even a sore throat—it happened! This work can be dangerous—working around helicopters; dangling from ropes off sheer cliffs; working in cold, fast water; or performing in winter avalanche conditions. Looking back, I'm lucky to be alive.

Emergency Medical Services—From Band-Aids to Defibrillators

Park rangers have been providing emergency medical care for the sick and injured in the national parks since their inception. Early rangers, with limited or no training, did what they could to help visitors when they got hurt or became ill. Today, many rangers are trained to perform at or up to the paramedic level of medical care. Over the course of my career, I saw a dramatic change in ranger emergency medical services and training.

As an intake trainee ranger at Gettysburg, I was not required to have any kind of first-aid training. I'm not sure what type of training the permanents had, but if there was a medical problem beyond simple Band-Aids, we called the local ambulance service. There was a basic first-aid kit in the patrol cars, but I don't recall ever having to use it. Cardiopulmonary resuscitation (CPR) was invented in 1960 but wasn't widely used outside of a hospital or military setting. Fortunately, I had received extensive first-aid training in the Boy Scouts and felt comfortable with that level of skill.

Working in Yosemite was a different story. There, I was expected to deal with traumatic injuries from traffic accidents, climbing falls, drownings, and other calamities. There were strokes, heart attacks, and medical emergencies I never encountered in Gettysburg. Here is a small sample of the hundreds of medical calls I participated in.

June 27, 1975—08-1700; remit, paperwork; called to Motor Vehicle Accident (MVA) east of Crane Flat (CF)—motorcycle hit a car head-on; Jack Fry and I transported a man and woman to clinic, two broken legs, concussion, fx ankle.

July 10, 1975—Called to WW, sow bear in trap, cub up a tree. Bob Cole and I were called to CF to transport a heart patient to the clinic; after lunch, report of lightning striking two hikers at Saddlebag Lake—one flown out. I escorted Bridgeport ambulance to Valley with an additional victim.

When I arrived in Yosemite, there was only one ambulance, located in the Valley. It was crude by today's standards. All we had in my district were our patrol station wagons. When someone got injured, we put them in the back of the station wagon on a small cot and drove like hell. Periodically, we would yell, "How ya doing back there?," and if they answered, everything was okay. If they were critical, we got another ranger to ride in the back and monitor the patient and drove faster.

It was Mead Hargis who, in about 1981, instigated getting a rudimentary ambulance for Tuolumne. We obtained a Ford van from the General Services Administration and added cabinets and shelving built at the carpenter shop. It turned out pretty good, and we used it for years. Meanwhile, the Valley District got a full-size, state-of-the-art Class I ambulance. Things progressed from there, and today the park has six Advanced Life Support ambulances.

June 20, 1976—Called out at 0500 to transport three injured in a wreck at Gin Flat—contusions, etc.; spent most of the day directing traffic and investigation; the car was over the bank and down in the trees, had to cut seven of them to winch it out with the help of the fire crew; got it out about 1600, three hours after the wrecker arrived; also report of two loose mules walking up the Tioga road from WW.

I was tied up with this accident most of the day. The car went over a steep embankment, got wedged between some trees, and was difficult to extract. We had to cut several small trees to get it out. About 10 people were involved, including the fire crew. Directing traffic on a busy summer day is not a lot of fun. As for the "loose mules"—well, it's Yosemite. What else can I say?

August 10, 1979—Called out at 0735 to motorcycle accident near Tuolumne Meadows store. Transported one injured to highway 395 and transfer to June Lake paramedics. Put ambulance back in order. Arranged a medevac from Vogelsang for a sick person, direct to clinic. Unloaded hay.

Motorcycle accidents were always bad. I once gave care to a Hell's Angel who crashed and broke his leg. Sprawled in the dirt in a great deal of pain, the "biker dude" was concerned only about his bike—"How's my bike, man?" was all he could ask.

His buddies didn't want to stick around. "He's okay, man," they said, brushing off his injuries. I tried to explain that their friend needed to go to a hospital, but they were having none of it. They picked him up, threw him in the back of a pickup, and drove off after signing the medical release form.

THE EVOLUTION OF A MEDIC

By now, I realized that I needed more advanced medical training if I was to perform this job at full capacity. Dr. Jim Wurgler, chief resident at the Yosemite Clinic, realized rangers were capable of doing more than basic first aid. In the winter of 1979, he and the nurses taught an emergency medical technician (EMT) class that met National Registry standards. Classes were held one night a week for 19 weeks. Basic EMT became the standard of care in Yosemite. Before this, a few rangers attended an advanced skills course offered by the military at Camp Lejeune, one of the first efforts to train park rangers to perform advanced skills in the field.

I was about to embark on a long journey that didn't end until I retired with 25 years as a nationally registered EMT. Continuing education, skills maintenance, and recertification never ended. It was a commitment that I took seriously and was rewarded with a variety of adventures and the satisfaction of helping people in need.

January 10, 1980—Rain, clearing by afternoon. Left for Fresno at 1430 to do my first hospital observation at Valley Medical Center (VMC), 1800-0001. Saw angina, massive laceration of the scalp (guy went through a plate glass window), an unconscious victim of a fight. A very busy place! Got to bed 0030.

The Valley Medical Center was a busy place. We called it the "Saturday Night Knife and Gun Club." This was my first time there for my EMT class. Later, I spent many hours there for my parkmedic training.

You never knew what was going to come through those sliding doors. I remember the guy with a scalp laceration—he had been in a bar fight and got tossed through a plateglass window. The doc peeled back his entire scalp like a rug from his skull—I had never seen anything like it. We all had plenty of war stories to share after our shifts there.

February 6, 1980—Studied in a.m. Called while at lunch: an Institute kid fell while skiing and injured her hip. I applied a HARE splint and took her to the clinic. No break, a pulled muscle. Took EMT test, not too hard. (A HARE splint is a device used to pull leg bones into alignment.)

July 14, 1980—Began the morning dealing with a mental patient, OD on drugs. Transported to the clinic and assisted with pumping his stomach, lavage and IV. Back to Tuolumne by 1800—just another day!

As these incidents indicate, we rangers could indeed perform at a higher level. Dr. Wurgler advocated for a program with an additional 80 hours of training and advanced skills. He and other colleagues worked with the Valley Medical Center in Fresno to establish what is now called the Parkmedic program. Parkmedics receive training in IV fluid therapy, drug administration, advanced airway care, and other advanced skills. Dr. Wurgler used to say that the difference between a paramedic and a parkmedic was a "k."

The Valley Medical Center was alleged to be the second-busiest emergency room in the state. It was the perfect place to train a group of individuals who would be working in a rural environment without close medical supervision. The course consisted of an additional 150 hours of classroom beyond the EMT level. Fifty hours of clinical time and 40 hours of ride-along were also required.

In January 1981, I began the twice-a-week eight-week lecture class, driving the 105 miles to Fresno over snow-covered roads and arriving back home after midnight. Lectures were followed by exams and skills labs. It was intense.

We were required to do 10 successful IVs, and I was very apprehensive about sticking a needle in someone's vein. Over time, I became more proficient and grew more confident in doing it. Dressed in scrubs, many patients thought we were doctors and didn't complain about our clumsy attempts at sticking them with a needle.

The docs would let us do just about anything under their close supervision. They were very supportive of the medic program and understood that we would have to do this stuff under demanding field conditions. I got to administer shots and push medications through the IV line. I was amazed to see how quickly a dose of dextrose brought a person out of semiconsciousness—just like the textbooks said it would!

There were gunshot wounds, stabbings, obstructed airways, unconscious people, heart problems, stroke patients, and lots of trauma. And then there were the "crazy" people. I met "Marie," who said she owned a reindeer ranch in Alaska that was 700 miles wide. "Doug" claimed he was a fighter pilot for 30 years but didn't look the part.

Shortly after arriving for a shift on April 7, I witnessed a 31-year-old man die on a gurney in Trauma One. His motorcycle hit a truck head-on. I also helped with a patient who stopped breathing. Death became stark reality—this wasn't a TV show. It was sobering to see this stuff up close and personal. I went home and told Donna what I had seen. It made both of us appreciate our good fortune. I gained new respect for doctors and nurses. How do they stay on their feet all day?

On April 15, I began my 40 hours of ride-along with the paramedics and firefighters on Truck Four, a 12-hour shift. We responded to seven calls that day, including a mattress factory fire, a stabbing, heart problems, and a diabetic seizure. I met "George," who told us he was on a commando raid. I ate with the guys in the firehouse and can attest they are great cooks!

This was excellent training, closer to my field experience than an emergency room setting. It was exciting riding on a large fire truck, screaming down the streets of Fresno, sometimes against opposing traffic. One time, I got to ride on a large hook and ladder rig. The fires were exciting, and large crowds formed. My job was to stay by the engine and keep people from stealing stuff. I really began to appreciate what these guys do every day. "Man down at Taco Charlies"—another call, another adventure. It was that kind of a place.

It's Always Something

No two medical calls are the same. Just when you think you've seen it all, on July 14, 1981, I was transporting a guy who fell out of a hammock and injured his back. His wife and four kids, following the ambulance, crashed into a tree and totaled the car. Fortunately, they weren't injured. On July 29, 1983, Mead and I responded to the Tuolumne Meadows Campground, where a young boy was choking on a grape. Despite our best efforts, he couldn't cough up the grape. We rushed the boy, on oxygen, coughing, and wheezing, 50 miles to the clinic, where the grape was removed with forceps.

Providing care to a patient with a pelvic injury near Glen Aulin.

Tuolumne was a busy place, and medical calls consumed much of our time. Due to our remoteness and numerous backcountry calls, we used the helicopter extensively. Many days, the helo made repeated flights to Tuolumne to pick up a medic and fly to some inaccessible scene. August 21, 1983, wasn't a typical day but wasn't unusual either. The day began at 0300 with a sick drunk puking his guts out. We went back to bed and were called again at 0500 for a lady with chest pains at Vogelsang. We flew her out at first light, then returned to Vogelsang to fly out a woman with a dislocated shoulder. I ended the day providing care to a woman at Glen Aulin High Sierra Camp who fell off a mule, nearly into the river. One dose of Demerol was ineffective, so the clinic ordered more. However, we carried only a small volume of drugs in our kit. I sent the helicopter back to Tuolumne for more medication. The drugs took effect, and with the help of bystanders, we moved her the 50 yards into the helicopter. It's impractical to carry or ride a person out on a horse when they are injured and time is critical.

November 27, 1983—Got a call at 1700 of a car over the bank on Sugar Pine hill—a fatality. Twenty-five y/o Vivian Burns was pinned under the car—dead—she was ejected, not wearing a seatbelt. Charlie and I jacked the car off of her and pulled her out. It was down about 100 feet. Then another vehicle went off the road at Rattlesnake. Took care of that. Home by 2100.

It was a Sunday, Thanksgiving weekend. The car skidded over a steep embankment in deep snow, landing on its roof. When I got down to the car, all I saw was an arm sticking out; the rest of the body was under the car. There was no pulse, and the woman was obviously dead. We had to dig through snow and jack the car up to remove the body. We placed her in a mortuary bag and hauled the body up in a Stokes litter. The car was retrieved the next day.

There is an emotional toll to be paid for these types of calls. I still remember the worst ones—they stick with you.

THE SMALLWOOD INCIDENT

May 17, 1984, was a beautiful spring day, one I would like to forget but never will. I had just moved my family to Tuolumne prior to the Tioga Road opening for the season. Ranger Mike Murray, my assistant, was also there, preparing his quarters and getting things in order. The road crew was removing loose boulders on a slide area about a mile east of camp.

In the Valley on some last-minute business, I got a radio call from park dispatch. I was instructed to go to the Awahnee Meadow helispot immediately and meet with Dr. Gary Fleishner from the clinic. There had been an accident in Tuolumne, and we needed to get there ASAP. The dispatcher said, "It is *not* your family." I couldn't imagine what had happened.

We landed in front of the ranger station, where Mike, Donna, and some road crew guys met us. A person, unrecognizable to me, was lying in the back of a pickup, strapped to a backboard. Mike was using suction to maintain an open airway. I immediately realized this was a dire situation.

Sam Smallwood was part of a road crew using explosives to break apart a large boulder that was hanging over the road on Blue Slide. After the blast and the "all clear" signal was given, two men went to inspect the results. Beyond the blast site, they found Sam lying facedown in the ditch, his face almost in the water. Sam's hard hat was missing. They called their foreman, who was nearby, stating that "a man's been injured."

Hearing the radio traffic, Mike responded to the scene, where he found Sam unconscious and unresponsive. There was a massive open wound in the center of Sam's forehead, his eyes were swollen shut, his right leg was twisted and deformed, and his breathing was rapid and shallow. Mike realized he needed help immediately and called dispatch and asked for a medic with more equipment to respond in the helicopter. Our ambulance was not yet in Tuolumne, and our gear was still in winter storage. Mike didn't have a great deal to work with, but he did the best he could. He radioed back to camp and asked Donna to bring the patrol car with all the medical equipment she could find in the rescue cache. Our girls, ages five and two, were in camp. Donna quickly found a carpenter working nearby and asked him to watch the girls. She drove to the scene and helped Mike.

Mike administered oxygen and had Donna suction Sam's airway with a bulb syringe, take vital signs, and relay them to dispatch. Dressings were applied to control the bleeding. Sam was stabilized on a backboard and loaded into the pickup. They drove to the ranger station while Donna maintained the airway and Mike started an IV.

Dr. Jim Wurgler at the clinic came on the radio and asked Mike if he needed a doctor on scene. Mike replied with an emphatic, "Yes!" That's when I got the call to return to Tuolumne.

Dr. Fleishner tried to intubate Sam to secure his airway. Sam vomited, and Mike and I worked to clear the airway. After another set of vitals, Dr. Fleishner said we needed to get to a hospital right away. Modesto was the closest trauma center, so we returned to the Valley to refuel. It was the only time I have ever experienced a "hot fuel" operation—the pilot kept the engines running while the fuel truck topped us off. In only a few minutes, we were off, flying west to Modesto.

Dr. Fleishner and I suctioned Sam's airway, used a bag-valve-mask to support his respirations, and took repeated vital signs for the entire one-hour trip. It's not easy doing this in a noisy, cramped helicopter, and I thought we'd never get there. We got Sam into the emergency room and turned his care over to the trauma team.

It was beginning to get dark, and we needed to get back to the park. Pilot Bill made the decision to go for it. The compass in the helicopter was out, and Bill asked me to navigate for him. We made it back just before sunset. It had been quite a day.

We received word that Sam died shortly after midnight. I suppose, given the injuries, it was inevitable. The ensuing investigation determined that Sam had been hit by a piece of flyrock traveling at supersonic speed. No one actually saw what happened, but evidence indicated that Sam had walked downhill from his truck to get a view of the explosion. Had he stayed behind his truck, the accident wouldn't have happened.

MAYHEM IN A TENT AND A FLIGHT TO REMEMBER

August 14, 1984, 0300 hours. Mead and I responded to a diabetic emergency in the Tuolumne campground. We found the patient in his tent, covered in self-administered glucose gel. He became combative when we attempted to start an IV. Wearing our headlamps, we rolled around in the tent trying to subdue him, all of us covered in sticky, green goo. Eventually, we got him to the clinic for definitive care.

September 1, 1984—Called to a possible CVA (stroke) at the VC; had driven his car off the road. Did an IV and flew at night to Modesto to hospital. Back home late.

The night flight was an extreme rarity. Modesto Medi-Flight was not available, so we flew the patient in the park helicopter. The incident happened late in the day, and it began to get dark while we were at the hospital. We lifted off in darkening skies, the dim glow of sunset to the west. It was a straight shot back to Yosemite flying due east. As darkness closed in, Bill, the pilot, radioed park dispatch and asked that the Crane Flat lookout turn on the big spotlight and point it west. All at once, we saw a bright pinprick of light in the east, where it was otherwise completely dark—it was the lookout and home. We flew at the beam and landed with floodlights at the heliport. I spent the night at Crane Flat and got a ride back to Tuolumne in the morning.

CARDIAC RANGERS

October 24 to November 9, 1984—ACLS class, Phoenix.

In 1984, the clinic purchased several LifePak 5 heart monitors/defibrillators. Dr. Wurgler felt that a small cadre of experienced park-medics could be trained to provide advanced cardiac life support (ACLS). Rangers Mike Murray, Paul Ducasse, Dan Horner, J. R. Tomasovic, and Charlie Fullam and I were chosen to take this training. Along with clinic nurse and tutor Cathy Shehee, we traveled to Phoenix, Arizona, for an intensive two-week customized cardiac course.

The class was arranged just for us with one instructor and met six days per week. Exams were given every three days, the first being 17 pages long. If you failed more than one, you were sent home. None of us wanted to be disgraced that way. We all studied after hours, some finding the information easier to grasp than others. Mike Murray and I often studied together, three to four hours per night, firing questions to each other even at the breakfast table.

We had to memorize about 20 cardiac medications, their use and dosage, and the algorithms for cardiac codes, and we learned to recognize and interpret electrocardiogram rhythms on the heart monitor and administer modalities of care. We learned how to use the defibrillator, run a code, and do perfect CPR. It was the most stressful, intense two weeks of my life!

All of this was designed for us to pass the national ACLS exam, also given to physicians, nurses, and other health care professionals—six park rangers up against the pros. A few of the docs actually failed and had to retest. It made us mere mortals feel better when we all passed with flying colors!

Being a parkmedic-cardiac was an enormous commitment in time and effort. We had to maintain our skills and know the cardiac protocols without hesitation. It was a great learning experience but very stressful.

June 16, 1985—A day to remember: MVA with one injury at Tenaya Lake, flew her to the Valley, used the heart monitor for the first time; then responded to an MVA near Mono/Parker Pass Overlook with four injuries, flew out two, one with Medi-Flight. Got two IVs. Also, a bicyclist was hit by a car at Daff Dome, flew her out.

June 19, 1985—Called out at 0430, another stabbing at the top of Yosemite Falls. They arrested a suspect at 0630. Went to Hodgdon but called by Jack Fry to MVA on the "S" curves. Two 80 y/o persons, placed heart monitor, A-fib on both! The lady vomited in the ambulance, a wild ride to the Valley. A long day.

The cardiac training was paying off. I'd come a long way from being a first-aider. I like to think that I helped a lot of people and maybe even saved a few lives. It's a very satisfying feeling.

Fire Management—"Put the Wet Stuff on the Red Stuff"

Firefighting, both wildland and structural, is a common duty for park rangers. Many large parks have volunteer fire brigades, often composed of employees from various divisions. These folks respond to structural fires in the park and often in nearby communities.

Equipping and maintaining a fire brigade and associated apparatus is expensive, and training to modern standards is becoming increasingly more demanding in terms of cost, time, certification, and personal commitment. In light of this, parks are being forced to reevaluate their structural fire programs. There's been a recent trend to disband and consolidate park fire brigades and contract this responsibility out to local communities. For example, Denali National Park no longer supports an in-house fire brigade at headquarters. Instead, structural fire response comes from the neighboring village of Healy.

Wildland fire is the most common type of fire that occurs in national parks. Many large parks have dedicated seasonal crews assigned to fight these types of fires. Wildland fire management is supported by a national command structure and receives the most funding and resources. These types of fires are occurring more frequently, increasing in size and becoming more widespread due, at least in part, to global climate change. Summers are becoming hotter and drier, and forests are suffering from disease and insect damage. Fire seasons are becoming more prolonged: fire season in California now seems to be year round.

I didn't have the opportunity to participate in many wildland fires because most of them were staffed by dedicated seasonal fire crews. What few skills I acquired were gained on larger project fires or in situations where a formal fire crew was not available. Most of my experience, responsibility, and training were in the realm of structural fire. I was a basic firefighter in Yosemite and a member of our local fire brigade and held Crew Boss wildland certification. Later on, I became the fire captain or "chief" of the fire brigades in Glacier and Denali.

There are a few fire incidents in my Yosemite diaries to share.

My First Fire

August 30, 1975. The Pohono Fire was my first experience at wildland firefighting. It really wasn't much as fires go—just a few acres in the rocky scree slopes at the west end of the Valley. It was difficult to extinguish, with fire creeping in crevices and popping up in unexpected places. I remember the warning that there might be scorpions, and I actually saw one. It was hot, dirty work, and I was tired. I slept in a government-issued paper sleeping bag that night and was aroused at 0530 for cold beans and franks.

There isn't much to say about the food, but it was part of the experience. Meals-Ready-to-Eat (MREs) are a staple early on in fires and other incidents. They are basically the same as military rations. Everything comes in a plastic bag, with small cans of interesting "gourmet" items: beans and franks, spaghetti and meatballs, and canned meat. Then there was the infamous fruitcake and pound cake. They were hard as a brick, but I actually liked them. There was powdered coffee in a packet and a cool little gadget called a P38 that worked as a can opener. There was always a "treat," such as a chocolate bar, chewing gum, or hard candy. The older versions also had cigarettes. There was a lot of trading and "high grading" going on, making for interesting meals. MREs have come a long way, and modern versions even have a method for heating food.

I spent most of the second day on mop-up, putting out hot spots with a Fedco, a portable tank worn on the back. After helping to sling-load gear out via helo, I hiked out, tired, dirty, and ready for a hot shower and a decent meal.

The Washington Fire

June 28, 1976—Day off, rode bikes; called out 1800 to a big fire near Smoky Jack/Aspen Valley; Kent, Terry, Connie, Tim, Red and I hiked into base camp in the dark, 2130 to 2230; went on the fire line at 2300, cut line until 0300; high winds caused the fire to jump lines, had to pull back.

In the bicentennial year of 1976, the park decided to name all wildland fires with patriotic themes, thus the name "Washington Fire." This was my first big fire, and I never got to go on another fire this large. It was an exciting experience. We were having a homemade ice cream party at our house when I got called out. Donna had made gallons of ice cream.

Our crew, outfitted in yellow Nomex fire shirts, green Nomex fire pants, hard hats, and eye protection, hiked about two miles in the dark with fire packs, shovels, and pulaskis to the fire camp. After checking in, we were immediately put on the line, working until 0300. We hiked back to fire camp and crawled into our paper sleeping bags. After what seemed like minutes, it was time to get back at it. Since this was a sizable, multiday fire, there were no MREs—food and most other supplies were flown in by helicopter. Having bacon and eggs, toast, and coffee delivered by air was a novelty.

We were back on the line at seven and worked all day. It was the hottest, dirtiest, most exhausting work I have ever done, before or since. I breathed my share of smoke and ash. In a short time, my sweaty face was streaked with soot and dirt. Only another firefighter could relate. It was exciting, things were happening all around, and you had to pay attention. It was also very noisy with flames roaring and crackling, limbs and trees crashing down, radios squawking, chainsaws buzzing, people yelling, and helicopters zooming overhead. I had never seen the destructive effects of a forest fire up close. Trees exploded, fire leaped to the crowns, and hollow trees became Roman candles, shooting flames 50 feet into the air. On night shift, the whole woods lit up, and you could see everything. Trees fell with a *woosh*, and you didn't hear them until the last second. A guy could get hurt out here!

Our job was to cut line, removing organic material down to mineral soil in a four-foot-wide path all around the fire. Using shovels and pulaskis, we formed a line, madly hacking at the ground nearly shoulder to shoulder until "bump up" was heard. Everyone moved a few feet to improve the line that had been pioneered by the first person in the line. Burnable materials were tossed into the fire. On hillsides, we constructed trenches to catch rolling pinecones and other debris. It's hot, dirty, backbreaking work.

The fire jumped the line several times, causing us to scramble to safe zones. Radios buzzed with excited instructions as the helicopter made repeated water drops on torching trees. We rushed to get lines around spot fires.

A crew of California Youth Authority inmates were brought in as additional resources. These crews are a low escape risk, specially trained for firefighting. We were told not to "associate with the cons," and we never intermingled with them.

On June 30, after breakfast minus the eggs (they got spilled off the helitack truck), we cut line on the east flank to contain the fire. I worked as a spotter for a sawyer who was dropping snags. Four of us nearly missed being hit by a falling burning tree. By now, the fire was almost 600 acres with 150 people assigned. This was some show!

On July 1, as I was digging line next to ranger Jim Lee, who should appear but Bob Johnson, carrying a heavy pack. Bob smiled when he saw how dirty we were and said, "Hey, would you guys like some ice cream?"

"That ain't funny, Bob," Jim said.

Bob had packed in a full six-quart, insulated container of Donna's homemade ice cream for us. He even had bowls and spoons. A small group of us devoured it, and nobody believed us when we told them we had homemade chocolate ice cream that day!

Things calmed down by July 2, and I was assigned mop-up duty, running a Mark III water pump, wetting down interior line most of the day. As evening approached, we were released from the fire, packed up our gear, and hiked out. Donna, Bob, and coworker Mary During met us with cold beer and goodies. After a long, hot shower and a good night's sleep, I was ready for the next adventure.

Fire Training

November 1, 1977—Fire school: ladders, SCBA (Self-Contained Breathing Apparatus); went to Wawona to prepare the house we will burn tomorrow; learned entry techniques, venting, locks, search and rescue. Experienced smoke without oxygen masks, crawled on the floor then did it with SCBAs.

Fire training is a constant necessity. Firefighting is dangerous work, and you have to know what you are doing. Our local Hodgdon Meadow fire brigade put on training for our spouses, who were often the only people around the housing area if a fire erupted. They were taught how to use a fire extinguisher and get water out of the local hydrant system. I was impressed by how seriously they took the training, and they appreciated being included and acknowledged for the role they play in keeping our little community safe.

Periodically, there was an opportunity to burn a structure that was slated for removal. An old government-owned house in Wawona was prepared for fire training. In those days, we generated smoke by lighting green hay or an old mattress. Today, there are machines that produce "smoke" that is safe to breathe.

We practiced being in a smoke-filled room, learning how to breathe oxygen near the floor. Later, we practiced using the SCBAs and searched for a dummy planted in the room. We had to locate the "victim" and bring it out of the building.

The building was ignited, and we practiced making an entry with charged hose lines. Fires are noisy. Things are popping and cracking, and there is near-zero visibility. It wasn't too bad at first, but as time progressed, the fire grew larger and more dangerous. I was on nozzle with a crew on the hose behind me, advancing upstairs to the second floor. I couldn't see a thing, just the orange glow of fire in the room. The guys behind me kept pushing, and I was getting piled on. This was no time to panic; you had to keep your wits and breathe slowly. It was extremely claustrophobic with the breathing apparatus and mask, helmet, and weighty turnout suit.

We practiced ventilation techniques, allowing smoke to escape from the house and clear the air. Finally, the fire progressed to a stage at which it was unsafe to be inside, and we let it burn to the ground. I had never seen aluminum roofing melt before—it was impressive. This was the first of countless hours of structural fire training I received over the years. In the coming years, I assumed an active leadership role as fire brigade captain and chief, duties that went with my job. I learned while doing, always trying to stay one step ahead to provide good training, good equipment, and good service.

Resource Management—Baffling Bruins

In the formative years of national parks, rangers were responsible for what is now called "resource management." They took care of "problem" bears, planted fish in high-country lakes, felled hazard trees, and fought forest fires. As visitation increased, park resources became vulnerable to overuse and a lack of understanding of complex natural interrelationships. However, managers didn't have the information needed to make sound decisions based on science and research. Resource management as a profession grew in the late 1950s and 1960s, becoming its own discipline based on meticulous research and sound science. With all the professionalism and specialization, park rangers are now often on the periphery in supporting roles.

Yosemite's visitation and backcountry use increased dramatically in the 1970s, with multiple millions of visitors necessitating the expansion of campgrounds, hotels, restaurants, backcountry High Sierra Camps, and other services. Often, these facilities intruded on natural bear habitat. At the same time, the bear population was also increasing to levels two to three times higher than historic 1920 estimates.

Over time, bears became habituated to human food and learned that they could obtain food that was improperly stored in vehicles and campgrounds. Property damage in 1975 was more than $113,000, mostly to vehicles. In one two-year period, backcountry bear incidents numbered more than 4,000.[4] Things were out of control, and something had to be done.

Park wildlife biologist Dale Harms was tasked with formulating a plan to gain control of the situation. He and his colleagues developed a five-part plan to restore and maintain bear activity to more natural conditions. The plan included public education, removal of artificial food sources, strict enforcement of feeding and food storage regulations, controlling problem animals, and research and monitoring.[5]

Park visitors were bombarded with bear information, starting at entrance stations. Park naturalists talked about bears at every program. The park newspaper featured an article about the problem and how to act responsibly in bear country. Bear-proofed dumpsters and food storage lockers were placed in campgrounds. Food suspension cables were installed in designated backcountry campsites. A special regulation concerning proper food storage was enacted, and citations for food storage violations increased dramatically.

Direct bear management actions were implemented, including capture and relocation of nuisance bears with euthanasia as a last resort. No one liked destroying a bear, but sometimes it had to be done. All of these efforts eventually resulted in a remarkable reduction in the number of bear incidents and correlated property damage and injury. "A fed bear is a dead bear" became the local mantra.

I arrived in Yosemite just as the bear management plan was being implemented and was trained to use immobilizing drugs and trapping devices. During the summers of 1975 and 1976, I was informally detailed to work bears as much as possible. As a "bear ranger," I spent many long nights chasing, darting, trapping, and moving bears. It was great fun!

TRAPPING TALES

July 17, 1975—Moved OB camper from CF; tranquilized a bear trapped at White Wolf (WW), 373 lbs., an old bear with bad teeth. Dale took it to North Mountain. This was the first time I got to "drug" a bear; rescue at Wilmer Lake, a woman transported out by horseback.

As part of the public education effort, we cruised the campgrounds each evening, making announcements on the PA system and checking on proper food storage. It helped prevent problems later on. People rushed to the car with questions: "No ma'am, there are no grizzlies in the park."

On July 17, I got to immobilize my first bear and assist with the workup. Our home at Crane Flat was the perfect place for doing bear workups. It was shady and quiet and had water and a garage bay for hanging the scales. Vehicles came and went during the night, and I often arose to find a culvert trap with a bear inside in my backyard. My kids got to see immobilizations and workups.

Morning shift checked the campgrounds. Often, there were reports of bears during the night or damage to vehicles. Broken windows were common, and even convertible tops got ripped. Each incident generated a Bear Information Management System report. Collected data gave the biologists a clearer picture of what was happening in the field, tracked trends, and identified hot spots.

A bear trap is constructed of steel culvert pipe about three feet in diameter, mounted on a wheeled frame with a hitch for transport. One end is fixed and contains a trigger mechanism where bait is placed. The opposite end is a door that is raised by a cable/crank system. The door, connected to the trigger by a rod, falls vertically like a guillotine. When the bear enters the trap to get the bait, it trips the release, allowing the heavy door to slam shut. It's kind of crude, but it works—usually. Sometimes, the bear got the bait without releasing the trigger. Traps had to be level for the door to fall correctly.

Traps have reinforced holes and screen for ventilation and to allow the use of the jab stick, a Lexan rod modified to hold a syringe. It's a daunting task, peering into a dark hole as the bear lunges at your face, spewing snot and saliva—and they don't use mouthwash. It was always disconcerting handling an immobilized bear. They are fully conscious, eyes open, aware of what you are doing—they just can't move their muscles to get you.

We used human food for bait, sometimes getting it from the Awahnee Hotel. It was pretty good stuff: prime rib and berry pie. Rumor has it that some of this food didn't always make it into the traps. Traps were baited and set at night, released the next morning if empty.

The largest bear we ever trapped was "Fat Albert," a 610-pound brute that had to be weighed on the truck scales in the Valley. I guess marshmallows really are bad for you.

BIG FURRY CRITTERS IN THE DARK

July 17, 1976—Paperwork; went to Tamarack bear hunting, missed a sow about 2330; darted her 0030; chased her about 200 yards through brush, stream and steep hill; she finally went down; crowd of campers helped carry her out and into the trap—200 lbs. She was previously tagged; home 0200.

While trapping was often productive, most of the time, I roamed the campgrounds on foot at night, free ranging darting bears. Free ranging means it's just you and the bear, with nothing to defend yourself except the dart gun and sidearm. I've had a few bears bluff charge me, but most just wanted to run away. Once darted, the chase is on, pursuing the animal over rocks, brush, and creeks in the dark. They are amazingly fast and cover a lot of ground quickly. We didn't want them go down and lose them. Stumbling across a large, brown, furry critter in the dark gets your adrenaline going.

I was "hunting" in Tamarack Flat Campground this night. It was after midnight when the bear appeared. I took the shot and gave chase as she ran through thick brush, across a small stream, and up a steep hill. My fitness routine was paying off!

I found her and needed help to get the 200-pound animal back to the trap and haul her away. Everyone in the campground knew I was hunting bears and was eager to assist. We rolled her onto the folding army stretcher, and I "allowed" the crowd to do the legwork. I took the opportunity to educate them about problem bears and why food storage regulations and camp cleanliness were so essential. They all had a story to tell when they got home, and I appreciated the help.

Things didn't always go as planned. Bob Johnson and I were hunting a bear in Crane Flat Campground one night. Bob darted the animal, and it ran across the nearby meadow, both of us in hot pursuit. It easily outdistanced us, and we soon lost it. Eventually, I stumbled across it lying in a small pool in Crane Creek. It was the only pool of water in the whole area. The bear had fallen in headfirst and drowned. We felt terrible, but sometimes "s—— happens."

A funny thing happened one night as Bob and I were hunting a bear in White Wolf Campground. We saw it several times, but it always seemed to be one step ahead of us. Also, that night, a concessioner-owned pack mule had gotten out of the corral and was ambling through the campground. We had seen it, but catching it was not a priority. As we were walking through one of the campsites, a man sitting up on the roof of his RV got our attention.

"Rangers," he said, "I just saw one of the biggest bears you'll ever see walk by my camp. He's right ahead of you." The loose mule was just ahead of us, and we fought to contain our laughter.

PORCUPINE BEARS

August 3, 1975—Went bear hunting, 2330–0400 at Porcupine Flat; bear was treed, came down, but dart gun failed due to low CO_2, so dart fell short; set the trap and bear came back and smashed a car window next to trap! A frustrating night. Saw one meteorite; back to work at 12 noon to do evals. Bear hunting again tonight.

I spent a lot of time at Porcupine Flat Campground. It was located in prime bear habitat and seemed to attract bears. I had been after this bear for some time and finally got a chance to dart it, only to have the dart fall short. The dart gun is a specially designed rifle powered by CO_2 cartridges. A dart consists of an aluminum tube—they come in various sizes—with a large needle on one end and fabric tail on the opposite end. A small .22-caliber charge fits in the tail. When the dart strikes its target, the impact sets off the charge, pushing the lubricated plunger forward, forcing the drug through the needle. They didn't always work.

On the night of August 4, 1975, ranger Rick Smith (yeah, "Ranger Rick") darted a bear at Tenaya Lake. This bear, known to us as "Shadow," was hard to capture, but Rick had finally scored. Rick was working alone and needed help to get the animal into the culvert trap. We often helped each other out during the long nights, keeping each other apprised of our successes or failures. It was a close-knit "club." This was also the night I discovered a burglary at the lodge that ended bear hunting for the night. I got home after six the next morning, another long day.

August 8, 1975—What a day; paperwork in a.m.; saw "Snoopy" at 1130 at Porcupine; I had time to load two darts and walk up to her; perfect shot in the rump, she went up a tree—dosed too light. Shot a second dart when she came down—it was deflected by the first dart! Chased and hunted her for 1.5 hours; gave up. While eating my lunch, she returned. Got another dart ready, darted her. She ran across road and went down; her head wouldn't go down so had to dart again—a "super bear"; bear techs did the workup. Got home 2100.

We gave names to bears. It was easier than trying to remember a tag number. There was Snaggletooth, Fat Albert, Scruffy, and Chicago Cub. Things are more professional today, and they don't give animals names—at least not officially.

Snoopy was a good little bear, but she kept coming back and getting into things. She had a gentle manner. She never charged people or became belligerent, yet she was my nemesis. I spent many hours chasing after her.

On this occasion, I spent most of the day at Porcupine. Snoopy was in the campground in broad daylight and treed when I darted her but came down because I had dosed too low. When I shot the second dart, it hit the first one, deflecting it. I couldn't have done that again in a million years. She returned, and I darted her again. I found her across the Tioga

Snoopy, a good little bear.

Road, but she wasn't completely down, so I had to dose her a third time. I was always reluctant to overdose and tried to use the minimum amount of drug. The biologist told me that some bears just don't seem to react to the drug. Snoopy was a "super bear," and I grew fond of her.

Drug dosages are based on weight—underestimate, and the bears don't respond; overestimate, and you kill them. Judging a bear's weight takes some experience, and I soon learned that bears often look larger than they really are. I erred on the side of caution, not wanting to kill an animal.

"Aw—They're So Cute!"

August 22, 1975—Took bear reports at CFCG, bear has a cut mouth and is bleeding; sow 316 with three cubs is back at WW in only five days; Bob and I spent most of the day with her, cubs up a tree, large crowd; we rigged a manual release on the trap when they came down but they wouldn't go in; we chased them around; I left scene at 1400.

Black bears produce an average of two or three cubs per litter. Triplets are not uncommon, and I once saw a mom with four furry little critters. Sows with cubs presented a challenge. It was all or nothing; we didn't break up a family group. It was usually easy to get the mom in first. Cubs were always eager to be reunited with mom and wanted to be close to her. We had a special trap with a partition that could be lowered, keeping the sow in the front end of the trap, allowing the cubs to enter the rear. The trap was released manually by pulling a rope once the cubs were inside. This required patience and luck. One time, things went terribly wrong when the door came down just as the cub tried to get back out. It was killed instantly, and visitors who were nearby were not pleased.

Working bears in a crowded campground was always challenging. Everyone wanted to see the bears and scrutinized our every move. I felt like I was "onstage" and tried to ignore some of the comments I heard. Most were fascinated by what they were seeing, but some thought they could do it better. After all, I had been doing this for only a few years.

Bear Wars

October 1, 1982—A bear(s) broke into Mead's tent and tore the door off the rescue cache. Cited two guys camping at Lembert Dome in a tent. Moved a dead doe off the road. Put food into Snow Flat for snow survey. Cut wood. Owl on the ranger station flagpole as the moon rose over Mammoth Peak—beautiful.

Bears become hyperactive in the fall, entering a state called hyperphagia, eating as much as they can before going into hibernation. After Labor Day, Tuolumne became a ghost town with minimal staff, so it was pretty quiet. Most seasonals lived in canvas tent cabins—wooden frames covered with canvas. Bears were looking for food and easily entered the flimsy tent cabins. There wasn't much we could do to keep them out. I've seen tent cabins totally trashed by bears—broken screen doors, torn canvas, refrigerators knocked over, and food and kitchen supplies scattered everywhere.

On September 29, 1979, I trapped a bear in our housing area. This was the bear that had raided Dick Ewart's tent a few days previously. He had been caught 10 days earlier and returned to Tuolumne from the other side of the park. Problem bears could be released only within park boundaries at predetermined sites with no public access. Bears were never released near developed areas. The biologists determined where each bear would be freed, accounting for local populations and time of the last release.

In 1976, 98 different bears were relocated 131 times. Bears have incredible homing instincts. Thirty-one percent returned to the location of capture. Even though bears were taken to the other side of the park, they often returned in a matter of days. Yosemite isn't large enough geographically and doesn't have a road network to effectively move bears. The average rate of return for a male was 38 days.[6] One bear traveled approximately 62 miles from its release site, and a tagged Yosemite bear was observed in Lake Tahoe, having crossed several major highways to get there. We often joked that the released bear would be waiting for us when we got home.

One last bear story. One snowy night in early spring, our neighbor borrowed a broom from us. A few hours later, Donna heard a noise at the door. Looking out the kitchen window, she thought she saw the neighbor, dressed in winter clothes, returning the broom. Donna opened the door and was face-to-face with a bear, standing upright just a foot away. Donna immediately slammed the door, and the visitor ambled away. The next morning, we discovered bear tracks going up and over our roof, the house buried under snow—just another day at Crane Flat.

Today's resource management professionals use a wide variety of technology that didn't exist during my time in Yosemite. Some bears are being tracked using satellite-based GPS equipment. The internet plays an important role in educating visitors, with ample information on food storage regulations, bear behavior, and videos on food storage techniques for frontcountry and backcountry users. Information about bear incidents is posted daily, and you can follow along with the bear team by reading their blog. Special "Speeding Kills Bears" signs have been installed in key locations in an effort to have drivers slow down and not hit bears that frequently cross park roads. More bear-proof food storage lockers have been installed in campgrounds and even at trailheads. Due to the team effort and hard work of rangers, interpreters, and maintenance staff, bear incidents are down 97 percent since the highest year of 1998.[7]

BACKCOUNTRY

There is nothing to be learned from the second kick of a mule.

—Mark Twain

Like many large western national parks, most of Yosemite's 748,000 acres is designated wilderness or backcountry. More than 800 miles of maintained trails lead to a wonderland of forests, high mountain meadows, lakes, streams, and rugged granite peaks. Each year, hundreds of thousands of people enjoy the backcountry after obtaining a free wilderness permit. Today, reservations are required for popular areas.

In the spring of 1977, I was offered a two-summer detail as a supervisory backcountry ranger. This was what I had always dreamed about when becoming a ranger, and I was thrilled.

I would be supervising the seasonal backcountry patrol rangers, working for ranger Ron Mackie, Yosemite's Wilderness Unit manager. Ron began his 37-year Park Service career in Yosemite as a seasonal trail crew worker in 1960 and became a seasonal backcountry ranger in 1965. No one knows the Yosemite backcountry better than Ron Mackie.

One of the requirements for this job was proficiency in horsemanship and stock use. I had never ridden a horse and didn't know much about mules. I would soon learn!

Yosemite periodically hosts a "horse school" to train small groups of rangers who work in parks where horses are used for patrol. This intense six-week course covers everything: grooming and care, stable maintenance, riding trained patrol horses for law enforcement duty, jumping, advanced equestrian maneuvers, and other skills. It is one of the most coveted training opportunities in the Park Service. Although the formal school was not scheduled this year, rangers Jim Lee, Mike Osborn, Bill Wagers, and Dean Paschel and I attended a modified version geared for backcountry rangers.

We began at the bottom. May 9, 1977, found me shoveling horse manure in the Yosemite stables. The next four weeks went by quickly. Our instructor, Walt Castle, supervised all park stock operations, and there wasn't anything he didn't know about horses and mules. Walt didn't mince words, expected you to give 100 percent, and didn't waste time. We worked hard to gain his trust and do our best.

We learned about feeding and watering, grooming, saddling, and bridling and studied horse anatomy, hoof care, and basic equine first aid. Finally, we got to actually ride, progressing from a walk to a trot to a canter.

Much of our training was done at the main corrals in the Valley. As training progressed, Walt led us on increasingly difficult "follow me" trips, taking us off trail over rough terrain, logs, rocks, creeks, and other challenges. My confidence in the saddle grew, although I occasionally hit the dirt. Jumping over low fencing was particularly unnerving, but we began to feel we could handle just about anything.

Along with formal training, we began to take short trips with the packers to do actual work. One day, Mike, Bill, and I accompanied packer foreman Rick Watson on a trip to resupply Snow Creek patrol cabin. We followed Rick and his mule string up the treacherous Snow Creek switchbacks. By the time we'd climbed more than 1,000 feet above the valley floor, the rain turned to wet snow. I soon learned how cold and miserable it can be to sit in the saddle all day. We saw fresh bear tracks, but the stock didn't seem to mind. Near the top, Rick stopped to adjust the load on one of the mules and got kicked in the thigh. Now, I had learned to cuss pretty good in the coast guard, but Rick did an admirable job himself. I can still hear that lightning quick *swoosh* as hoof connected with leg. It was a good lesson for all of us: the hind end of a mule is no place to dawdle. We made it back to the barn, cold, wet, and sore, but it was a great first experience on the trail. My "real" backcountry job was about to begin.

MERCED LAKE

May 27, 1977—Mackie and I flew into Merced Lake to check on a reported break in of the patrol cabin. Turned on the water, took shutters down. Ron hiked out, I stayed, got hot water, washed dishes and cleaned up the place. Mike Cobbold hiked in to help; contacted campers at the lake, compliance checks; fished.

Merced Lake patrol cabin serves as a valuable contact point for hikers and stock users due to its location at 7,300 feet near the junction of Merced Lake Trail and Lewis Creek, a short distance from the popular Merced Lake High Sierra Camp. Built in 1927 to provide long-term shelter for backcountry rangers and snow surveyors, the single-story cabin is constructed of stone and logs with a shake roof. The cabin is 560 square feet with a small tack room on the southwest corner.

Compared to the seven other patrol cabins, which are very austere, Merced Lake cabin is like the Hilton Hotel, pretty plush by backcountry standards. It has a small kitchen with a propane cookstove, a comfortable living area with a fireplace, and a bunk room. A propane-fired water heater serves the interior kitchen sink and outdoor shower. There's also a propane-powered refrigerator. Most of the other patrol cabins are one room with a woodstove for cooking and heat. A horse corral and storage shed complete the picture. The cabin is located near the headwaters of the Merced River and a series of lakes where fishing opportunities abound. The trail system leads to a wonderland of rivers, lakes, and high mountain meadows. It's a delightful place to spend a summer.

Opening up a cabin for summer use requires some preparation: shutters must be removed, mouse poop swept up, dishes washed, and corrals and fences inspected and repaired. There's always firewood and kindling to be split and winter debris to be disposed of. Keeping these historic

Merced Lake patrol cabin.

structures in good condition was part of our job, and we took it seriously. I enjoyed doing minor repairs, splitting firewood, fixing the corral, and other manual labor. It's satisfying to look back at your accomplishments at the end of the day.

I almost blew this cabin up one time. Ranger Dean Pascal and I were getting the cabin ready for summer. We had to change propane bottles, stored outside in the tack room, and relight the pilot on the propane-powered refrigerator. Dean connected a new tank and turned on the gas. However, he didn't tell me he had done it. We were yelling at each other, "Are you ready yet?" I didn't hear his reply and went to light the pilot light in the fridge. There was a loud *kawoosh* as the built-up gas ignited. The cabin walls bowed out, and the windows creaked. I had singed eyebrows. Dean ran in and said, "Are you all right?" I had been knocked on my ass but was okay. We escaped a calamity, and I'm glad I'm not the one to go down in history as that idiot ranger who blew up the Merced Lake cabin.

GENTLE JOHN OF MIGUEL MEADOWS

June 22, 1977—Left Valley at 0800 with John Hartman, riding our stock to Miguel Meadows. I was on Otis; my mule was Biscuit. Lunch at the top of Yosemite Falls—quite a view. Continued up Yosemite Creek, looking at trout in clear pools; lots of hikers; got to Tioga road via old trail, then to White Wolf, a distance of 15 miles, and corralled the stock at Harden Lake; stayed with Bryans at WW.

This was my first real pack trip. John Hartman and I rode our stock from the Valley to John's summer quarters at Miguel Meadows, a distance of about 32 miles. We took three days, stopping overnight at White Wolf, then on to Hetch Hetchy with a side trip to Smith Peak for lunch. After a night in the bunkhouse at Hetchy, we rode our horses and mules up the interminable switchbacks to Miguel Meadows.

A schoolteacher in the off-season, John worked 33 seasons for the Park Service, serving at the North Rim of Grand Canyon, Zion, and Yosemite. John spent most of his time in Yosemite's seldom-visited north end. He and his wife Charlotte and four daughters lived in an isolated cabin at Miguel Meadows, accessed by a rough, steep, four-wheel-drive road from Hetch Hetchy dam.

A quiet man, John liked to work alone. Ron Mackie thought I was the only person who could get along with John, so I spent much of my early time with him. Ron was right, as John and I got along well. John taught me how to pack a mule using the complicated diamond hitch. A "hitch" is made using a long lash rope and ties the load to the pack animal. Many packers prefer the intricate diamond because it makes a tight, neat load that stays put all day if properly tied. After I became somewhat proficient at "throwing a diamond," we competed to see who could make the neatest equal-sided diamond, the hallmark of this trademark hitch. John introduced me to the north end of the park and, as we got to know each other, began sharing his secrets, revealing the old army trails and shortcuts he had discovered roaming this remote area solo for many years, taking me to places few have seen.

NORTH END PATROL

July 1, 1977—Up at 0500 and off to Miguel Meadows; Packed the stock while Charlotte cooked us breakfast; rode to Lake Eleanor; went up Kibbie ridge, posted boundary and went out of the park, past Shingle Springs, then on to Kibbie Lake; went cross country to Sachse Springs, then on to Styx Pass with view of Lords Meadow; back into the park at Boundary Lake. Posted boundary there and camped for the night at Little Bear Lake. Mosquitoes were wicked. Had a good supper and swim in the lake; brief shower at 0200.

July 2, 1977—Up early, saw Spotted Fawn Lake; took old army trail to Inferno Lake—beautiful; cross country to Huckleberry Lake, then on to Twin Lakes, posted boundary. Went to Bear and Snow Lakes, Montezuma mine—very windy and cold, some snow drifts. Back into the park at Bond Pass—cold there. Down Jack Main Canyon, saw dead horse bones from when it got struck by lightning. Saw Grace Meadow, stayed at Wilmer Lake cabin—a 27-mile day!

This was the first of many north boundary trips with John. Our purpose was to contact hikers and stock users, check wilderness permit compliance, break up illegal fire rings, pack out trash, and generally "show the flag." We also replaced damaged or missing boundary signs and checked trail conditions. John liked to make side trips and cross-country jaunts, and this trip was no exception. Many of the lakes mentioned above are off the main trail and accessed only by going off trail, picking the way through rocks, brush, and steep terrain. They are small gems, surrounded by flower-filled alpine meadows and thousands of acres of granite. The north end of Yosemite doesn't get a lot of use, and it wasn't uncommon to travel for several days without seeing anyone. The few adventuresome souls we encountered were surprised and somewhat relieved to see us.

The "dead horse bones" mentioned in the journal entry is a bleached partial skeleton of a horse and is a trailside landmark in Jack Main Canyon. The story I heard was that the horse and rider were struck by lightning, killing the horse but sparing the rider. Supposedly, the bolt blew the shoes right off the horse. Even if not true, it's still a good story. I used to think about this when I was riding up on some exposed crest as storm clouds gathered—made me nervous.

John liked to get an early start, so it was up at five and on the trail by 0630 on Independence Day. We encountered several skinny dippers at Beehive Lake and took a bear incident report. Since Otis, my horse, lost a shoe the day before, I did some walking, which was quite nice for a change. We arrived at Miguel Meadows in late afternoon, and I headed home to Crane Flat.

Horses and mules were an integral part of my work, and I rode a variety of horses during my two-summer assignment. Peter, a white-blazed chestnut thoroughbred, was a fine horse. He was a good walker, but I made the mistake of putting him into a gallop once and was terrified until I got him reined in. He had won a couple of competitive races before we got him, and it was the fastest I've ever gone on a horse.

Tenaya, a big Appaloosa with huge feet, could really step off the miles. His biggest fault was that he would take off for the barn if given the least chance. I always had to hold his reins or keep him tied. John and I were fishing one evening, allowing the horses to graze in the meadow nearby. John had placed hobbles on Tenaya's front legs to keep him from taking off. Tenaya had other thoughts. We heard some crashing in the brush behind us and saw Tenaya crow hopping up the slope, headed for Miguel Meadows. After running furiously to catch him, I kept him tied up. I just couldn't trust him after that.

Otis was a tall chestnut horse with a long, flowing tail. I logged many miles on Otis, and he was a good companion. Sitting atop Otis with his long mane and flowing tail, I felt like a real cowboy in my ranger hat, boots, and spurs. Otis made me look good.

Biscuit was my favorite mule, and I was lucky to have her. She was black and brown with long, floppy ears. She was short and easy to pack and always patient with my clumsy attempts to throw a diamond. A friendly critter, she came into camp from grazing to nuzzle me and bum a treat or see what I was doing. She was a sweetheart and a good companion.

The mule carried most of my gear: extra clothes, sleeping bag, cooler, food, an axe and shovel, oats, and alfalfa cubes. In my saddlebag, I carried

Packing up with my old friend Biscuit.

fence pliers, some wire, a few nails, a rain hat cover, an extra radio battery, and a small lunch. I ate so much dried salami that summer that I still can't stand the smell of it!

When you spend a great deal of time with animals, you begin to form a bond with them. You learn each other's quirks and personalities, and they can sense your mood. Some of the best moments I had in the backcountry were interacting with my stock. I needed them, and they needed me. I sometimes went for days without seeing anyone, and it was good to have a friend on those long, lonely trails. We had many conversations, and unlike my wife, they never disagreed with my opinions!

BUCK CAMP AND THE DAY IT RAINED OATMEAL

July 18, 1977—a day of solitude on the trail to Buck Camp from Merced Lake. My job was to ride to the remote ranger stations, learn the country, help with projects, pack in supplies, repair drift fences, and do whatever needed doing. Since I was their supervisor, I tried to spend time with each seasonal ranger.

There's a tricky piece of trail just above the Merced Lake cabin. The narrow path is blasted out of the granite cliff, a sheer drop of nearly 100 feet into the swirling blue water of the river below. I never liked this stretch, tense in the saddle, ready to bail off if the horse or mule stumbled. I breathed a sigh of relief when it was behind me.

Red Peak Pass is located in the heart of the Clark Range, the spectacular 11,000-foot-elevation trail being the highest maintained trail in Yosemite. I stopped frequently to let my horse take a breather as storm clouds gathered over the unending switchbacks, and I couldn't help thinking about those horse bones in Jack Main Canyon. Shortly after I made this trip, a mule died on the trail, a real dilemma. It's not easy to dispose of a dead mule at 11,000 feet in a place that is nothing but rocks and boulders. The solution was to blow it to smithereens with dynamite, accomplished by Walt Castle and the trail crew. I heard there wasn't a piece larger than a postage stamp left.

I camped that night at Lower Ottoway Lake, a small alpine tarn at the base of Red Peak. There was a small meadow with lush grass for the stock to graze. I hadn't seen anyone all day and had the entire basin to myself. The quiet was deafening, not a blade of grass stirring. At dusk, a hatch of insects allowed me to fool dozens of small trout that I caught and released back into the crystal-clear water. As suddenly as it began, the hatch was over, the lake surface turning into a sheet of glass. As the sun sank below the surrounding peaks, the lake reflected their perfect mirror image, orange and pink alpenglow. I enjoyed these quiet evenings alone, sleeping under a tree beneath the stars, the occasional tinkling of the bell on the horse and mule grazing nearby. It was good to be alive in this place of grass and clear water, flowers and critters, and a billion stars in a cold, black sky. It was why I wanted to become a ranger.

July 19—After a quick stop for lunch at Lower Merced Pass Lake, I rode on to spend some time with ranger Mike "Oz" Osborne at Buck Camp ranger station located in the uncrowded, breathtaking south end of the park. The rustic cabin sits next to a fenced meadow filled with corn lily, aster, and coneflowers. Water is piped in from a nearby spring, and there is an outdoor shower on the back porch—a real luxury.

I helped Mike fix his water line, which had gotten plugged by a stone. After locating the obstruction, we spliced in a new section and had our showers.

Mike showed me around his neighborhood the next day, contacting a few fishermen and hikers near Chiquito Pass and nearby Chain Lakes. We replaced some signs, broke up fire rings, and hauled out trash. Mike was due for some time off, so we packed up and got a late start for the Valley. It was nearly dark when we made camp at Buena Vista Lake. For some reason, the horses were restless, and we didn't get much sleep.

Rising early the next morning, I decided to make some coffee and hot oatmeal to take off the morning chill, firing up my trusty Svea camp stove to boil water. After a few minutes, I noticed that the stove was making an unusual hissing, surging sound. Flames began to erupt around the fuel tank as the noise grew louder. Sensing disaster, I said to Mike, "Get back, I think it's gonna blow." With that, there was a loud *boom*. The stove and cook pot flew about 50 feet straight up, scattering twisted pieces of stove, cook pot, and oatmeal into the air. What goes up must come down as hot shards of metal and oatmeal rained down on us. The stock, tethered nearby, went berserk, mules kicking, horses bucking, gear scattering everywhere. Luckily, I didn't have my head over the pot when it blew, or this might be another story. I looked at Mike, he looked at me, and we both let out some cuss words and began to laugh. To this day, whenever I see Mike, I ask him if he wants some of my special oatmeal, and we both bust out laughing.

WILMER LAKE PATROL CABIN AND THE LONELY NORTH END

August 1, 1977—Layover day at Wilmer Lake* cabin. John and I rode to Tilden and Mary Lakes; horse party at Tilden. Saw five fawns, one just born. Went cross-country to Otter Lakes, got stormed out. Back to cabin ten minutes before a storm hit. Took a swim in a beautiful deep pool on Falls Creek. *Also known as "Wilma Lake."

Staying in a patrol cabin is a luxury. If the Merced Lake cabin is the Hilton, Wilmer and the other cabins are Motel 6. Nonetheless, they are a welcome sight after a long day, especially in bad weather.

Wilmer Lake patrol cabin was built in 1947 to provide shelter for winter snow surveyors and ranger patrols. The log cabin sits on a knoll overlooking nearby Wilmer Lake and Falls Creek. A hitching rack is handy to tie up stock while unloading onto the covered porch. An outer "bear door" studded with sharp nails deters curious bears. Shutters protect the windows.

When entering a backcountry cabin, you are greeted by a cool, dark interior with a musty odor of wood smoke and bacon grease, a place that has been closed up for a while. Removing the shutters allows you to see what you are doing. Most of Yosemite's cabins have a wall-mounted "chuck box," or kitchen. The door folds down to form a counter. There's always an eclectic variety of food: an assortment of canned goods, Spam, tea and coffee in tins, some ramen noodles that no one eats, rancid peanut butter, candles, matches, and lantern mantles. If you're lucky, there's a stump of booze left over by the last patrol.

There's a small table with uncomfortable folding chairs. Each cabin has a logbook used to record details of your trip, trail conditions, wildlife sightings, and other musings. I've spent many nights reading these historic documents, and there are some fascinating stories inside.

Two sets of metal army-issue bunk beds with terrible springs line the back wall. Thin mattresses hang on wires to keep the mice out. It's still better than sleeping on the ground. Mice are a given in cabins, and tales of combat between mice and rangers are legendary. You haven't lived until you've had a mouse run over your face in the middle of the night.

A woodstove provides for heat and cooking. Cabin protocol is to leave a match-ready fire for the next person—it has saved lives in cold weather. Three matches in the hanging Coleman lantern are always there when you need them.

An assortment of pots, pans, and wash basins hang from nails on the log wall. Water buckets must be left overturned to keep the mice out. There's a broom, a mop, an axe, and a saw. Luxury items include a few paperback books and a worn deck of cards. Home sweet home.

Wilmer Lake cabin was destroyed by an avalanche during the winter of 1985–1986. It's sad to see this historic structure meet such an end.

A welcome respite after a long day. Wilmer Lake patrol cabin, 1977.

August 8, 1977—Cold this morning, in the 30s; crossed Rancheria, saw remains of old cattleman's cabin. Dropped into Bear Valley, had lunch at Kerrick Canyon. Then up the meadows to camp on the boundary at Peeler Lake. Cold swimming but I was filthy so it was worth it. Rode about 28 miles today.

John was an early riser, up by 5 a.m., stumbling around in the dim light, humming a tune while graining and grooming the stock. I, on the other hand, nestled deeper into my sleeping bag, especially on frosty mornings. I slept on a "packer's bed" using my horse pads sandwiched between the canvas manty used to cover the pack load. It rarely rains in the Sierra in summer. I didn't carry a tent but slept under the stars and never got wet.

John was satisfied with a biscuit and handful of trail mix for breakfast. I *had* to have coffee. John was a Mormon, so I made him hot chocolate. I scarfed down a bagel or some fig bars, not wanting to delay our departure.

Breaking camp, we packed our mules, checked our saddlebags, and left no trace of our presence. On the trail by 0630, our day had begun.

NEVER LIE TO A RANGER

On August 24, 1977, longtime seasonal horse patrol ranger Maynard Medefin and I rode into Grant Lakes to check out a report of three kids camping with a gun and a dog. Finding the dog was easy—a puppy running around off leash—strike one. They didn't have a wilderness permit—strike two. They said they didn't know anything about a gun. I knew it was there somewhere. I asked for the truth; no one confessed. They were instructed to pack up and leave, and I was ready to take the dog when I just happened to lift up a sleeping bag stretched out on the ground. There was the rifle, a loaded .22—strike three, you're out. I arrested the kid who confessed to owning it, handcuffed him, and had him walk out in front of my horse. I told him if he tried to escape, I would run him down. It must have been a strange sight to the hikers we encountered, a kid in handcuffs and a dog draped over my saddle. One guy asked me, "What did he do?" and I replied, "No wilderness permit. Where's yours?" He couldn't get it out fast enough!

SIX INCHES OF "PARTLY CLOUDY"

I loved to be in the backcountry in the fall, and in September 1977, Donna and I made a four-day pack trip into Benson Lake, a beautiful gem surrounded by granite cliffs and a broad, sandy beach. I got to show her what the country was like and what I did back there. Chief ranger Bill Wendt felt it was important for rangers' spouses to understand what the job was really like and encouraged these experiences. Despite being sore from riding, Donna enjoyed it thoroughly.

She got to make one last trip with me in September 1978. On September 12, we left Miguel Meadows, posting the boundary near Kibbie Lake, camping for the night. Threatening weather on September 13 forced us to ride 15 miles to the Huckleberry Lake snow survey cabin. I asked park dispatch for a forecast. They said it was to be "partly cloudy." A violent storm came that night with thunder, lightning, and then rain turning to snow. Snug and warm in our tiny cabin, we were unaware of what was happening outside. Opening the door in the morning, we were astonished to see a world of white. "Partly cloudy" had turned into six inches of heavy, wet snow! It was beautiful but also a bit disconcerting. We had a decision to make: continue on with poor trail conditions or turn around and go home. The weather forecast from park dispatch called for slowly improving weather. We decided to go for it.

Everything was frozen as we packed up, the lash rope and manty frozen stiff. The stock got some extra grain that morning, as I knew it would be a long day. We headed north, gaining elevation, the rocky trail obscured by snow and running water. Rain, snow, and low clouds finally gave way to weak sun as we neared aptly named Snow Lake. We had to cross a nearly 10,000-foot pass here to drop into Jack Main Canyon. I hadn't been up this way all summer and was shocked to discover a large snowfield on the lee side of the pass. This was not good. We had to figure a way down this obstacle or turn back. After much hand wringing and with lots of uncertainty, I decided to try to get the stock down the snowfield.

Donna stayed at the top with the mule while I led the horses down the steep incline, about 50 yards long, slipping and sliding all the way in my riding boots. I went back to the top and told Donna to go down to the horses. I then let the mule go by herself. Fully packed, she sat down on her haunches and slid the whole way down to the rocks, landing on her feet. I was so relieved—I knew Walt would kill me if I did something this stupid and injured an animal. Breathing a big sigh of relief, we continued down the snow-covered trail to Wilmer Lake cabin for the night.

All went well the next day, the sun shining warmly as we made our way back to Miguel Meadows. The hot coffee at the trail crew camp in Paradise Valley was a welcome treat.

"You Guys Are Tough!" A Trip to Yellowhammer

September 26, 1980—Up at 0445, had breakfast and off on our trip. Got to Hetch Hetchy about 0630, loaded the mules and off by 0830. Rode up the switchbacks to Lake Eleanor for lunch. Saw a three-foot rattlesnake. I got stung by yellow jackets up on Kibbie Ridge. Had to repack Soda five times as she kept bucking and shifting her load. Got to Sachse Spring at dark, stayed in the cabin.

September 27, 1980—Up early and cooked breakfast. Lunch at Lord's Meadow, contacted hunters there. Rode on a little used trail up the north fork of Cherry Creek, took duck (rock cairns) trail into Yellowhammer Lake cross country. Camped at the lake, a rough trip in.

September 28, 1980—Took the duck trail out of Yellowhammer, lost it, and went cross country. Spent four hours coming down a steep cliff into Cow Meadow. We had to stop and build rock slab ramps to work our way down. We met some hunters at the bottom who had been watching us and said we were "tough" to make it down there! Made us feel good but we had our doubts!! Rode to Huckleberry in the dark.

This was my last boundary patrol trip with stock. I had encountered bees on the trail before. While climbing up the steep trail toward Bond Pass, the horse stepped into a yellow jacket nest. I didn't realize it until the mule started bucking and the horse lunged forward. A cloud of angry bees attacked, hurrying us along up the trail.

Bob and I still talk about our excursion into Yellowhammer Lake, located in a remote area outside of the park. Walt Castle told us that he had worked as a packer on a water project there in his early teens. He said, "You guys'll never find it." The challenge was on!

We had a topo map, but there was no marked trail into the lake, which lies in a basin of thousands of acres of open granite slabs and cliffs. The country was littered with glacial erratics and gnarled, stunted juniper, hundreds of years old. We followed a faint shadow trail marked by occasional rock cairns. It was slow going, losing the way often. This was open granite, a place where few have traveled. Suddenly, there was the old cabin with Walt's initials carved in the door frame. We camped there, enjoying the solitude.

The next day, we continued on, still in the national forest. The map showed a trail in Cow Meadow that connected with the park boundary. We were out of the park in unfamiliar territory and had to go cross-country to hit Cow Meadow.

Slowly winding our way on open, slick granite, we came to a rock face that sloped down to the meadow far below. There was no trail, so we had to find a way down or turn around. Walking the horses and leading the mule, we gingerly made our way down the slick granite to a series of natural ramps that permitted the stock to jump down to the next level. I remember the sharp clink of steel horseshoes on stone, an occasional *zing* when the horse slipped, scrambling to gain its balance. It was scary and slow going.

At last, we got to a place where we were forced to build a ramp down to the next level. Tying the stock to some small gnarled trees, we lugged large pieces of granite to build a step so the horses could negotiate their way down. All of this was done wearing our slick-soled cowboy boots and spurs!

As we cautiously made our way down, we could see some guys with binoculars watching us from below. Back in the saddle on the valley floor, we rode over to the guys who greeted us with total awe. "You guys are tough. I can't believe you guys came down that cliff." They went on with their praise, and I said, "Oh, yeah, we always come down that way."

Many rangers never get the chance to work in the backcountry in a large national park. I was fortunate to ride nearly 1,000 miles in my years there. Sometimes, I could ride for days without seeing anyone. It got

Ranger Bob Johnson leads a pack string down Jack Main Canyon.

kind of lonely back there at times, but I enjoyed the solitude. I will never forget the pure joy of riding on the lonesome trails in the north end with only the sound of the breeze sighing through the gnarled, wind-polished, ancient, white-barked pines and the grating *kraak kraak kraak* of a Clark's nutcracker welcoming me to his world. The warm, sunny days and cool nights; the high alpine meadows sprinkled with colorful wildflowers; the imposing granite peaks; the jewel-like lakes; and my faithful horse and mule will always be some of the best days of my life.

WINTER

Winter is nature's way of saying, "Up yours!"

—Robert Byrne

After the chaos of summer, most of us looked forward to winter. It was a time to regroup, do training, work on neglected projects, and get ready for the next summer. Weekdays were usually pretty quiet, but weekends were often chaotic. Thousands of people from the central valley and Bay Area came to the mountains to enjoy the snow.

Winters are long in the Sierra, usually beginning in October with snow on the ground in the high country until late May. Crane Flat, at 6,200 feet of elevation, averaged 250 inches of snow per year. In the record winter of 1982–1983, we got slammed with 360 inches. The most common winter entries in my diaries are "shoveled snow," "sat at chain control most of the day," and "investigated car wreck."

Crane Flat was a major destination for cross-country skiers and snow addicts. On weekends, the parking lot was full, and often our driveway was blocked with cars. People asked to use our bathroom—after all, they were paying for it with their taxes! Badger Pass ski area across the valley attracted thousands, and I was grateful to not be involved in the chaos of vehicle accidents when it snowed at the end of the day. Ranger Rick Smith once described the scene as "an explosion in a macaroni factory."

We had our share of mayhem too. I soon learned that Californians are not the best winter drivers. It seemed to always snow on weekends when the park was crowded. We all spent countless hours investigating car wrecks, flagging traffic, and assisting the tow truck driver with clearing the roadway.

Then there was chain control. In the mountains, deteriorating conditions often necessitate the installation of snow tire chains. We posted chain requirements at established turnouts where people could safely install their chains. Regulations went from "Chains Advised" to "Chains Required" to the extreme of "Chains Mandatory—No Exceptions." Like many Yosemite rangers, I spent hundreds of hours monitoring chain compliance. If we left the chain station, people ignored the signs, often getting stuck or causing an accident up the road. It's no fun arguing with people all day about the need to put on chains. Many folks didn't know how to install chains, didn't want to get dirty, or didn't have them. I asked one guy why he was putting chains on the front wheels of a rear-wheel-drive car. He replied, "They're easier to put on the front."

The Big Storms

February 9, 1978—Spent five hours shoveling out the driveway to get patrol car out, pulled it out with Land Rover. 24 inches new snow since 4 p.m. yesterday. Eight-foot piles along our sidewalk; tree tops snapping off.

February 10, 1978—Snowed all night and all day. Over 50 inches since Sunday. Donna and I spent the entire day shoveling off the roof. Bob slogged in to dig out the Tucker, no luck, drove him part way out on the snowmo. Four trees down from here to the gas station. Main road is still closed, snow to 2000'.

Huge, moist storms coming off the Pacific Ocean sometimes slammed the Sierra for days, snow piling up in feet. We struggled to keep up, clearing a tunnel into the house, sometimes shoveling the roof lest it

Winter at our house. Daughter Kelly in foreground.

collapse. When the interior doors began to bind, it was time to shovel. When the clothesline went under, Donna hung laundry on clothes hangers from a rod over the woodstove. As winter wore on, snow built up to the level of some of the windows, forcing us to close the shutters to avoid breaking the glass. It was like living in a snow cave.

When it snowed like this, we closed the road to all traffic. It made everyone's job easier and gave the plow crews a chance to catch up. The big rotary plows were the only way to keep the road passable. A rotary plow is a large, self-propelled machine with an auger in front and an impeller that shoots snow out of a directional chute. It can shoot snow more than 100 feet in any direction. It's like your home snowblower on steroids, mounted on a huge diesel-powered truck. Rotaries are used in deep snow in western mountains and to clear airport runways. Sometimes, we couldn't get in or out of our driveway for days until the monster plows "blew us out."

The big guns—rotary snowplow working its way to Crane Flat.

"Death March" to Tuolumne

March 4, 1982—Dick Ewart and I left from Mirror Lake in the Valley for Snow Flat at 0745. We climbed the 109 switchbacks to the top of the Valley rim on the Snow Creek trail. At the top, put on skis and skied to Snow Creek cabin for a quick lunch (1345) and continued on to Snow Flat. Got there at 1910 hours using headlamps, following markers on the trees to the cabin. I was as exhausted as I have ever been, severely dehydrated. It was cold and uphill all the way, about 5000' elevation gain. Almost too tired to eat, I finally got some hot food and water in me and felt better. This was a long day.

This was the biggest trip I've ever made on skis. Winter ranger Anne Macquarie had to leave early, leaving husband Chas alone in Tuolumne. The chief ranger decided that rangers would rotate in to relieve Chas. Since I was the sub-district ranger, I got to go first and set the example.

Ranger-naturalist Dick Ewart volunteered to accompany me to Snow Flat patrol cabin. We left the Valley floor and began the arduous 2.6-mile hike carrying heavy packs, gaining 2,600 feet in elevation. Reaching the snow line, we put on our skis.

Snow Flat cabin, at 8,858 feet, was another seven miles, all uphill. We took turns breaking trail in the deep snow. It was exhausting work, sinking in to our knees, stopping frequently to rest and rehydrate.

Continuing to slog upward, the snow getting deeper, we crossed the Tioga Road as twilight settled in. For the final mile, our headlamps illuminated the reflective markers leading to the cabin. I was elated to see the cabin after 12 hours of grueling travel.

The cabin was almost buried under 12 feet of snow. We had to enter the cabin using the loft door, descending the ladder to the interior below. Then we shoveled out the outhouse and stovepipe. We lit the lantern, built a fire, and collapsed on the bunks, totally spent. After melting snow, we drank Tang and forced ourselves to eat, alleviating the symptoms of dehydration and early stages of hypothermia. It had been a long, exhausting day.

Dick left for the Valley the next morning, and I continued on to Tuolumne, breaking trail under a beautiful blue sky. I met Chas, who skied a few miles west breaking trail. I was glad to get to my cabin and get a fire going. Hot dogs and beans never tasted better.

I spent the next seven days in Tuolumne, shoveling out buildings, splitting firewood, hauling water on a sled from the river, and skiing. Chas invited me for dinner at his quarters, a one-mile ski. It was great to be back "home" in the Meadows, and I rejoiced in skiing on snow that allowed me to skim across broad expanses of open terrain. I skied to Tioga Pass and called Ferdinand on the phone—he was delighted. The Tuolumne River was mostly frozen over with beautiful blue ice, large pillowing snowdrifts, and gurgling water. Peaks in the Cathedral Range faded from orange to purple to gray each evening in the alpenglow. There's nothing like skiing alone under a full moon, the meadows and peaks lit up like daylight, dead quiet, just the hiss of the skis on cold, crystalline snow. I heard a pack of coyotes yipping one evening. A pair of owls were hooting back and forth—mating season. It was magic. I was reluctant to leave but missed my family too.

The return trip, beginning on March 12, was much easier, the trail already broken and mostly downhill. I left my cabin before 8 a.m., picked up Chas's outgoing mail, and headed west. Changing conditions caused me to stop and rewax my skis several times. After a late lunch at Tenaya Lake, I trudged up the old cutoff road to Snow Flat cabin, where I spent the night.

It was warm enough for gooey purple klister wax, a cross between Vaseline and bubblegum, when I left the cabin the next morning. Later, mohair climbing skins helped control my descent on the steep trail. After a quick lunch at Snow Creek cabin, I made my way toward the Valley rim. The big surprise was seeing Donna at the Snow Creek bridge. She had lugged a cold beer up for me too! That's the kind of partner she is.

Spring was fast approaching, and only one other ranger made the trip. For me, it had been a test of my physical and mental strength, and I proved to myself that I could do more than I thought possible. It was an unforgettable experience.

Spring!

March 20, 1984—To Sonora, very warm. Spring is here! Meadow is melting, even a hint of green. Dandelion flowers out at Hodgdon.

We grew weary of seeing white all winter and looked forward to spring. Our girls loved running barefoot in the green grass of the San Joaquin Valley. There were even orange trees!

Spring arrived at Crane Flat when the "peepers," small frogs, appeared in the meadow. They grew quiet at our approach but began trilling again if we stood still. The resident great gray owl attracted birders, and I often saw him perched on a snow stake on my way to work each morning. It was like seeing an old friend.

Snow Surveys

No Road Too Steep, No Snow Too Deep.

—Tucker Sno-Cat Corporation

In the arid West, where water is king, the demand for water for agriculture, hydroelectric power, recreation, and commercial and domestic use is unending. Nowhere is this more evident than in California, which produces more than 90 percent of the fruit, vegetables, and nuts in the United States. Hydroelectric power accounts for 21 percent of power generated in this most populous state.[8]

Sierra snowpack forms the bulk of the state's water supply. Large dams and reservoirs store this water, which is distributed by a complex system of irrigation canals. The idea of correlating snowpack with irrigation forecasts was conceived by Professor James Church in 1895. Measuring the snowpack began in 1923. A network of snow courses, managed by the Department of Water Resources, gives hydrologists and water management specialists the information needed to make decisions regarding seasonal runoff, water storage capacity, irrigation potential, flood control, and overall water supply.

Yosemite rangers began collecting snow data for local use in 1912 and has been a cooperator for more than 80 years. Following in that tradition, I was one of a handful of rangers trained to do snow surveys. Our district encompassed the upper Tuolumne River drainage and parts of the Merced River drainage. Surveys on our six snow courses were done monthly from January through April. I enjoyed doing this work immensely, as it broke up the winter routine and got me into the winter backcountry. No two trips were ever the same, with equipment break-downs, variable weather, snow, and trail conditions—for me, all the trips were enjoyable.

FIRST TRIP

My 16-year career as a snow surveyor began on January 20, 1976. It was unusual, as we drove pickups behind a snowplow to Olmstead Point, 15 miles west of Tuolumne Meadows. From there, we used snow machines to travel to Tioga Pass and Snow Flat. In this book, "snow machine" is synonymous with "snowmobile." It was my first time driving one of these "crotch rockets," and I logged hundreds of hours on them in subsequent years. The paltry 19 inches of snow at Snow Flat was the first indication of two years of extreme drought in California. I have measured more than 144 inches there in January.

SNOW FLAT IS SNOW FUN

March 24, 1980—Left on snowmobiles for Tuolumne snow survey. Easy, fast travel on hard crust. Mackie and I got to Snow Flat at 1030 and started the course at 1100. Finished at 1600—there is 24" of ice. We broke several tubes, and had to build a fire in the cabin to melt candles to wax the tubes. 136" average. This was one of the most arduous snow courses we ever did. Tubes constantly icing up. Started Tenaya course but gave up as tubes keep freezing. Saw a coyote on talus. In Tuolumne at 1800. Will return to Tenaya course tomorrow.

In contrast to my first trip, as this diary entry illustrates, taking snow samples was not always easy. In fact, this was one of the most difficult surveys any of us had ever done. It took most of the day to obtain 10 good samples. We broke several tubes and struggled to keep them from icing up.

A set of tubes consists of eight aluminum-alloy cylinders, each three feet long and one and a half inches in diameter. The tubes have slots to permit visual inspection of the sample core and allow the driving wrench to be clamped on. Engraved in one-inch increments, the tubes are calibrated to give a reading of snow water equivalent (SWE), the amount of liquid water equivalent for the volume of snow. Tubes are screwed together in numerical order, the bottom one with a sharp cutter to bore through ice.[9]

Once assembled, the tube set is driven vertically into the snowpack until it hits the ground. You learn to "feel" the ground, and there must be some dirt or grass on the bottom of the sample to indicate you've reached the bottom. After recording the outside depth, the tube is extracted with a snow core inside. Tube and core are then weighed using a calibrated spring scale attached to a cradle. SWE is calculated using an average of 10 samples.

March 29, 1983—Left on snow survey—again! Good travel to Snow Flat, arrived at noon. Took the snow course, relatively easy today with a 211.5" average. Shoveled 6 feet of snow off the roof. Left for Tuolumne at 1600, had to shovel on May Lake hill, broke a steering rod into a U shape! We got it re-straightened—"bush mechanics." Reached the Tioga road at 2200. Arrived at Tuolumne at 0045— exhausted. Got to bed at 0200.

The year 1983 was a 100-year record snow year in the Sierra. Tuolumne received 720 inches of snow that winter, and our house at Crane Flat got buried with 360 inches. This was our second trip to Snow Flat after an unsuccessful attempt on March 23. With an estimated 18 feet of snow, we labored to shovel our way into the buried cabin. Finding and shoveling out the outhouse took more than an hour!

This diary entry references a broken steering rod. On extended trips, we used the Tucker Sno-Cat, a tracked over-snow vehicle sometimes known as a "weasel." These machines are used in Antarctica, ski resorts, and other places where over-snow travel is required. Affectionately known as "the Tucker," our machine was on permanent loan from the

No snow too deep—the Tucker Sno-Cat.

State of California for snow survey work. It also came in handy for winter rescues and emergency maintenance work.

It's a pretty simple machine: stick shift, flathead four-cylinder gasoline engine, hydraulic steering, and four independent steel tracks on pontoons. There is a series of rods and U-joints that control the steering system. Although it went just about anywhere, care had to be taken not to over-torque the hydraulic system and linkages. "Bush repairs" were common, and we carried enough spare parts, belts, hoses, nuts, bolts, and pins to practically rebuild the thing. The machine could transport six people. A towed large metal sled mounted on skis carried all our equipment.

We were still doing snow surveys in June, and the Tioga Road, usually open by Memorial Day, didn't open until July. Spring revealed substantial damage: roof overhangs were sheared off, pipe fittings were broken, backcountry bridges were destroyed, and seasonal quarters tent frames looked like kindling. We told the chief of maintenance, responsible for all road work, there was a lot of snow in the high country, and he said, "Oh, we'll handle it." I said, "No, you don't understand: there is a *lot* of snow up there." When the plows started east at Crane Flat that spring, they made only 100 feet the first day!

Enjoy Your Breakfast, Tom

Some snow courses are designed for aerial surveys. Specialized markers are photographed from the air, and the photos are examined later to determine snow depth. On April 20, 1978, I had the opportunity to join an aerial snow survey with Bill Murrey and Don Paulsen, California Department of Water Resources employees. It was my first time flying in a small, fixed-wing plane. We took off early from Pine Mountain airport and flew east over the north end of the park. It was spectacular, and I got to see all the country I had explored by horseback the previous summer.

After landing near the town of Bridgeport on the east side of the Sierra, we got a ride to a small café for breakfast. Following Bill and Don's lead, I enjoyed a hearty meal of greasy bacon, eggs, potatoes, and coffee. Then it was time to get to work.

In order to photograph several courses that day, the plane had to do low, tight circles to get good shots of the markers. Pushed back into my seat, pulling several "Gs" and watching the ground spin around as we orbited the marker, I quickly became aware of an odd feeling in my stomach and began to get warm and sweaty. That breakfast was coming back up, and Don handed me a "barf bag," which I immediately filled. It wasn't the last time I would have this experience, and I think Don and Bill were somewhat amused to see a green ranger in the rear seat. They later apologized for not letting me in on what was "coming up."

Last Trip to Winter Wonderland

March 25, 1985—The last snow survey of the year. It had dumped snow for five days with high winds and deep cold. We struggled to do the Dana Meadows snow course at 9,600 feet in whiteout conditions, eyelids freezing shut, the wind knocking us off our feet. The steering mechanism in the Tucker broke, forcing a retreat back to Tuolumne for bush repairs. We completed the course the next day and headed for home with 42 inches of new snow. An avalanche released while doing the Tenaya Lake course, coming through the trees into the meadow where we were working. It took two more days to get home with breakdowns and shoveling our way through mountainous drifts.

I didn't know it at the time, but this was to be my last "old-fashioned" snow survey in Yosemite. In 1984, nearly 90 percent of lands within the park were designated wilderness, where mechanized equipment is strongly discouraged. In 1990, the decision was made that future snow surveys would be done using the "minimum tool" doctrine. Today, rangers and resource management staff use skis and snowshoes to access the snow courses. Helicopters may be used if avalanche conditions make travel unsafe.

New technologies, such as satellite-linked Sno-Tel sites, dot the Sierra, replacing many snow surveyors who need to validate data only periodically. The era of wrestling balky snow machines and traveling in the beloved Tucker is over. I suppose it's for the best, but it sure was fun.

Tuolumne—"Meadow in the Sky"

From the first time I saw Tuolumne Meadows in 1974, I knew I wanted to be a part of it. It's unlike any other landscape in Yosemite. A series of subalpine meadows stitched together by the meandering Tuolumne River, ringed by rugged granite peaks and glacially polished granite domes, the place has an aura of wonder and delight. It's been suggested that John Muir got his inspiration for forming the Sierra Club while camping in Tuolumne.

I got my chance to work here in 1979 when I was assigned as the assistant sub-district ranger under ranger Steve Hickman. Fortune smiled again in 1981 when I was promoted into the sub-district ranger position. It was a big leap in responsibility for me and set the path for the rest of my career.

Tuolumne is a prime destination for thousands of visitors each summer and is second only to the Valley in infrastructure and operational complexity. Besides the historic ranger station, built in 1924, there is a barn, rescue cache, visitor center, High Sierra Camp lodge, mountaineering school, concessioner stables, store, service station, maintenance facilities, and housing for more than 100 employees. The campground, with more than 300 sites, is always full. Hiking and backpacking opportunities abound with the John Muir and Pacific Crest trails skirting the meadows. It's a busy place, and I was "mayor."

It's a big job to get such a complex ready for summer operations. The following sections describe the process from opening to closing and what it was like to live and work in such a special place.

MOVIN' IN

After a winter of investigating car wrecks and enforcing chain control, I eagerly anticipated getting back to Tuolumne. I wanted to escape the confines of the district office and run my own show. When the plows got to the meadows, I was right behind them.

For the first week or so, I was the only one there. I shoveled out buildings, removed window shutters, and got the ranger station ready for business. As others arrived, work began in earnest.

Major tasks include erecting seasonal tent cabins, activating water and sewer systems, and getting the corral ready for stock. A large assortment of equipment and supplies is brought to the high country: cash registers, park newspapers, maps, and office equipment. The ambulance and fire truck were prepared for service along with the emergency equipment and medical supplies. Radios, firearms, vehicles, and even new flags came out of winter storage. I was always glad to see the horses and mules arrive with a truckload of hay.

May 26, 1982—Packed up and went to Tuolumne—hooray! Moved into our cabin and gear into RO. Mead and I shoveled out Ferdinand's cabin with the help of a loader. Moved rescue cache and shoveled out Fred's tent. Locked up the ski hut; took down avalanche signs. Moved wood from cabin closets. Fair and warm, tired.

Moving Ferdinand Castillo into his quarters at Tioga Pass was an annual ritual. Usually, it took hours to shovel into the front door and remove window shutters and get the entrance kiosk ready for business. Ferdinand was always eager to return to his beloved pass, and it was good to have him there to watch over things.

Life in camp was pretty austere early in the season. Having potable water and the ability to take a shower was most important. It took time to thaw out pipes and get the sewer plant functional. There usually wasn't water until early June. On June 13, 1981, I noted it was 19°F and the pipes had broken. We hauled water in large milk cans from nearby Tioga Pass Resort. I took lots of sink baths and a few dips in the river to get clean after a hard day's work. It's amazing how a hot shower lifts your spirits!

Camp "Springs" to Life

May 21, 1981—Went to Tuolumne with a load of household goods. Took Ferdinand to Lee Vining with the remit, he got groceries, etc. Helped Donna move beds, she's cleaning the cabin. Swept out four tents.

It was always good to see the seasonal staff again: Fred, Smitty, Roger, Sarah, Adele, and many more. There was a general air of excitement in camp. Everyone was eager to go to work, old friendships renewed. I was particularly glad for the help and didn't feel so alone if something happened. There was so much to do—keys, badges, and radios issued and scheduling, readying the campground, and firearms qualifications for the rangers. Donna pitched in, sweeping out tent cabins, splitting kindling, filling woodboxes, and laying the first fire in stoves. It made folks feel welcome, and they appreciated the thoughtfulness, especially as most arrived late in the day after a long drive.

With more people in camp, the "bear wars" began. Just out of hibernation, they eagerly scrounged for food. We were all scrupulous about food storage, but bears still broke into tent cabins looking for food. Trapping and darting bears was not what I wanted to do at the end of a long day, but it had to be done.

Living and working in Tuolumne was one of the best-kept secrets in the park. People were devoted to the place, and many had worked there for years. There was a camaraderie not found in other parts of the park. Lasting friendships formed, and people worked as a team. In those days, whole families came for the summer. One year, there were 10 kids in camp. It felt a bit like summer camp.

My philosophy was to hire the best people and give them latitude to make decisions, think for themselves, and let them do their jobs. As a result, they performed to their full potential and made my job easier. It's a solid way to build trust and loyalty, and people wanted to return year after year.

The Evolution of Our Summer Home

My assignment as assistant sub-district ranger in 1979 forced a major change in our housing arrangements. Crane Flat remained our primary residence, but we moved to Tuolumne in the summers. In our seven years there, we lived in a variety of seasonal housing.

Our first "house" was a canvas tent with hard wooden siding, erected over a concrete slab. The front half of the structure had a small wood-stove for heating and cooking, a small refrigerator, and a sink with "extra cold" running water. A picnic table in the front half served as the dining area of the "great room." The rear of the tent was for sleeping with either bunk beds or a makeshift double bed. All the seasonals had this type of accommodation. Only the sub-district ranger and naturalist supervisor had small cabins.

Living in a tent structure had its moments. One day, an intense thunderstorm rolled directly over camp with hail, wind, and lightning. Donna was in the front of the tent when there was a bright flash followed by an immediate loud clap of thunder directly overhead. A giant blue spark exploded from the sink spigot, hitting the frying pan in the sink. The bolt had struck the exposed water line outside the tent. No one was injured, but it's still a topic of conversation in our house!

Donna was pregnant with our first child that summer, and I lobbied management to improve our quarters for the next season. We would have an infant, and I wanted something warm and sturdy. As a result of my persistence, a new "hardtop" design was to be constructed and tested for future use. If it worked well, it might be used for rangers who arrived early and stayed late, eliminating the annual chore of putting up and taking down canvas.

A new frame, sheathed in plywood with an insulated metal roof, was constructed in the spring of 1980. I scrounged a five-gallon electric hot water heater for the "kitchen" sink. Having hot water in the house with a new baby was a real blessing.

When I became the sub-district ranger in 1981, we moved into the historic permanent ranger cabin built in 1924. It was a frame structure with a woodstove, a kitchen, and a larger sleeping arrangement. This cabin was used in winter by snow survey crews. The winter rangers lived in the visitor center with no indoor plumbing. Melting huge amounts of snow for water was very labor intensive. People were constantly moving in and out of these buildings for summer and winter operations. There had to be a better solution.

Plans for a new winterized cabin were finalized in 1982. Donna and I eagerly participated in the design. A drilled well eliminated the need for winter rangers to melt snow for water. The cabin had indoor plumbing: sink, toilet, and shower. The house was super-insulated, with electric heat and a modern, efficient woodstove. There was also an electric range, a refrigerator, and a root cellar for bulk food storage. A loft provided additional space for storage or sleeping. It was pretty luxurious by Tuolumne standards!

Marilyn Muse and husband Jim Harper were the first winter residents, and the cabin worked exceptionally well. My family moved in the following spring, and this was our summer home until I transferred to Glacier. We were very grateful for the conveniences in the shoulder seasons, especially with two small children.

Our Family Grows

November 11, 1979—Our long-awaited baby is here!! Went to Sonora at 0300, it was raining and snowing so we took the Land Rover Arrived at hospital 0415. Our baby arrived at 1312, by Caesarian. Her name is Kelly Ann, 7 lbs. 7 oz. 19.5". I was in the OR for the whole thing. Quite a day. I came back to Crane Flat 2130, very tired but very happy.

I include this entry because it's one of the most momentous events in our lives. In the busy summer of 1979, we were expecting our first child. Donna was a trooper through it all, shoveling snow, splitting wood, living in a tent, and hiking countless miles. She even climbed the backside of Half Dome on the cables! It was a 60-mile drive to the hospital in Sonora in the dark, and, of course, it was snowing.

November 11, 1982—Katie Beth Habecker born at 0759, 7 lbs. 5 oz. All went well. I spent most of the day at the hospital. Made lots of phone calls. Picked Kelly up at Peterson's about 1730—she wasn't too excited to have a little sister. Home for supper, built fire, and to bed, very tired but happy.

Yes, you read it correctly: our second child born on the same day as the first, three years later—another momentous event in our lives. It was a good year.

Raising children in a national park is a unique undertaking. Crane Flat was rather isolated; there were no other children in the area. Our kids had contact only with adults and matured quickly. Living in the park, they were exposed to opportunities that most children never experience. They got to see bears being immobilized; built snow caves; got to ride on horses, snowmobiles, and boats; learned to ski at age three; and grew up with a profound appreciation of the natural world. They didn't understand what a unique childhood they had until they went away to college. The girls soon realized that their experiences were far different from others and began to appreciate the special world they grew up in. Their lives have been enriched beyond measure thanks to growing up in the parks.

"Rangers of God" and Sir Edmund Hillary

October 7, 1982—Left at 0800 and trailered to Tenaya to ride to Sunrise High Sierra Camp. No water there. Rode on to Cathedral Pass and Lakes, then to the Meadows, a total of 15 miles in six hours. Saw 55 people, a lot for this time of year as the weather is good.

An enjoyable perk of working in Tuolumne was the opportunity to patrol on horseback. Visitors love seeing a ranger on a horse; it's what they envision we all do. It's been said that "no one pets a patrol car," but people are drawn to a horse. Riding across the meadows and trails allowed me to clear my mind and relieve some stress.

Sitting on a horse gives a perspective unseen in a patrol car. People were totally unaware when I quietly rode into their camp. One fine day as I was riding through the campground, I heard someone say, "Don't ride the animals, brother." I stopped, looked around, and heard it again: "Don't ride the animals." I saw a rather unkempt man in a group of "nontraditional" visitors looking at me. I said, "Sir, I'm a ranger, and riding this horse is part of my job." The man said, "I'm a ranger too. A ranger of God." We had an agreeable chat about animal cruelty and parted ways amicably.

You just never know what's going to happen next. One day, Steve Hickman and I were chatting in the ranger station when we got word that someone was trying to climb nearby Lembert Dome. The report was that the person was ill equipped and didn't seem to know what he was doing. Steve and I went to investigate.

A short drive from the ranger station, Lembert Dome is a massive granite monolith that rises gradually at the base, then gets very steep very quickly. It is not a place usually climbed, but people can easily scramble up the first 50 feet. After that, the slope rapidly increases, as does the danger of falling.

Arriving, we saw a young man dressed in jeans and T-shirt about 100 feet up the slope. He was tied into a cotton clothesline-type rope and was pounding large spikes into a crack with a hammer. This guy was not Sir Edmund Hillary! We shouted up to him, telling him he really should come down, that he was in a precarious position and in imminent danger of falling. He said something about knowing what he was doing, "I'm okay," and so on. Our concern for his safety didn't seem to faze him.

We knew this guy was going to fall—it was only a matter of time. A small crowd gathered to watch. Steve and I came up with a plan. In a loud voice, I said, "Steve, you should go back to the rescue cache and get the body bag."

Steve said something like, "Yeah, looks like we'll need it."

Then I shouted up to the guy and asked him for his name and address and next of kin. This got his attention.

He said, "Why do you want that?"

I replied that *when* he fell, it would make it easier for us to identify his remains. There was a long silence, then the would-be mountaineer slowly began to inch his way back to the ground—crisis averted.

And Too Soon, It's Over

September 7, 1981—Went riding with Smitty, our annual ride before he leaves. Looked for an 18 y/o boy who is mentally disabled, found at Ghost Forest. Also, there was a hasty search for an overdue hiker who was found. Took an auto-burg report. Someone drove across the Meadow right across from the RO—why do people think they can just drive anywhere? Checked folks out, everyone is leaving to go back to his or her real life.

It was an end-of-season tradition for Smitty and me to take a leisurely horseback ride before he left for his home in San Jose, California. You've seen Tom "Smitty" Smith's name many times in this book. Tom migrated from South Bend, Indiana, to San Jose, where he taught high school and eventually headed the park management program at West Valley College. Smitty is responsible for many young people making a career in parks and recreation. Beginning as a seasonal backcountry ranger in 1973, he and his family spent summers at the isolated Buck Camp ranger patrol cabin. He became a frontcountry horse patrolman and worked with me in Tuolumne. He and wife Mildred became surrogate grandparents to our kids and remain two of our most treasured friends. I valued Tom's counsel and appreciated when he took me aside to tell me I was doing something dumb. I have fond memories of our time together on these rides.

September 5, 1983—Labor Day and people are clearing out. Smitty, Adele, Maureen leaving. Went to Snow Flat to do some work on the cabin. Home late 2030.

In what seemed like no time at all, it was time to pack up and leave. Donna and I began a tradition that we carried with us to other parks. In August before everyone started to leave, we hosted a "Thanksgiving" dinner for the staff, complete with turkey and all the trimmings. It was our way of saying thanks for all the hard work everyone had done. It was a time for everyone to come together and celebrate the season, have an evening of fellowship, and wish each other well.

Labor Day was my favorite holiday. Visitors left in droves, campgrounds emptied out, and a constant stream of traffic exited the park. The next day, Tuolumne was a ghost town. I was always sorry to see the seasonal staff leave. They worked hard for little pay, and the job couldn't be done without them. Suddenly, there were only a few of us left, waiting for the big snow that would close the road for the season.

October 13, 1980—17°F this morning. Pipes are frozen. Patrolled to Tioga. Began taking corral down, cleaned out the barn. Fixed window pane in fee office. Split wood for snow survey at ranger cabin.

Closing the area for the season was the reverse of spring opening. Everything that was hauled up for summer had to be removed for winter storage. I was always sorry to see the stock go back to the Valley. There was firewood to split and stack for winter operations, Snow Flat cabin had to be stocked for winter use, and snow survey equipment had to be checked. It was a race against time, as it could dump snow at any moment.

November 8, 1981—Closed Tuolumne as a storm is predicted. Put up avalanche signs, dropped side road chains, locked shutters and moved out.

November 9, 1981—Of course—it didn't snow and the road opened at 1300. I'm getting tired of this!

Once all the work was done, there wasn't much to do but watch the weather forecast and wait for snow. One quiet fall day, ranger Ken Kehrer and I, bored and with nothing to do, engaged in shooting confiscated bottle rocket fireworks at each other—not OSHA approved or very professional behavior, but you had to be there to appreciate it.

November 8, 1982—Snowing at 0500, ate a quick breakfast and closed the road for winter at 0915. High of 21°F. Snowed all day, moved out and home at 1700. Took Ferdinand to Buck Meadows and could barely see to drive home. Home at 1930, all closed up.

Closing the road for winter was the last task. This was made more difficult by erratic weather that dumped just enough snow to force a closure, then get warm and melt things out. There was a constant battle about keeping the road open as long as possible with pressure applied by east-side businesses. I just wanted to swing the gates and go home.

It was imperative to get everyone out when it snowed. This involved driving to every parking lot, trailhead, side road, and turnout to make sure everyone was gone. An October 1981 storm was unusual because it included thunder and lightning. I stopped at a large RV parked in the lot at the visitor center. It was dark, snowing hard. I knocked on the door, and just as the man opened it, a bolt of blue lightning lit up the entire sky, immediately followed by a deafening explosion of thunder. I said to the man, "It's time to go, sir." He turned white and said, "Yes sir, yes sir, we're going right now." I couldn't help but smile as I escorted him over Tioga Pass to safety.

FERDINAND—MR. TIOGA

What a lucky guy.

—Ferdinand Castillo

If you ever entered Yosemite by the Tioga Pass entrance during the 1960s through the early 1990s, chances are good that you were greeted by a short man dressed in an impeccable uniform, wearing his ranger flat hat. He was the only park employee with just his first name on his nametag: "Ferdinand."

Ferdinand Joseph Castillo was born in San Francisco in 1917. Orphaned at age four, he was raised by the Dominican Sisters in Ukiah,

California. Trained as a teacher, Ferdinand taught for a year, then enlisted in the U.S. Marine Corps in 1942. He served three years in the Pacific theater and later in the Korean conflict. He was a true patriot.

As a teacher, Ferdinand had summers free and became a career seasonal park technician in 1954. His 40-year career was mostly as a fee collector at Yosemite's Tioga Pass entrance. He greeted each carload with a smile and sometimes a corny joke and made them feel as if they were the most important people of the day. He became a legend, with generations of visitors returning to see the "guy at Tioga Pass."

Ferdinand's many idiosyncrasies included keeping foot traffic off wildflowers, asking visitors to stop for the raising and lowering of the flag, and paying the fees for nuns and marines. A weather buff, his weather observations and "forecasts" were folksy but often accurate. He hoped against all hope that good weather would prevail so that he could remain at Tioga Pass for as long as possible. Tioga Pass was truly his home.

Ferdinand's money till was always spot on, and he hated the term "fee collector." Instead, he liked being called a ranger. He had a canned spiel about paying an entrance fee and retaining the "permit"—never to be called a "receipt." His extended dialogue with visitors, causing long lines of traffic to back up, eventually became his downfall.

When bikers arrived at the gate, he made them—even Hell's Angels—pay their fees and line up so that the traffic counter would count their motorcycles. He called them "lean-backers" and let us know via radio that "six lean-backers just entered the park." Thanks, Ferdinand.

"Coffee, double cream, double sugar. Meat sandwich on white bread" was Ferd's standard order when one of us went to Tioga Pass Resort, just down the hill. We never paid for anything for him; either he had a tab going or the owners comped the food. I took him to Lee Vining occasionally for groceries and a cooked meal, but he had plenty of food and goodies that visitors dropped off. Folks gave him fresh trout, fruit and vegetables, and baked goods—way more than he could ever eat. He was a pack rat and never discarded anything, and I often threw food away when he departed for the season.

June 5, 1980—Went to get Ferdinand and took him to the pass. About 8–9' of snow in Dana Meadows, 10–15' cuts on the east side. Went to

TPR for coffee, they are digging out. Shoveled out Ferdinand's quarters with help of the Cal Tran's loader. Got shutters off kiosk. Checked out the RO, VC, etc. put up "thin ice" signs on Tenaya Lake.

Never an easy task, it was my responsibility to see that Ferdinand got moved in and out each season. He was eager to come in spring and reluctant to leave in fall. He was never ready to leave despite my repeated warnings to get things packed and organized. He was sure that the station would remain open regardless of dire weather forecasts. Sometimes, I spent hours getting his things packed and securing the station while a blizzard raged outside. At times, we barely made it out, with high winds, poor visibility, and snow piling up. I confess I got angry with him, and he once admitted he was "stubborn." He never swore, and the worst thing I ever heard him say was, "Crimeny crap."

ONCE A MARINE . . .

One last Ferdinand story captures the essence of the man. At 6 a.m. on November 11, 1980, park dispatch called me inquiring about road conditions. It was raining at 6,000 feet and probably snowing at higher elevations. I called Tioga Pass. When Ferdinand didn't answer the phone or his radio, I knew something was wrong. Then I remembered that he always attended the Marine Corps birthday bash in the Valley, a lavish affair held at the Awahnee Hotel by the head of concessions, a former marine. Where could Ferdinand be?

Concerned, I informed Bob of the situation, and together we drove up the Tioga Road to investigate. It was snowing at 7,000 feet, the road turning slushy. Driving on, we began to see faint footprints in the snow. There were no other cars, the footprints a mystery. On a long straightaway just east of White Wolf, 12 miles from Crane Flat, we saw a solitary figure, head bowed, walking in the middle of the road. It was Ferdinand, dressed in light shoes, no hat or gloves, wearing his heavy olive drab military-style coat. We were stunned to see him.

I don't know what possessed us at the time, but we decided to have a little fun and maybe teach him a lesson. We drove slowly by him, waved, and kept on going. Looking in the mirror, we saw him stop, hands on hips with an astonished look on his face. Maybe it was cruel, but we couldn't help laughing as we turned around, picked him up, and gave him some coffee from our thermos. He was laughing too: "Crimeny sakes! What a nerve," one of his favorite sayings.

After attending the party, Ferd had gotten a ride to Crane Flat. He walked right past my house without asking for help, certain that he would get a ride to Tioga Pass, 47 miles away. He'd walked all night in the rain and snow, but no one came. "I could have made it," he said, and maybe this tough little marine could.

THE LAST GOOD-BYE

Things began to unravel for Ferdinand after I left for a new job. By 1990, his age was catching up to him, and he slowed down as visitation increased. His lengthy interaction with visitors resulted in complaints about long lines and wait times at the entrance station. In 1993, he was reassigned to the much-slower-paced Hetch Hetchy entrance. In other words, he was ratholed where no one would complain about him.

Always hopeful of returning to Tioga Pass and with letters and newspaper articles of support, Ferdinand passed away at the age of 76 after the summer of 1993. I think he died of a broken heart.

In the summer of 1994, I flew from Alaska to participate as part of a mounted honor guard in a memorial service for Ferdinand. A small plane circled overhead, scattering his ashes over Tioga Pass, the place he loved. If there's an entrance station to heaven, Ferdinand is there.

Ferdinand was the first person I met when we drove into Yosemite that September day in 1974, and he was the last person to say good-bye when I left, exactly 11 years later. Both of us stood at the pass in the cold and wind, hugging and weeping. He was my friend, and I will never forget him.

MOVIN' ON

People ask how rangers transfer to a new job. Many think we receive "orders" like the military and are gone. It's not like that. Essentially, you can stay in one place if you desire. However, if you want to advance your career, you usually have to move.

Early in my career, transfers were generated from the Washington Office using an annual skills survey everyone completed. Parks with job vacancies received a list of eligible candidates from an archaic sorting system of punch cards. I received several job offers out of the blue but wasn't ready to leave. This system evolved into service-wide vacancy announcements sent nationwide from parks with job openings. You applied and waited for a call that never came. Today, this is all done by computer.

By the early 1980s, our lives had changed, and we were ready to move on. Our two daughters were approaching school age. While Yosemite was a great place for a green ranger to learn the ropes, making arrests, treating injured persons, and investigating car wrecks were taking their toll. I wanted more experience in resource management beyond darting bears.

In February 1985, I applied for the vacated Lake McDonald Sub-District ranger position in Glacier, located at park headquarters in West Glacier. The job involved resource management duties, including bald eagle management, river and lake patrol, grizzly bear management, and structural and wildland fire responsibilities. There was an elementary school right in town. It was just what we were looking for, and the long wait began.

A busy summer went by. I met Robert Redford and other dignitaries at the ceremony for the dedication of Mount Ansel Adams held in Tuolumne Meadows. I tried to stay focused on my job, but Glacier was always in the back of my mind. Through the ranger rumor mill, I learned that I had made the list of "highly qualified" candidates. Maybe I had a chance.

July 29, 1985—Off today. Ron Bryan and I went to Granite Lakes fishing, each caught six—very windy. Returning, I learned that Glacier NP had called to offer me the Lake McDonald position, which I immediately accepted! I can't believe it! A dream-come-true. We will be leaving this place I love. We are both very thrilled. Went home to Crane Flat, emotionally drained!

The next five weeks passed quickly. I trained my interim replacement. Seasonal staff were leaving. I realized, sadly, that I would never see most

The last good-bye with my friend Ferdinand, September 4, 1985

of these fine people again. There was a good old-fashioned farewell pot-luck, complete with campfire, at Tuolumne. All our friends and neighbors were there. We were very moved by their generosity and warm wishes.

The day came to turn in my keys and badge and sign the paperwork. Our moving van came; all our worldly goods fit in a third of a semitrailer. Bets were taken on whether the Land Rover would make it to Montana (it did). One final dinner with best friends, one last night in our little house by the meadow.

On September 4, our van pulled out, and we said our final good-byes. Teary eyed, we drove through Tuolumne for the last time, said a few quick good-byes, and drove to Tioga Pass. It was snowing as Ferdinand and I said what would be our final good-bye, crying and awkwardly wishing each other well. Our Yosemite adventure had ended, but a new one awaited in Montana.

PART III

Glacier

Crown of the Continent

If it isn't God's backyard, He certainly lives nearby.

—Robin Williams, while shooting a movie in Glacier, August 2014

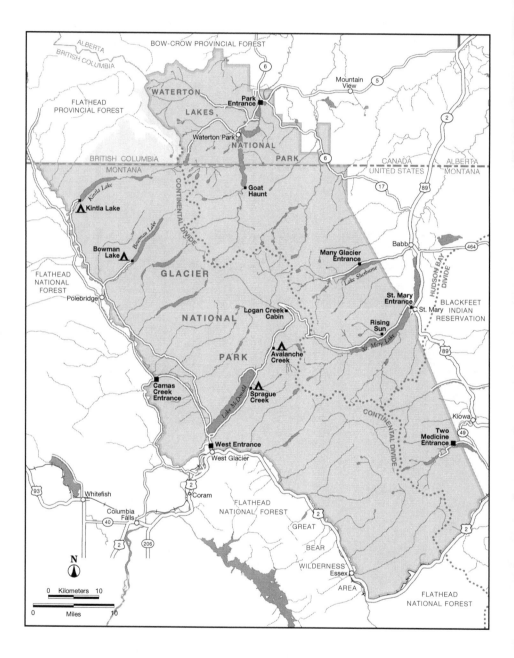

NEW BEGINNINGS

With Yosemite in our rearview mirror, we drove north, the rugged Sierra to the west, and crossed the sagebrush flats of eastern Oregon and southern Idaho. At the Lochsha River in Idaho, we retraced the trail of Lewis and Clark, crossing into Montana at Lolo Pass.

At a turnout north of Missoula, we got our first view of Flathead Lake. It was very windy, the sapphire blue waters whipped into a frenzy of whitecaps. The 30-mile-long lake looked like an ocean. Snow-capped peaks of the Mission Range and emerald green forests completed the scene. We immediately fell in love with Montana!

Two hours later, we crossed the bridge over the Middle Fork of the Flathead River and saw the sign: Glacier National Park. We made it despite the jesting that our Land Rover wouldn't.

It was Saturday, and no one was around at park headquarters. We found a ranger, Gerry Bell, who told us we weren't expected until next week. After some frantic phone calls, Gerry received authorization to have us stay two nights at the Apgar Village Lodge on the shore of Lake McDonald. Like the iconic view of Yosemite Valley, our first view of the 10-mile-long lake didn't seem real—it looked like a painting. There were spectacular snow-covered peaks of the Livingston Range soaring up to the Continental Divide, jade-green forests, and the glacially carved valley cradling the deep blue lake.

We were eager to explore and took a Sunday drive up Going-to-the-Sun Road. It was snowing as we climbed, and the road was getting hazardous. Rounding a curve, a large grizzly bear stood up on its hind legs right in front of our car. It was the first "grizz" any of us had ever seen, and we were impressed. Gerry was astonished when we told him about the encounter and said, "You've only been here a day and already saw a grizzly. Most folks *never* see one!"

THE PARK

Tucked away in the northwestern corner of Montana, hard against the Canadian border, Glacier is often called the "Switzerland of America." Spectacular mountain scenery, huge lakes and rivers, glaciers, abundant wildlife, and historic landmark hotels distinguish this crown jewel of the park system. Established in 1910, the million-acre park shares a boundary with Waterton Lakes National Park in Alberta, forming Waterton-Glacier International Peace Park.

The glaciers, of course, are the main attraction. If you want to see one, you better visit soon, for they are disappearing fast. In 1850, there were nearly 150 glaciers in the park. Today, there are only 26, remnants of once-vast fields of flowing ice. Scientists estimate that all the park's active glaciers will disappear by 2030. Sadly, Glacier has become the poster child for the effects of climate change.

Going-to-the-Sun Road, a national civil engineering landmark and one of the most spectacular scenic drives in America, traverses the heart of the park, crossing the Continental Divide at Logan Pass at an elevation of 6,646 feet. If you prefer to hike, there are 745 miles of maintained trails and 65 designated backcountry camping sites to choose from. Just watch out for the grizz.

Wildlife abounds: deer and elk, bighorn sheep, mountain goats, moose, mountain lions, black bear, wolves, and, of course, grizzly bears. Wolves and grizzlies give Glacier a true wilderness atmosphere found in few other parks.

First Impressions

Our moving van arrived, and we settled into our new home. It was a far cry from the CCC-built house at Crane Flat. This was a modern ranch-style house, built as part of the Mission 66 program that pumped millions of dollars into park infrastructure between 1956 and 1966. Hundreds of employee housing units and other infrastructure were built during that decade, using common housing floor plans with few variations from park to park.

The three-bedroom house had an open living room and kitchen, a full basement, an attached garage, and an outdoor patio with a spacious backyard. We were now living at park headquarters among dozens of other people. The housing area was adjacent to the offices and maintenance shops. There were lots of kids, and my girls were pretty excited to finally have playmates. The park's community center hosted all kinds of park and community events, and the small town of West Glacier, with the elementary school, post office, and seasonal businesses, was a short walk across the river bridge. The towns of Columbia Falls, Kalispell, and Whitefish, each less than an hour away, offered all amenities. It was odd at first to find ourselves living at the edge of a vast wilderness with "civilization" minutes away. Suddenly, life was less complicated for us.

I was excited to be here and begin my new job. The next few weeks were a blur of meeting new people, seeing the country, and learning how I fit in. Lou Hendrix, West Lakes district ranger, showed me around. In the North Fork Sub-District, I met ranger Jerry DeSanto, one of the last "old-time" rangers. Jerry was a local legend who relished being away from the hustle and bustle of headquarters and roaming the wilds of the northern part of the park. He once had been mauled by a grizzly on one of his patrols. Soft spoken, he welcomed me to the staff.

Walton Sub-District was next. Sub-district ranger Charlie Logan showed me what he could of his mostly wilderness domain and the Middle Fork of the Flathead River. Walton is located on the southern tip of the park near the rail stop of Essex. Charlie was an experienced ranger, having worked in Rocky Mountain National Park before coming to Glacier. A first-class mountaineer and skier, Charlie was the go-to guy for any technical rescue work. He finished his career in Glacier, eventually moving up to the West Lakes District ranger position. He is highly respected by his peers and is one of the finest rangers I've had the pleasure to work with.

As a headquarters ranger, I had frequent contact with management, something uncommon for me in Yosemite. Superintendent Bob Haraden, a veteran Park Service employee, began his career as a civil engineer in the 1950s. A taciturn Maine native, Bob made the tough decisions and sought advice from others. He was one of the last old-time superintendents and well respected.

Chief ranger Chuck Sigler had come up through the ranks and ran a tight ship. He had been a helicopter pilot and smoke jumper in his early years. Chuck always presented a relaxed, calm demeanor, and I never saw him angry. It didn't matter what you did as long as your uniform was perfect. After I got to know him, Chuck told me how I had been selected for the job. He said, "We kept seeing your name show up on the highly qualified candidate list, and you always scored in the top two. When I saw your name again, I said, 'We better hire this guy, he really wants to come here.'" Chuck was a gentleman who treated us fairly, and we tried to do a good job for him.

The two most important people in my own staff were Dan O'Brien and Gerry Bell. These two permanent rangers supervised a combined total of 28 seasonals. Dan specialized in wildland fire and was highly ranked in the national incident command structure. He supervised the fire crew and SAR team. He also directed the bear team, which was responsible for getting bear information out to the public, patrolling trails, and posting trail closures. Dan was the man when it came to trapping or immobilizing bears. I relied on him for advice about many things; he also had a wealth of local knowledge.

Gerry Bell supervised the road patrol operation, entrance station fee collection, and campgrounds—a big job. As a marine, Gerry saw intense combat action in the Pacific. A "fitness nut," he put us young guys to shame and played racquetball with a passion. Gerry knew everyone and all the local politics and intrigues. He quietly took care of business, always one step ahead of me. I didn't have to worry about much with these two guys doing their jobs so well. As a new sub-district ranger, they made my life much easier.

We settled into our new world. Six-year-old daughter Kelly started first grade at the West Glacier School. Katie, three years of age, enthusiastically attended a local preschool right in the housing complex. Donna busied herself with setting up the house and began making new friends.

For the first time in my career, I had my own office. The West Lakes District office was located in a beautiful old log structure, built in 1924, as the original park headquarters. I scored a spacious corner office with a view of the mountains and the river just down the hill. It was only a few blocks from my house, and I could go home for lunch.

At first, I was wary about working at park headquarters. I had always worked mostly alone in a small office setting with a few close friends. Suddenly, I found myself amid the hustle and bustle of offices and shops and 100 other employees. There were people coming and going, phones ringing, and meetings to attend. Gradually, I began to adjust and found myself liking the activity. As the headquarters ranger, I was pulled in many directions and got involved in things that rangers in outlying districts were not exposed to.

When I accepted the job, I didn't realize how multifaceted it was. This was the busiest sub-district in the park. There was the usual SAR, law enforcement, and EMS. I was responsible for patrol of 32 miles of park road from headquarters to the Continental Divide at Logan Pass; fee collection at two entrance stations and four campgrounds; structural fire protection for more than 100 offices, homes, private inholdings, and businesses; and a large historic hotel. I supervised a bear management team, backcountry operation, boating safety on Lake McDonald, and river patrols on the North and Middle forks of the Flathead River. And, oh yes, I was to serve as the park representative on the Kalispell Regional Hospital's air ambulance board of directors. This was far more complex than my Yosemite position.

It was fall, and, as in Yosemite, there were things to do to prepare for the long winter ahead. We stocked cabins, removed buoys and floats from the lake, and placed boats and bear traps in storage. The fire trucks were chained up, ready for ice and snow.

When conditions warranted, we closed the Going-to-the-Sun Road. It was a similar procedure to the Tioga Road process, but there was far less pressure to keep this road open. Few local businesses operated in winter, and the road wasn't a major traffic corridor. Because of avalanche danger, the road crew removed roadside guardrails each winter to allow avalanches to blast over the road without destroying the log barriers. Once this was done, the road remained closed. There were few visitors way up in Montana at this time of year, so things were pretty quiet.

EARLY MORNINGS ON THE MIDDLE FORK

October 27, 1985—The first day of hunting season: Dan and I on patrol at 0630. Checked access points to Nyack and along the railroad ROW (right-of-way). Went to a hunter's camp, an elk went into the park. Drove them to Flathead road, no elk. Fed the horses. Rechecked Nyack. Beaver cuttings in the river. Beautiful warm day.

Opening day of hunting season was a big deal. There were many elk inside and outside the park, and hunting pressure was intense. The town golf course attracted a resident population of elk that attracted a resident population of hunters. It got pretty crazy.

Railroad maintenance roads provided easy access to hunters looking for elk that came out of the park and crossed the river. If a hunter shot an elk and it ran into the park, regulations required them to contact a ranger who would verify where the animal was shot and supervise retrieval of the carcass. This wasn't easy, as it required crossing the river by canoe to get to the park side. Once the shooting started, elk ran into the park for safety. Dan showed me all the access points and traditional trouble spots. I spent long hours cruising the highway and railroad right-of-way looking for hunters.

I've always loved this time of year, and autumn in Glacier was spectacular. Larch trees, a deciduous evergreen, turn golden yellow and cast off their needles. The hillsides were a patchwork of shades of yellow larch, aspen, and birch, interspersed with splashes of bright red mountain maple and ash. Cottonwoods along the river glowed in the sun. Early snow dusted the peaks. The morning air was crisp and clean.

Boundary patrol days saw me up before sunrise, sitting along the swirling green waters of the Middle Fork, watching the dawn creep down the craggy, snow-covered peaks of the Livingston Range: Stimson, Threesuns, Loneman, and the sharp elf hat of St. Nicholas glowing rosy pink in the distance. As the air warmed, light fog rose from the river, and I could hear the sound of whirring wings of a flight of mergansers skimming over the water on their way to breakfast. Meadows covered in frost glistened in the new sunlight. If I was lucky, I might hear the distant bugle of a bull elk looking for a mate in some quiet glade over in the park. Time for a cup of coffee from that thermos. I loved this new place, so different from the Sierra.

I found the rescue cache and structural fire gear in total disarray. Equipment was antiquated, disorganized, and not up to modern standards. I asked my boss for money to fix things and got $5,000 from the chief ranger's account. I sought Charlie Logan's advice and had John Dill send photos of Yosemite's state-of-the art rescue cache. I went to work: new "blitz packs" that contained all the gear for a technical rescue, inventoried and weighed for helicopter ops, and upgraded medical gear and a drug pack for my use as a medic. I purchased some new climbing ropes and modern hardware, headlamps, and new avalanche beacons. I purchased a generator and portable lighting for night operations and got all the avalanche response gear marked and consolidated in rescue-ready packs.

Fire turnouts—helmets, coats, bunker pants, boots, and gloves—hung on hooks, all mixed together. How could anyone find their stuff when the alarm sounded? This was unacceptable. I built lockers for each person, labeled gear with their names, put fresh batteries in flashlights, and purchased personal locator beacons for each firefighter. Folks were pleased to find their equipment all in one place, ready to respond. I spent most of the winter picking away at this massive project and was satisfied with the end result. It was a good start on my belief that one should leave a place better than one found it.

EAGLES ON MCDONALD CREEK

November 12, 1985—Took Supt. Haraden and Supt. of Waterton Lakes NP down McDonald Creek in a canoe. Counted 454 eagles, including an albino. It was 0°F when we started. Saw a grizzly track on the shore. Cold but a great experience for all.

Each fall in the early 1980s, hundreds of American bald eagles congregated along McDonald Creek to feast on spawning kokanee salmon. It was an artificial fishery, the salmon migrating from Flathead Lake where *Mysis* shrimp had been introduced. Hundreds of visitors came to watch the spectacle. Our job was to try to maintain viewing opportunities for people without disturbing the birds. It was easier to manage eagles than people.

Park biologists conducted weekly eagle censuses by canoeing down McDonald Creek. On this cold day, I was tasked with taking two superintendents down the creek in a canoe. Although I was an experienced canoeist, I was apprehensive of dumping this precious cargo into the creek.

Placing a transmitter on a bald eagle.

It was a cold, clear morning, mist rising off the water, ice on the shore, as we quietly drifted down the creek, hundreds of eagles all around us. It turned out to be a great experience for all.

I participated in more counts, used telemetry equipment, and helped put a transmitter on a bird. It was the type of resource management experience I was seeking. A few years later, the shrimp and salmon populations crashed, and the fall gathering of eagles in Glacier was over.

A Day to Remember

January 28, 1986. There are days in our lives that we all remember where we were and what we were doing: the assassination of President John F. Kennedy or the attacks on 9/11. Many will remember the day the space shuttle *Challenger* exploded after liftoff.

I was in town on a day off when someone told me that the space shuttle had exploded, killing all on board. Stunned, I immediately went home to watch the tragedy unfold on TV. Then the fire siren sounded—fire at the West Glacier School. I couldn't comprehend what I was hearing. Fire at the school! My daughter was there! It was a punch in the gut.

Our fire brigade arrived on scene within two minutes. The building was almost fully engulfed in flames. Smoke poured out of the roof, flames shooting out the windows. How could a fire get this large so quickly?

All the kids were safe in the school yard thanks to quick-acting staff who had escorted them past flames through smoke-filled halls. With everyone accounted for and the building fully involved, our strategy was to keep it from spreading to nearby structures. It was all over in an hour—our school, the pride of our community, a pile of ashes.

The entire community was in disbelief. The state fire marshal determined that the fire started in the kitchen when a faulty electric stove failed to shut off after a teacher finished a project melting wax. The fire had spread into the overhead space, undetected until the smoke alarm sounded.

That night, we talked with our daughter Kelly, who was understandably upset about her experience of crawling on hands and knees past flames and dense smoke. Were her friends okay? Where would she go to school now? The park offered its community building for a makeshift school. Our kids went there for the rest of the school year.

The local school district declared that the West Glacier School would cease to exist. Our kids would be bused to other schools. Our community questioned this decision and rallied to rebuild our school. Meetings were held. Everyone felt strongly that we needed a school in our community and that there would be no busing kids over treacherous winter roads. What could we do?

My wife Donna, a professional educator, read the Montana School Code and discovered a section outlining the procedure for forming a new school district. The die was cast. Together with many others, she set about to make it happen. Through bake sales, bingo nights, and donations, we hired an attorney to guide us through the process. It was big news. Articles appeared in the local papers. One day, I came home to lunch and found a TV crew in our living room interviewing my wife. Our phone rang constantly. Donna became the spokesperson of these "radicals" from West Glacier who were defying local authority.

There were hearings, decisions, and appeals. Finally, county commissioners determined that we met all the legal requirements and approved creation of West Glacier Elementary School District Eight. Construction on a new building began in the spring of 1987.

YOU GET PAID TO DO THIS?

January 30, 1986—Dan, Elwood, Jack Potter, and I went to Essex to the Silver Staircase with Charlie to practice ice climbing—my first experience at this—crampons, ice axe, ice screws. It was a lot of fun. I climbed an 80' frozen waterfall! And rappelled off—didn't think I could do it but I did. Rain and snow, home 1800 hours.

Ice climbing was a totally new experience for me. I hadn't lived in a climate consistently cold enough to produce massive ice forms. Standing at the bottom of the vertical turquoise blue frozen waterfall, it looked impossible—there was no way I could get up that thing. I had never worn crampons or used an ice tool, but Charlie, ever the patient instructor, talked me through it, and I found myself really enjoying this new experience.

February 4, 1986. Glacier was very proactive in keeping its rangers well trained and prepared for any situation. On this day, all of the park's rangers skied into Autumn Creek from Marias Pass on the Continental Divide. It was cold and windy as we set up camp in an aspen grove and honed our winter camping skills.

It got even colder as evening approached. Someone suggested we build a fire. Chuck wasn't enthusiastic about that idea—we weren't in a designated camping area. As it got colder, we stamped our feet and moved our arms. Someone said, "Screw this, let's build a fire." We all joined in, gathered wood, and soon had a proper bonfire going. It felt great, and Chuck even admitted it was "probably okay." Someone had a bottle of whiskey that got passed around, and the bullshit stories began to fly—it was so much fun!

It was 8°F the next morning when we broke camp and skied to our training venue. I learned how to use an avalanche beacon (SKADI), construct survival shelters, and package an injured person for transport on a makeshift sled—all skills I later used in real rescues. In a later session, we built snow caves and spent the night in them.

Ice climbing on the Silver Staircase.

Spring Arrives

April 5, 1986—studied ACLS and reviewed Avalanche Plan. Spent all afternoon on GTS road. Made two bicyclists leave above the closure (Loop). Lots of people out enjoying the spring weather. Three boats on the lake, open water with a few "bergs" evident. Saw seven elk and seven goats. Stopped a truck with a rifle in the back rack.

With warm weather, bears emerged from their dens. Dan and I did a snow survey on Mineral Creek and found fresh grizzly prints in our ski tracks on the return trip. Locals knew that bears frequented avalanche chutes looking for carcasses or anything else to eat. People were out in droves, enjoying the park.

As the snows of winter melted, streams and rivers rose, and waterfalls thundered. A few hardy boaters appeared on the lake. Wildlife became more active: goats lost their shaggy winter coats, elk and deer grazed tender shoots on the hillsides, and black bears appeared on roadsides, looking for fresh dandelions. Yes, bears eat lots of greens. Traffic "bear jams" began to happen, something I'd never experienced in Yosemite. I was enthralled by all this wildlife; animals were everywhere in large numbers. Bear cubs and mountain goat kids frolicked in the warm sunshine. Things were greening up, tiny leaves bursting forth on the birch, a few tentative glacier lilies peeking out of the duff. Avalanches roared off the steep cliffs. The park was coming alive, and I enjoyed my first springtime in the Rockies.

The Snowy Torrents: Avalanche Training

May 8, 1986—avalanche training all day. Did SKADI work, ran probe lines and had dogs from the Sheriff's Office on-scene. Beautiful sunny day. Saw a large black bear and snowshoe hare.

It was my responsibility each spring to arrange for avalanche rescue training for the road crew working on the Going-to-the-Sun Road opening. I'd had some very basic avalanche rescue training in Yosemite, but this was a whole other level. I read everything I could and asked Charlie for help.

Spring snow removal on Going-to-the-Sun Road is a massive undertaking, taking months to clear the road for public travel. The upper road is prone to frequent avalanches and rockfall. It's a dangerous place to work, and several workers have been killed over the years. Large pieces of heavy equipment have been swept over the side—there is still a road grader down there in the brush if you know where to look for it.

Everyone was required to wear and be proficient with an avalanche beacon, a small device that sends an electronic signal that can be detected by rescuers. We practiced finding and retrieving buried transceivers and a dummy using long aluminum wands called probes. In subsequent years, I arranged for the ALERT hospital helicopter to fly in a trained avalanche dog and handler and simulated a multi-casualty burial. The dog found the buried dummies within minutes, an impressive feat.

My days were filled with performing safety inspections of the hotel, opening campgrounds, meeting key concession staff and private inholders, responding to false fire alarms, attending bear management training,

A probe line doing avalanche rescue training above the Going-to-the-Sun Road.

and getting familiar with my "fleet" of watercraft. I finalized an agreement with the local hospital to provide a sponsoring physician and serve as our base for the parkmedic program, which was new to them. Shortly after getting the program authorized, a visitor flagged me down and told me his wife was having a miscarriage. I did an IV right there along the road, got her stabilized, and had her flown out on ALERT. The emergency room docs were skeptical at first, but once they saw what a medic could do, they were very excited to have advanced life support in the park.

THE POTLUCK THAT WASN'T

June 13, 1986—Worked 13-2100. Patrol and office. Went to first seasonal potluck but got called out for a carryout at Avalanche Lake: a 200+ lb. woman with fractured ankle. Out at midnight, home 0130, tired.

While at my first Glacier potluck, I received word that a woman had fallen at Avalanche Lake and needed a rescue. It was a short potluck for some of us! I stood up on a picnic table before a large crowd of seasonals and announced I needed 10 people to do a carryout. Someone said, "Who is this guy?" thinking I was joking! They quickly learned that this was the real deal and responded enthusiastically.

After hiking the six uphill miles to the lake, we got the woman into the litter and started back down the trail. I was glad there were at least 10 of us as we stumbled over rocks and roots in the dark and got her down to the road. Why do carryouts always seem to involve heavy people?

The summer wore on. An 81-year-old visitor died of a heart attack on a tour bus. There were the usual motor vehicle accidents, traffic tickets, and minor mayhem. Donna and I hiked the popular Highline Trail to Granite Park and saw moose, mountain goats, bighorn sheep, elk, and two grizzlies—nothing at all like the deer and chipmunks in the Sierra.

As summer was winding down, I grew a bit bored. I hadn't adjusted from the frantic pace of Yosemite. I was waiting for the "big one." As it turned out, I didn't have to wait long.

OVER THE WALL—THE REED FATALITY

August 2, 1986—Checked out a site for swift-water training. A car wreck at 2130, car 500' over the side, one dead. Out until 0400. Had to slide down the hillside to the car, couldn't find the body at first. The car was wrapped around a tree.

The narrow, two-lane Going-to-the-Sun Road hugs the rugged cliffs, winding its way over the Continental Divide. Surprisingly, there have been few accidents over the years; those that have occurred have mostly been due to inattention. However, high speed and alcohol can lead to deadly consequences. This was the first recorded visitor traffic fatality on this famous road.

On August 2, 43-year-old Ross Alden Reed left his home in Alberta, Canada, and crossed the border to meet friends in the Flathead Valley in Montana. He never made it.

At about 2130 hours, I received a call from the Comm Center informing me that seasonal rangers Loren Fredin and Peg Holwick were at the scene of an accident where a vehicle had crashed through the guardrail and was down an embankment. They needed help immediately.

It was dark when I arrived with additional rescue crew and technical climbing gear. Several sections of wooden guardrail were lying in the road. Ranger Brian Kenner, who had arrived previously, and Ranger Holwick located the vehicle over the cliff but no driver or other persons.

As I rappelled down the retaining wall, I began seeing pieces of the car and found the vehicle wrapped around a small tree 550 feet down the embankment. There was evidence of alcohol consumption. Mr. Reed's body was found 350 feet down the slope straddling a broken section of guardrail. There were no signs of life.

I remained with the body while the others went back to the road to formulate an extrication plan. The first tow truck that responded was too small. The extrication would require a much larger rig and closure of the road. Alone in the dark, waiting with the body, I found some huckleberries and ate them. Not an issue in Yosemite, it dawned on me that this was grizzly country and that I was sitting near a large pool of human

Over the wall—the Reed fatality.

blood. All of my senses were on full alert. Fatalities never "freaked me out." People handle death in a variety of ways. I went about the business of taking care of business.

A Stokes litter was sent down, and I managed to get the body in it. Secured to the raising system, I clipped in and radioed for the crew on the road to haul. As I "walked" up the retaining wall with the Stokes, I heard shouts, "Whoa! Stop!" —not something you want to hear while dangling from a rope with a body in the dark. After a pause, the lift proceeded. When I topped out, I learned that the anchor for the lift was Dan's truck and that when the load went vertical, the truck slid sideways into the retaining wall.

Alcohol and speed were factors. A motorcyclist told us he had nearly been run off the road by the convertible. There were no skid marks, so brakes hadn't been applied. My calculations showed that the car had been traveling at a speed beyond which it could make the curve. The car was removed on September 13, requiring several hours of road closure.

A Trail Ride Goes Bad—The Jacobsen Fatality

August 7, 1986—Began working on Reed fatality report. Called out at 1145 to horse accident at head of the lake. Three people were thrown off a concessioner-led horseback ride. One was in critical condition. An on-scene physician did an IV, I applied MAST pants, oxygen, monitor, etc. ALERT flew her out. She died during the night. Others are in the hospital.

It was a beautiful day for a horseback ride. Sixty-four-year-old Geraldine Jacobson from Minnesota was visiting friends in the Flathead. The group of five decided to go to the park and take a concessioner-led trail ride. They booked the morning ride to Paradise Valley, leaving the McDonald Lake corral at about 9 a.m. All went well until the return trip, when something went terribly wrong.

Seasonal ranger Michael Ober was unhooking a horse trailer at the government barn near the Lake McDonald Ranger Station when he heard the clatter of hoofs on the paved road nearby. He saw two riderless horses run by, followed by a woman hanging on to a galloping horse, yelling, "Whoa, whoa." Michael began hearing radio traffic about a horse accident and responded toward the scene.

A Park Service road crew was working with a loader near the junction of the trail with Going-to-the-Sun Road. When the group of riders approached, the horses became skittish and began to shy. As the wrangler began to dismount, his horse started to run, dragging and kicking him in the ribs. Immediately, the other horses turned and bolted, running back the way they had just come. Two of the riders bailed off; three others hung on.

The horses raced full speed down the road toward the ranger station, ending near some private inholdings. A 12-year-old boy and an 18-year-old girl got thrown off. Geraldine held on, her horse running flat out. After about a mile and a half, Geraldine was thrown, landing in the middle of the gravel road.

I began hearing radio traffic about a horse wreck near the head of the lake and responded from headquarters with lights and siren. When

I arrived, Michael was treating the two youths. He told me that a doctor was attending to the third rider. Michael had requested an ambulance and the ALERT helicopter and directed me to Geraldine's location.

When I got to Geraldine, a physician was attempting to start an IV in her hand. Geraldine was unconscious but breathing, and the doctor had placed an oropharyngeal device to maintain her airway. Gerry was bleeding from her head and had shallow respirations, and one pupil was dilated. The doctor, who had been visiting a friend nearby, told me he thought she had a basal skull fracture. I applied MAST, started oxygen, and placed her on the heart monitor. There was a pulse and electrical activity, but her condition was dire. She needed to get to the hospital immediately.

We transported her to the Lake McDonald Lodge, where care was turned over to ALERT medics who intubated Gerry and started another IV. She was flown to Kalispell Regional Hospital and passed away there that night. One rider was hospitalized, the other treated and released.

I began my second fatality investigation for the week. There were interviews, evidence collection, photographs, witness statements, and, later, a board of review. Since this incident involved the park concessioner, it was especially important to do things right. I met with the local U.S. attorney regarding a potential lawsuit. I don't recall if lawsuits were filed. In the end, it was a tragic day for a group of friends who just wanted to have a nice time in the park.

Seasonal ranger Michael Ober did a tremendous job at this chaotic scene. Three people were injured in three different locations. Michael made the right call, allowing the doctor to treat the most severe injury. Michael had the presence of mind to get advanced care rolling his way.

Michael and I became good friends. A backcountry ranger for many years, Michael showed me remote areas of my district that I otherwise would have missed. Although he's now hung up his flat hat, his dedication to the job and protecting park natural resources showed how much he loved Glacier and how he will always be a part of it.

These fatalities were big news. Things like this just didn't happen in Glacier. Some wag at headquarters half jokingly said, "This kind of stuff never happened until you got here." In a perverse sort of way, I was grateful for the action. By Yosemite standards, it had been a slow summer, and I was a tad bored and hadn't learned to slow my pace. I was confident in handling these intense situations; it was what I was used to.

It wasn't all bad. I began working with a horse, Cub, and did some mounted patrols through busy Apgar Village and the campground. Visitors loved seeing a ranger on a horse, and the chief ranger encouraged my initiative. I rode into Trout Lake with Michael and saw the site of the famous grizzly attack detailed in the book *Night of the Grizzly*. I began learning how to row an inflatable raft for river patrols down the North Fork and enjoyed this new challenge. I found that boat patrols on Lake McDonald were a great way to get away from the crowds and relax a bit.

Fall and hunting patrols began—I had come full circle. Chuck called me periodically and said, "Tom, do you have time to take a little ride?" Of course, I always had time for the chief, and he and I would drive up the road and chat about things. He needed to get out of the office even more than I did, and I really began to appreciate his advice and quiet demeanor.

I saw my first wolf tracks and a mountain lion on a hike into Dutch Lake with resource specialist Bill Michels. Bill was a jack-of-all-trades and knew the park well. He specialized in fisheries and water quality. He always was one of the first to respond to fire alarms and pitched in when we needed help on big events. Bill and his wife Sheila became good friends, and we travel to the Flathead to visit a few times a year.

Too Close for Comfort—A Bear Mauling on Elk Mountain

April 25, 1987—Began cleaning the boat. Outfitted patrol car. Drove above the Loop and cited a bicyclist (Saturday). Saw goats. Warm today. Called out at 2345 for overdue hiker at Fielding who had been stalking grizz sow with cubs. Charlie Logan investigating.

This was my first experience with a bear mauling fatality. Charles "Chuck" Gibbs and his wife were returning from a hike near Ole Creek when they spotted several grizzly bears high on Elk Mountain near the southern boundary of the park. Gibbs, a semiprofessional photographer, wanted to get a "really good" photo of bears and told his wife Glenda that he would meet her at the trailhead. After waiting for her husband for four hours, Glenda became concerned and went to the Walton Ranger Station to report Chuck overdue. It was getting dark as Charlie hiked into the area and fired three rifle shots to attract attention. With no response, he returned to the station and asked me to assemble resources for a search the next day. We mustered at daylight on April 26 with 25 searchers and two tracking dogs. An air force helicopter facilitated getting us high up onto the mountain to begin the search. After two hours, we found Gibbs's body 50 yards from a gnarled 30-foot tree. There were claw marks 15 feet up the tree. The bear apparently pulled him down, there was a struggle, and Gibbs staggered away. Gibbs had multiple bites and lacerations on his head, arms, and legs. There was no predation. The .45-caliber semiautomatic Colt pistol (unlawful at the time) that Gibbs was carrying was still in its shoulder holster, unfired.

We recovered Gibbs's camera equipped with a 400-mm lens and sent the film to Kodak to be specially processed as evidence to help reconstruct the incident. The photos revealed that Gibbs had been following a sow grizzly with three cubs much of the afternoon. She was fully aware of his presence; photos showed her looking back at him. As he continued to approach closer, she became more agitated as evidenced by photos of her laid-back ears. Finally, she must have had enough and apparently charged him. He attempted to climb a scrawny tree but was pulled down and mauled.

This was before digital photography, and I wanted to establish a time frame for the incident. One photo showed the Amtrak *Empire Builder* passenger train as it passed westbound far below. I contacted Amtrak and got the exact time the train had passed that point. I made a cardboard silhouette of a bear and used Gibbs's camera and telephoto lens to focus in on the cutout at the approximate distances from the bear in his photos. Measuring from camera to bear in relative size, we determined he had been only a few yards away when he took the last photo.

The incident made national headlines. The park superintendent chose not to destroy the animal, determining that the bear was being harassed and was only trying to protect its young. Mrs. Gibbs strongly supported this and told us that Mr. Gibbs felt that bears could sense that he meant them no harm and would never want a bear destroyed because of his actions.

Déjà Vu—Motorcycle over the Wall

June 4, 1987—Called out at 2100 to a motorcycle wreck at Triple Arches. Brad Cox went over the guardrail and went over 200' down the hillside. Had to rappel down. Got home at 0300.

Déjà vu. Bradley Cox, 32, from Calgary, Alberta, was traveling with a friend on Going-to-the-Sun Road when he lost control of his motorcycle on a series of sharp curves known as the Triple Arches. Cox's bike stopped at the guardrail, but Cox vaulted over the edge, landing 275 feet below.

Again, ranger Loren Fredin was first on the scene. Loren and two visitors climbed down to Cox, who was still alive with shallow breathing and a faint pulse. Loren began CPR, and I got the call to respond.

After gathering rescue equipment, I arrived at the scene 47 minutes later. While I was en route, Fredin told me that Cox had stopped breathing and had fixed and dilated pupils. I did a radio phone patch to the hospital and told the doctor that it would be impossible to continue CPR in this terrain while attempting to raise the person in a litter. The doc told me to place the heart monitor and call him back.

I rappelled over the side, placed Cox on the monitor, and observed asystole—no electrical activity. Cox, who was not wearing a helmet, had an open skull fracture and was obviously dead.

Again, we went through the process of raising the body and retrieving the bike. My investigation showed that Cox had exceeded the critical design speed of the curve and lost control. Another fine day in the park that ended badly.

Back in the Saddle

July 13, 1987—Eric and I rode into Lincoln Lake: put up bear cables (used to hang food), fixed the campground sign and put screen up on the outhouse. Rode 18 miles, a long day but fun. Had trouble loading Frosty. Home 2000.

Eric Morey appears many times in my diary. Eric was a second-generation ranger, his father Bob a legend in Yellowstone and Glacier. Growing up in those parks, it was only natural that Eric would follow in his father's footsteps. Eric is the consummate outdoorsman, expert with firearms and stock, and taught me what little I know about elk hunting.

Eric worked seasonally, then got a permanent job and went on to a successful career, retiring as a district ranger in Yellowstone. I've worked with a handful of exceptional rangers in my career, and Eric is one of them.

July 26, 1987—Up at 0500 and at the barn 0545, met Gerry and trailered horses to Jackson Glacier overlook. On the trail at 0915. Rode to Gunsight Lake/Pass, lunch at Lake Ellen Wilson. Caught some fish, then on to Sperry Chalet for a drink of cold lemonade, then out to Lake McDonald. Home at 2000 hours, tired but a beautiful day.

Gerry Bell was retiring and wanted to make this special trip with me. We hadn't spent much time together in recent months, and this was a great day. Gerry and Dan kept the sub-district functioning smoothly, and I really appreciated their hard work and steady hands. The trip over Gunsight is one of the most scenic in the park, with spectacular alpine scenery, vivid wildflowers, and cold blue lakes. Mountain goats are commonly seen in this region. Gerry was thrilled to show me one of his favorite areas of the park, and it was good to spend the day together. It's hard to believe I was getting paid to ride a horse in such a beautiful place.

These Things Don't Happen in Glacier— The Sniper Incident

October 20, 1987—Off today, fair and cool. Called out at 1645 re: a sniper took a shot at a government pickup truck and hit the driver in

*the stomach, up near Logan Creek. We shut down the road and made
a quick search but found nothing. Up until 2300 making plans for a
law enforcement search of the area using dogs and helo.*

No one expects to be shot at in a national park, but it happened in
Glacier in October 1987. Maintenance foreman Earl Armstrong and his
passenger, Andy Schildt, were driving back to St. Mary on Going-to-the-
Sun Road late in the afternoon on October 20. A short distance west of
Logan Creek, Earl heard a loud noise and felt a stinging sensation in his
stomach. He had been hit by a bullet fragment after it passed through the
left door of his government truck. Earl was not seriously injured, radioed
for help, and pulled into a turnout a quarter of a mile from the shooting.
There, he was interviewed by ranger Bellamy, who collected bullet fragments that were lying on the front seat. This set off a chain of events that
will go down as one of the most bizarre events in Glacier's history.

The fact was that someone had been shooting at Earl and others
over the course of the past five days. Several visitors had reported hearing gunshots in the upper McDonald Creek valley over the past week.
We increased our patrols of the area but never heard shots and couldn't
pinpoint their reported location. On the morning of October 20, as Dan
O'Brien was driving in the area, he thought someone in a passing vehicle
had shot at him. Dan stopped the driver, who said he hadn't heard anything and didn't have any firearms. Later in the day, Earl was shot, and
things rapidly changed.

We immediately closed the road and interviewed people who were
exiting. No one had seen or heard anything. Dan, Charlie Logan, Jim
Bellamy, and I drove to the scene as daylight was fading. After parking
the truck, Dan and I made our way through the brush along McDonald
Creek to an observation point while Charlie and Jim proceeded on in
their pickup. Jim had fortified his truck with a piece of plate steel next
to the door and window. Jim's plan was to drive back and forth and draw
fire. Charlie, who was in the back of the pickup, bailed out along the
roadside to a hidden location where he could observe Jim's actions. Jim
made several trips, but no shots occurred. It was a brave thing to do, and
he later received the Department of Interior Valor Award for his actions.

Two rangers each at Lake McDonald and St. Mary roadblocks secured the road all night. Law enforcement specialist Bob Burns, along with chief ranger Sigler and Jim Bellamy, led a late-night strategy session to plan for the next day. Two local FBI agents were called in, along with a Kalispell Police Department officer and his dog. A helicopter was placed on standby for a possible aerial search.

We gathered at 0600 the next morning to review our plan. At dawn, a strike team of six rangers, FBI agents, and the dog team began searching for the shooter. It was cold and just getting light as we waded across icy McDonald Creek to begin our sweep. It was rough going, with thick brush, rocks, and limited sight distance. This was grizzly habitat, and we were ready to react, armed with handguns and 12-gauge shotguns. As we spread out in a line, I couldn't help thinking to myself how closely this resembled hunting for rabbits when I was a kid—except this time, I could get shot. I was on full alert, hyperaware of my surroundings.

Ranger Roger Semler thought he heard three shots in rapid succession farther up the valley. With adrenaline pumping, we slowly advanced toward the area, fully aware that any of us could be shot at any moment. Roger spotted a person about 100 yards upstream, armed with a long gun, throwing rocks into the river. Quietly advancing, shotguns at the ready, the man disappeared into the brush. Bob Burns was with the dog handler. Suddenly, the German shepherd grew tense, ears erect, alerting on something ahead. The subject was looking in our direction, only about 20 yards away. He had spotted the dog and seemed confused by its presence.

Seizing the moment, Burns yelled, "Federal officers, drop the gun or we'll shoot!" The man dropped his gun and was instructed to put his hands behind his neck and drop to his knees and then to his stomach. As a group, we all rushed in and took control of the man. Charlie kicked the loaded .22-caliber magnum rifle away. Dan placed the man in handcuffs and searched him. The man told us he had a handgun in his vest pocket, and Dan retrieved a loaded .22-caliber semiautomatic pistol and secured the rifle. It was over in less than a minute. Agent Thueson read the man his rights and escorted him across the creek to the road.

Cecil Sutherland, 32, from Dix, Illinois, was dressed in a gray hoodie, blue jeans, and hiking boots. His camp, located nearby, was quite simple.

He used a poncho for shelter with only a blanket for sleeping. We found more than 250 rounds of .22-caliber ammunition and four empty ammo boxes. He had lots of clothes, four knives, a bayonet, and a hatchet. There was very little food and no evidence of a campfire. After some questioning, Sutherland alluded that there might be a dead animal somewhere in the vicinity. Charlie discovered a dead deer with two bullets inside. The deer's throat had been cut and part of the rear quarter removed. Sutherland had apparently eaten the meat raw, not wanting to start a fire that might disclose his location. We told him he was lucky a bear hadn't found the carcass and killed him as well. Sutherland didn't say another word and was taken to jail by the FBI agents. This was a federal crime because it occurred in a national park and also involved assaulting a federal employee.

Sutherland appeared before the federal magistrate that same day and pled guilty to the charge under Title 18, U.S. Code, Section 1114, Assault with Intent to Commit Murder. He was later tried, convicted, and sentenced to 15 years with no parole for the federal crime.

Local media went wild, and the story made national TV news. Things like this just didn't happen in a national park. As word spread, at least six persons came forward with information that they too had been shot at. One man had heard a gunshot and thought that we allowed hunting in the off-season. Local tire dealers called to tell us they had repaired several tires with bullet fragments inside from people who had driven in the park. Forensic tests proved they came from Sutherland's rifle. Other holes were discovered in vehicles as well. One person said she actually saw a man with a rifle across the creek but didn't think much of it. No one thought to report any of this to us until the news broke.

But that's not the end of this story. Ranger Eric Morey realized that he had spoken with Sutherland during an illegal camping contact on October 8. Sutherland was sleeping in his car when Eric approached. He looked startled to see a ranger and agreed to move into a campground. A few days later, Eric found Sutherland's vehicle in a turnout, evidently abandoned. He broke into the car and found a note indicating that the car was out of gas and that the owner was headed south and had abandoned the car. He even signed the title. Eric impounded and inventoried the vehicle and secured it in lockup. A large quantity of ammunition and a large sheath knife were discovered during the inventory of the vehicle. Items found became crucial in the events to follow. Eric had been talking with a murderer and didn't know it.

The proper handling of evidence became crucial as new events unfolded. We were contacted by police in Dix. Sutherland was a suspect in the brutal murder of a 10-year-old girl there. He had slit her throat with a knife. Traces of dried human blood were found on the hilt of the sheath knife recovered from Sutherland's vehicle. Forensics examiners matched this blood with that of the girl. Tire tracks at the scene of that crime were also in question. Four different tread patterns from one vehicle were found at the murder scene in Illinois. Two Dix detectives, a state crime lab expert, and a deputy district attorney flew out to process Sutherland's vehicle. In our auto shop, we spread sheets of white paper on the floor and inked the tires. The four different tread patterns matched

The arrest of Cecil Sutherland, the Glacier sniper.

those at the murder scene. The car was secured for further evidence processing and hauled away in a rental truck under control of the Illinois police.

Sutherland was subsequently tried in Illinois and convicted of murder. He was sentenced to life in prison with no parole. Eric testified at the trial regarding his role in securing the evidence. Sutherland is serving his term in solitary protective confinement at the Illinois State Penitentiary. It seems that even criminals don't like child murderers. The largest law enforcement episode of my career was over. Very few rangers get to investigate such a dangerous and complex incident. We worked together as a team to locate and arrest the individual and evaluate and process the evidence and worked with outside agencies to bring the case to its final conclusion. This case was cited in future training sessions as a textbook example of proper evidence handling. Our team received a Department of the Interior Unit Citation for our work. This event demonstrates that anything can happen in a national park.

OVERWHELMED

August 5, 1988—Called out at 0200 to respond on Hwy. 2 just outside park entrance to a two-car head-on MVA. I was first on scene, there were two dead and two injured. I did two IVs, called for ALERT. Used extrication to get bodies out. Home 0415.

I still vividly recall this accident. It was deadly quiet when I arrived on scene. It took a moment to realize what had happened—there was broken glass, gasoline and oil, and debris everywhere; the cars were almost unrecognizable, in a crumbled heap in the middle of the highway. This was a high-speed, head-on, high-impact crash. I immediately called for help, but it took a few minutes for the troops to show up. I was all alone, in the middle of the night, trying to sort out the living from the dead in the twisted wreckage. I did a quick triage and did two IVs by headlamp on the two survivors.

It seemed to take forever, but I heard the park fire siren and knew that help was on the way. Dan and others arrived with the fire truck and extrication equipment. We continued treating the injured and washed down the flammable fuels. An ambulance and the ALERT helicopter arrived for a night landing in the middle of the road. The Montana Highway Patrol arrived and took over the scene. It was a mess.

A Hot Summer Erupts—The Red Bench Fire

It had been a hot summer, forests were tinder dry, and lightning-caused fires were beginning to pop up. The park contracted a fixed-wing aircraft to do aerial fire patrols. On September 3, Bill Michels and I were flying on fire recon when I spotted a small fire that had just started near Cerulean Lake. Although we had fire lookouts, they could see only a limited area. A one-hour overflight was the best way to see this rugged country. Bill Michels was the go-to guy for this job. He knew the park from the air and didn't get airsick! I was proud of myself because I spotted the Cerulean Lake fire before Bill did.

> *September 6, 1988—A fire began in Red Meadow just outside the park near Polebridge. It got to the river, then jumped into the park, forcing people to flee for their lives. 100' flames, a firestorm at Polebridge, thousands of acres burned in a matter of hours. I posted trails closed in the park—we are shut down. Worked until 2200.*

Most people will recall the catastrophic wildland fires that burned more than 700,000 acres of Yellowstone National Park in the summer of 1988. Fewer have heard of the fire that blew up in northwest Montana late that summer.

Then it happened: a dry lightning storm with hot, gusty winds. A small curl of smoke drifted up from the dry grass of Red Meadow, near the small hamlet of Polebridge, just across the river from the park. Within minutes, the fire exploded and advanced to the east, jumping the river into the park. At 38,000 acres, it became one of the largest fires in Glacier's history.

Within three days, more than 700 firefighters were battling the monster blaze. One firefighter was killed by a falling tree, and 19 others were injured. There were helicopters and fixed-wing slurry bombers, dozers, and other heavy equipment. A large tent city fire camp mushroomed in nearby Red Meadow.

The fire roared across the river, burning the only bridge (the old wooden pole bridge that gave the area its name) into the park. It swept through the ranger station complex, razing the historic barn and other structures. The ranger quarters miraculously survived. In total, the fire consumed more than 25 structures in the park and on private lands.

September 8, 1988—There was real concern that the southward advancing fire, gobbling up the tinder-dry beetle kill forests, would burn park headquarters and maybe even the town of West Glacier—it was that serious. I was tasked with developing an evacuation plan for headquarters and the adjacent housing area. Residents began packing belongings. Park staff packed up critical records and other valuable resources and moved them to Kalispell. We watched as the smoke column to the north grew to resemble a nuclear bomb cloud. Apocalyptic orange light from sun-filtered acrid smoke enveloped the area, and ash fell when the wind shifted. No one got much sleep, phones were constantly ringing, and news media arrived. There is a weird sense of dread and uncertainty knowing that your home might disappear in a matter of hours.

On September 9, after presenting the evacuation plan to park management, Jim and I drove to Polebridge to survey the damage. We crossed on foot into the park on the twisted steel remains of the old bridge that were lying in the river. I was stunned. The ranger station, barn, and outbuildings were gone, smoldering ash. Only the ranger quarters survived. Everything was coated red by a slurry drop of fire retardant. There were burned-up tools, twisted water pipes, and the charred remains of unrecognizable things. A sign near the propane tank, "Danger No Smoking or Open Flame," still stood, mocking the carnage. We stood there in silence, taking it all in. It looked like a scene from Dante's *Inferno*. The fire had passed and was now burning eastward toward the mountains in the park.

September 10, 1988—Fire is 30,000 acres. Went to a briefing. Did odd fire related jobs all day. Some blessed rain in evening and snow at Logan Pass! Drove up there to see it. Cooler.

The Red Bench Fire blows up in Glacier National Park.

Just in time, the weather turned in our favor. It began to snow in the high country and rain at lower elevations. Temperatures began to drop, and fuel moisture rose. We got prolonged rain, then snow. Most crews were demobilized by September 19.

Gerry had retired, and now Dan was leaving. He took the job of fire management officer at Indiana Dunes National Lakeshore. I was glad for his promotion; he had been here a long time and needed to move on. However, I was also sorry to see him go. He was such a competent ranger who went about his duties without fanfare and got the job done. His absence left a big hole in my operation. Thankfully, both he and Gerry left in winter and not the busy summer. I got the paperwork rolling to advertise their jobs via service-wide vacancy announcements.

NIGHT RESCUE ON HOWE RIDGE

January 8, 1989—Patrol in a.m. Skied to Rocky Point, broke trail. Called out at 1945, Dave Bristol, a skier, was injured on the top of Howe Ridge. Roger, Jim and I went up in the dark on snowmobiles almost to the top. Had to ski up the rest of the way. Found Dave lying in the trail with possible fx leg. Packed him into the rescue sled and got him down the mountain, out at 0140. We got stuck several times on the way up, had to unhook the sled, man-haul it, etc. It was snowing hard. Got home at 0245.

January began with a nighttime rescue on Howe Ridge near the head of Lake McDonald. Bristol's partner made it down to the emergency phone at the ski hut and called 911. With Dan and Gerry gone, Jim Bellamy asked North Fork Sub-District ranger Roger Semler to respond. It's a long drive to headquarters from Polebridge, so our response was delayed. Jim, Roger, and I eventually made it to the trailhead with two snowmobiles, medical gear, and a rescue sled.

It was a true "dark and stormy night" adventure with heavy snowfall and high winds. The narrow trail up the ridge wasn't designed for snow machines, and we fought our way through knee-deep snow. We got bogged down many times and struggled to find the sinuous trail, abandoning the machines near the top, skiing the remainder using head-lamps, and pulling the sled by hand.

We found Dave Bristol in the middle of the trail, lying in his sleeping bag on foam pads. His partner had made him as comfortable as possible before leaving for help. I immobilized Dave's leg and checked him over. He had caught a ski on a root and wrenched his knee. We packaged him into the sled and made our way gingerly back down to the snow machines, belaying the sled with ropes.

The rescue sled had a Lexan face shield to protect a patient's face. I told Dave that we would be as gentle as possible but that this wasn't going to be an easy trip. We hitched the sled to a snow machine and started down the mountain. Imagine yourself lying in a small sled, your face inches from a snow trench, being pulled by a roaring snow machine in a snowstorm in the dark. That was Dave's experience, and it must have been a terrifying trip. He couldn't see anything, so I spoke with him frequently to soothe his fears and let him know of our progress.

We got down to the road after 1:00 a.m. and met a waiting ambulance. Dave had arthroscopic surgery that day and made a full recovery. He paid us a nice compliment in an article in that week's *Hungry Horse News*.

Scott

Hiring a permanent ranger involves a great deal of time and paperwork. After a service-wide vacancy announcement is issued, there is a waiting period for the applications to be received and rated. The selecting official, me in this case, then begins the laborious process of reviewing the applications, developing a list of the most highly qualified candidates, and conducting phone interviews. It all takes months.

March 13, 1989—Jim, Bob Burns, and I had a conference—decided to hire Scott Emmerich for the GS-7 position. Bob made the phone call. Snow by 1600, snowing hard.

There are decisions in a supervisor's career that can determine success or failure. I've always tried to recruit and hire the best possible person for the job, especially a permanent career position. Having good, smart, reliable staff makes your life a whole lot easier.

Scott Emmerich was one of my seasonal patrol rangers in Tuolumne in the summer of 1985. He worked a variety of jobs in Yosemite, hoping to land a permanent position. I met him on several occasions and immediately liked him. When I got the chance to work with him in Tuolumne, I was even more impressed. Scott's circuitous route to Glacier included an MBA, seasonal work in Glacier and Yosemite, and a stint with the U.S. Customs Service.

When Gerry Bell retired, I knew Scott would be an ideal replacement. Although there were other fine candidates, Scott stood far above the rest. He was intelligent, enthusiastic, very physically fit, and a skilled outdoorsman; he had a wonderful sense of humor and made friends easily. I was more than pleased to offer him the job.

After I left Glacier, Scott was selected as the North Fork Sub-District ranger at Polebridge. Leading by example, he inspired his staff to new heights of performance. People returned year after year to work with Scott. He built good relations with a local community that didn't always appreciate the park or the government in general. Scott received the prestigious Harry Yount Award for outstanding ranger in the entire Park Service. He was a parkmedic and took my place as a member of the ALERT board. Hiring Scott was one of the best things I ever did in my career.

Scott spent the rest of his distinguished career in the North Fork. He retired in 2014 and finally got to spend time with his wife Jan and daughter McKenna. In August 2018, at age 61, Scott passed away after a courageous, nearly three-year battle with brain cancer. He was one of my best friends, and I'm fortunate to have known him. I miss him terribly.

THE WOLVERINE AND THE POWER OF THE PRESS

April 3, 1989—Off today, snow. I didn't get the Tetons job, got the gong letter today. A wolverine attacked a deer which then ran out on to the ice on the Lake and couldn't move. Called out to investigate.

What seemed like a simple call turned out to be quite controversial, raising a furor in the local community. A wolverine had apparently chased a doe out onto the ice on frozen Lake McDonald. The deer was crippled and couldn't move, having been hamstrung by the wolverine. It was a sad situation but nature's way.

Hungry Horse News editor Brian Kennedy heard about the incident on his scanner and was present when I called in to headquarters for advice. The decision to dispatch the suffering animal was above my pay grade, and I wanted guidance from the experts. I already knew the answer would be to let nature take its course because that is Park Service policy. I also knew this would be in the paper and would be unpopular.

The deer died the next day, and the wolverine, coyotes, ravens, and magpies made it disappear quickly. The article appeared in that week's paper, complete with a photo of the hamstrung deer with a drooping neck and blood on the snow.

In the next edition's letters to the editor, I was personally castigated for not shooting the deer. How could the ranger be so heartless? How could he let this poor animal suffer? I was upset about all this because I knew I had done the right thing. If I had shot the deer, I would have been wrong to interfere with natural processes. Although seldom witnessed, this type of thing happens every day in nature. This time, it just happened in a public place.

Brian Kennedy came to my defense in the next paper. His editorial explained that he had been present when I received instructions to leave things alone. I was carrying out Park Service resource management policy. I felt better and received a lot of moral support from park staff. They knew I had been raked over the coals just for doing my job.

It was a hectic spring. With Dan and Gerry gone and Scott not yet on board, it was up to me to do all the seasonal hiring. I spent many hours poring over applications, doing interviews, and completing appointment paperwork. I was able to hire Gary Moses to fill Dan's permanent position. Gary's wife Amy was the new public information officer, and Gary had career status. He had an excellent résumé, and I quickly offered him the permanent slot. Gary turned out to be much like Scott, a super-achiever and good all-around ranger. Gary spent the rest of his career in Glacier, also attaining the coveted Harry Yount Award. That's all you need to say about the superiority of Gary's work. He and Amy are enjoying their retirement in the Glacier area.

Scott arrived and I was glad to have some help. He and Gary hit the ground running as I knew they would. Before we knew it, summer was on us with the usual mayhem—bear jams, DUI arrests, and minor searches.

RANGER HEAVEN—BELLY RIVER

September 29, 1989—Donna and I left for our much-anticipated trip to Belly River. Hit the trail at Chief Mountain Customs at 1030, had lunch at Three Mile CG. Arrived at the ranger station at 1230—beautiful blue sky, sun and golden aspen. Hiked to Elizabeth Lake, caught two grayling and one rainbow. Back to the cabin at 1845. Cleaned and cooked the fish for dinner. A beautiful night, the Milky Way was out in all its glory!

The Belly River patrol cabin sits in a broad meadow in a scenic mountain valley with Mount Cleveland, the highest mountain in Glacier, dominating the skyline. The log ranger station, barn, and outbuildings are historic structures. Buck and rail fence encloses the horse pasture, while the river flows just a few yards from the cabin. Groves of golden aspen ring the meadow. It's what a backcountry station should look like.

Our trip to this beautiful place was memorable for another reason. It was snowing with fog and low, brooding clouds when we began our hike out on October 1. Passing a long stretch of willow and alder, snow swirling about, we heard it—a low growl, deep and guttural. I knew what it was immediately. Donna was frightened as well. She whispered, "What should we do?" I told her to just keep walking and don't run. The grizzly, unseen and no more than 20 feet away, was just letting us know he was there, getting too close to his personal space. Your heart races, senses on full alert—it's a humbling experience. I've always wondered how often I've been close to bears without knowing it. I'm sure it's happened plenty of times, and maybe it's a good thing not to know.

We should have been making more noise—surprise encounters end badly. Never run from a bear—you will be perceived as prey. Instead, keep facing the animal without making eye contact while slowly backing up, talking in a quiet voice. And by all means, always carry bear spray when hiking in bear country. There's lots of detailed information available at park visitor centers, in pamphlets, and on the internet. Better still, ask a ranger!

BAD ENDING OF A GOOD MORNING

April 22, 1990—Out of Logan Creek cabin by 10. Picked up roadside trash. Went down an inholder road and found a man who was in process of attempting suicide by drug overdose. Flew him out on ALERT—what a day.

There isn't much of a diary entry for this incident, but I've never forgotten it. It was a beautiful morning after an overnight with my family in the cabin. I went on patrol when we got back down to headquarters and was the only person on duty this Sunday afternoon. There had been a BOLF (Be On the Lookout For) for a car with a person who was reportedly suicidal. I checked secondary access roads and went down to an inholder cabin along the lake—a place I rarely went—and was astonished to see the car parked there. I called it in to dispatch and cautiously approached the car. There was a man inside, head down, seemingly asleep, a bottle of vodka and a pill container lying on the seat. He didn't respond when I rapped on the window, so I opened the door and tried to get him out and assess his condition. He immediately became combative and tried to slug me. We rolled around on the ground, almost going into the lake when I finally subdued him. I handcuffed him and sat him down until backup finally arrived.

We did a quick medical assessment and called for the ALERT helicopter to land at Lake McDonald Lodge a mile distant. Later, from his hospital bed, the man thanked me for saving his life, giving him another chance—a beautiful spring day for me, a terrifying experience for one troubled man. I was glad I could help him.

Lion on the Beach

July 23, 1990—At about 1130 got a call that a mountain lion had attacked a 9 y/o boy at Apgar beach. I stabilized him and flew him out using a Forest Service helo. He was severely clawed about the head, eyes, and arms. I stayed in the hospital with parents until 1530. Wedum shot the cat in the afternoon.

It was a typical summer day at the Apgar beach on Lake McDonald with dozens of people enjoying the sunny weather, kids skipping rocks on the lake, and people picnicking and strolling along the stony beach. Nine-year-old Scott O'Hare from Dayton, Wyoming, and his friend Chad Flanagan were playing near the water when Scott was suddenly bowled over by a mountain lion that jumped on him from behind. The boy fell facedown with the lion on top of him, biting and clawing his head. Scott remembered a naturalist program he attended earlier where it was recommended to play dead if attacked by a bear and don't fight back.

Chad was running up the beach toward the picnic area when he heard his friend's scream. He turned to see a mountain lion on top of Scott and yelled for help. Chad's father Mike ran toward Scott, thinking he was being attacked by a dog. When he saw the long tail of the cat, he realized it was a lion. Mike charged toward the lion, causing the cat to leave Scott and run toward him. He kicked at the cat as it ran by. The lion then leaped at Scott's seven-year-old sister Aminda but ran away when she screamed.

Scott's parents and Mike Flanagan scooped up Scott and brought him to the nearby Apgar Visitor Center to report the incident. A visiting doctor administered first aid and attempted to stop the bleeding.

I responded to the scene within minutes. Scott was covered in blood and had numerous lacerations and puncture wounds. His back and scalp had claw marks. There was an injury to his eye. I called for the ALERT helicopter and was told it was on another call. I told the Comm Center we needed to get this boy to a hospital immediately, and they arranged for a local Forest Service helicopter to meet us at the landing pad at park headquarters. I took Scott and his mother to meet the helo and began treating his wounds. A short time later, we were at Kalispell Regional Hospital, where Scott underwent four hours of surgery. Lacerations on his scalp totaled 10 to 12 inches, and he had cuts and puncture wounds on his arms, legs, and back. The greatest concern was Scott's eye injury. He was taken to the hospital in Missoula, but I believe he lost the use of his eye.

While I was at the hospital, the bear team, led by ranger Neal Wedum, arranged for a local cat hunter with dogs to track the animal. It didn't take long to find it. The animal was shot less than 100 yards from the beach. The cat weighed 40 pounds and was taken to Bozeman for a necropsy. It was a juvenile and very scrawny. A piece of fabric was found in the lion's stomach. This incident made national news. I was glad I could help this young boy and his family. It's why I became a ranger.

YOU'RE GOING WHERE?

By 1990, with no prospects for advancement in Glacier, I began looking for greener pastures. I saw a vacancy announcement for the North District ranger position in Denali. Donna and I had talked about going to Alaska, and this was an opportunity too good to pass up. It wasn't a remote "bush" position, it had a good school nearby, and Ken Kehrer, the chief ranger, had worked for me in Tuolumne. He knew my work—maybe I had a chance. Although Donna was working at the school and loved her job, we decided to go for it.

> *September 28, 1990—Went to a supervisor's meeting in Essex and presented the summer's activities to the group. At 1600 I got a call to go to the chief ranger's office—I was told I got the job in Denali!!! Boy, what a day—it finally came true. My head is swimming. Had a champagne toast with the folks.*

Everyone knew that I had applied for the job. When I got the radio call to see the chief ranger, Scott got on the radio and said, "Bye Tom." My supervisor, Jim Bellamy, met me in the street and gave me a big hug. Good neighbor Sheila Michels saw us and knew we were leaving. Donna's parents happened to be visiting at the time. Her mother asked, "How far north are you going to keep going?" Daughter Kelly was not happy. She loved school, had a good friend, and didn't want to leave. Katie was ambivalent.

The next few weeks were filled with travel preparations and vacating my job. I briefed Charlie Logan, who would be assuming my position. Scott took my position on the ALERT board. I was leaving the place in good hands.

We received paperwork for the move and travel orders for outside the United States, or "OCONUS"—for travel through Canada. I made reservations for the ferry trip to Haines, Alaska. This was already becoming a different move.

November 16, 1990—My last day of work. Our party began at 1730 and went to after 2200—the most people I've ever seen in the community building. It was a big "roast" and very good to see so many friends. We got home 2300, exhausted.

Our "going away" party was quite an event. The Community Building was packed, Scott the master of ceremonies. Of course, there was the inevitable roast, and I was presented with many gag gifts, including a bent boat prop and a fur-lined jock strap—what could that be for? Scott told my girls that when we got to the Canadian customs station, they should yell, "This man's not my daddy. We don't know who he is!" I love you, Scott.

Our moving van arrived on November 18. It had a logo with an Eskimo driving a dog team running the full length of the van. It was a company that specialized in Alaska moves. Everyone in the community came to see it. The van would travel to Seattle, then onto a barge to Anchorage, and then trucked to Denali. It's always disconcerting to see all your "stuff" drive away.

November 25, our last night in Glacier. A nice dinner with Scott and wife Jan. An ice storm struck, but I was able to thaw our vehicles in the auto shop and pack our belongings. We were exhausted, ready to leave after a week of emotional good-byes with good friends and planned for an early departure.

At 0515, as we started out of the housing area, two patrol cars with lights flashing and sirens blaring escorted us out to the highway. Scott and Gary, ever-faithful friends, saw to it that the whole neighborhood knew we were on our way. We were very honored and sad to be leaving this place and good friends, crying as we drove down the road. Good-bye Glacier, hello Alaska.

North to Alaska

Denali National Park and Preserve

There are strange things done in the midnight sun.

—From "The Cremation of Sam McGee" by Robert Service

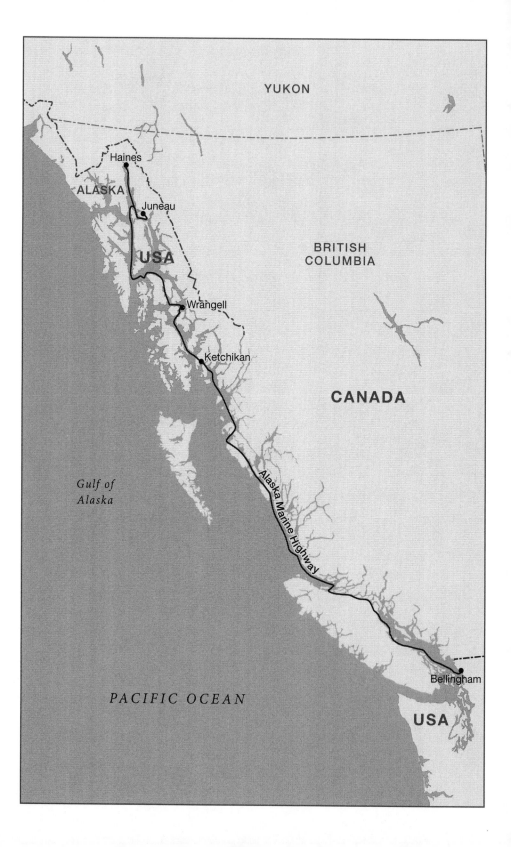

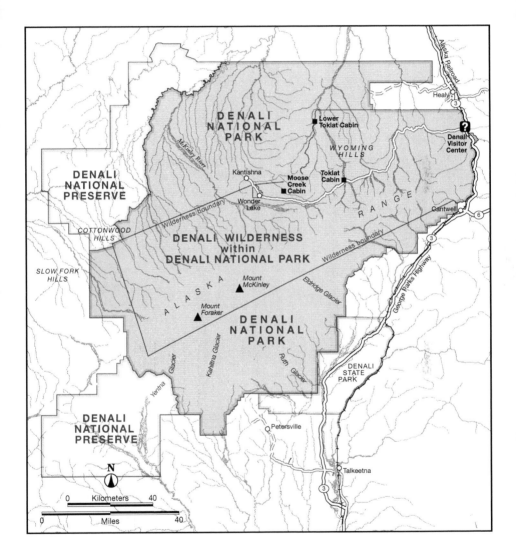

Alaska Bound

As a kid, I dreamed about going to Alaska. I'd read Jack London's stories about White Fang, gold mining, and the mysterious aurora. I loved watching Sargent Preston of the Yukon and his faithful dog King on TV. I enjoyed Robert Service's poetry tales of deep cold and mushing on the trail. When I was about 12, I wrote a story for school revealing that I wanted to become a bush pilot or maybe a trapper in Alaska. I had dreams of going there someday and living in the bush.

The national parks in Alaska were mysterious places to me. I had met a few lucky individuals who had worked there seasonally and was fascinated with their stories of bears, big rivers, vast forests, riding in airplanes, and living in remote cabins. In 1980, President Carter signed the Alaska National Interest Lands Conservation Act—the most significant expansion of national park land in history—and I was determined to go.

Our trip to Alaska began with the purchase of high-quality winter clothing for all of us—coats, gloves and mittens, and insulated snow boots. In Bellingham, Washington, we boarded the Alaska state ferry *Columbia* after fueling the truck with ethanol and the Mercedes with diesel.

November 30, 1990—Got our tickets and boarded the ferry. Underway at 2000, good-bye CONUS! (Continental U.S.) Raining hard. Had supper in the snack bar. Explored the ship, slept well.

Alaska state ferry *Columbia*.

It was getting dark and raining when we first saw the ship. At 418 feet in length and accommodating 499 passengers, it was huge! Under the direction of the loading crew, we drove our two vehicles into the bowels of the ship, where they were chained down to the deck with other cars, trucks, and semis. Vehicles were loaded in order of departure, first on, last off, the placard on our windshield indicating our destination: "Haines," Alaska.

We settled into our cozy cabin—four bunks and a lavatory. After stowing our few belongings, Donna and Katie went forward to check out the observation deck while Kelly and I went aft. There was just the two of us. As the deckhand cast off the line, the huge ship slowly eased from the pier. Standing in the rain, I looked at Kelly and said, "Kelly, this is real. We're going to Alaska." It was thrilling and scary at the same time.

December 1, 1990—Continued up the Inside Passage. Had eight-foot seas crossing Queen Charlotte Sound, the ship rolling and rocking but we didn't get sick—many others were. A mixture of rain, snow, clouds and sun. Had dinner in the ship's restaurant. The scenery is really neat.

We woke up the next morning to a world of blue ocean, small islands, and dark forest. Unlike most of the Inside Passage, Queen Charlotte Sound is a stretch of water exposed to the open sea. We happened to pass through on the tail end of a Pacific storm. The ship began to pitch and roll, waves crashing against the sides, wind whipping spray off the tops of the waves. Our cabin was near the galley, and we heard dishes crashing to the deck. It was difficult walking in the narrow passageways, lurching from side to side. Fortunately, none of us got seasick. The ship was not crowded this time of year, with plenty of room in the observation deck to play cards, relax, and simply watch the scenery go by.

December 2, 1990—A few passengers and vehicles disembarked at Ketchikan, our first stop. We took advantage of the time to step off the ferry onto Alaskan soil, calling Glacier to tell them we were in Ketchikan—it sounded so exotic!

Off the tiny fishing village of Wrangell, we waited five hours for the high tide before going through the shallow Wrangell Narrows. It was fully dark when we got under way, the kids in bed for the night. Donna and I went forward to watch as the *Columbia* cruised slowly up the channel. A crew member shone a light on each reflective marker and channel buoy as the channel narrowed— just like my coast guard days. At times, it looked like we could reach out and touch the cliffs. The ship slowly threaded the needle of the narrows and emerged into broader waters.

Traveling farther north, each day grew colder, noticeably shorter, and more desolate. There were few signs of human habitation—no houses or lights, power lines, or roads. Occasionally, a small fishing village with boats moored in the cove glided into view. Doubts about my decision drifted in. What had I gotten us into?

The ferry trip was the forced rest we needed after all the hoopla of saying good-bye. I teased Donna that this was the cruise I'd always promised, just no sandy beaches.

December 3, 1990—Our last day on the Columbia. Stopped in Juneau for an hour, early morning. Continued up Lynn Canal to Haines, our final stop. Saw porpoises, seals and orca whales. Got to Haines about 1430 and checked into got our motel. It was snowing and 9°. Had supper at the "Bamboo Room" of the Pioneer Bar. A beautiful harbor, giant mountains and, real glaciers.

Lynn Canal is the upper portion of the Inside Passage. It terminates at Skagway, 13 nautical miles beyond the town of Haines, Alaska. The stop in Juneau was short and didn't allow time to see the state capital. Many people think Anchorage is the capital of Alaska, but it's Juneau— and you can't drive to it. Welcome to "Alaska Weird."

The ferry docked in Haines, a small town of 1,700 that connects to the road system through Canada into Alaska. Dozens of fishing vessels lined the harbor, bounded by large mountains and glaciers. We got our vehicles, disembarked, and drove to the Captain's Choice Motel, where I had made reservations prior to the trip. It had just stopped snowing, and there was a good three feet of snow in the parking lot. It was 9°F and getting dark; nothing was plowed out. We had to wait for a front-end loader to clear a space for us to park.

We found a little restaurant, the Pioneer Bar, and had dinner. The place was, we were soon to learn, typically Alaskan, a bit rough around the edges. It was chilly and dark and not especially clean, with a wood floor, cigarette smoke filling the air, and country music on the jukebox. I recall sitting in our booth and seeing ice on the *inside* of the windows.

December 4, 1990—It was snowing when we woke up and began the nearly 800-mile drive north to Denali. Hundreds of American bald eagles decorated the trees like Christmas ornaments just outside of town at the Chilkat Eagle Preserve, where they congregate by the thousands along the Chilkat River to feast on spawning salmon. There were moose lounging on the town's airstrip.

The U.S./Canadian customs station at Dalton Cache was a lonely place this time of year. If ever there was a "middle of nowhere," this was it. We were the only people waiting to cross. The customs officer asked our destination and where we were coming from. I told him we were moving to Denali from Glacier National Park, Montana. His eyes brightened, and he said, "Do you know Jerry DeSanto?" I replied that I did and that Jerry had recently retired. He knew Jerry from his previous customs post at Moose City on the North Fork. It was like old home week after that, and he wanted to chat. Donna, waiting in the car behind me, thought something was wrong. Maybe one of the kids had listened to Scott! After a few minutes, we were admitted into Canada with best wishes in the new job.

Forty-five miles north of customs, we crossed into fabled Yukon Territory and arrived at Haines Junction 61 miles farther on. We had lunch in a little café and chatted with a few folks who were driving our way. It's a lonely road this time of year, with only a few businesses still open, and it was good to know someone else was going in our direction. We saw only about 10 other vehicles for the remainder of the day.

We turned left at Haines Junction onto the famous Alcan Highway. This two-lane, then–mostly paved road is the only highway that connects Alaska to the Lower 48 states. If you're going to drive to Alaska, this is the road you will take. Carved out of the wilderness in less than a year during World War II, it is the lifeline to the far north. The scenery was spectacular with the majestic St. Elias Mountains and 19,000-foot Mount Logan to the west and the Dawson Range to the east. We passed through a small part of massive Kluane (kloo-WA-nee) National Park, a vast, snow-covered country with forests, open tundra, frozen lakes, distant ice fields, and large glaciated rivers. The Alcan is perhaps the most beautiful drive I've ever taken.

It got colder by the hour and was getting dark by late afternoon. I was in the lead, driving the pickup, when I noticed Donna, following in the Mercedes, flashing her headlights. I stopped and ran back to ask what the trouble was. She said the car was missing, bucking, and almost stalling. I wasn't sure what to do, so we just kept on driving.

Night comes early in these parts at this time of year with only six hours of daylight. This was wild country with no sign of civilization: no houses or businesses and no other vehicles for hours. It was pitch dark and the deepest cold I have ever experienced. And our car was acting up—we could be in real trouble. Driving on, I noticed the Mercedes had stopped, headlights flashing frantically. When I got back to Donna, the car had completely stopped and would not run. We were in a tough spot: this was dangerous cold, and we were all alone, in the dark, and not exactly certain of our location. We decided to put the girls in the truck with me and attempt to tow the car. Donna would stay in the car and steer while I towed it. If that didn't work, we would abandon the car and drive until we could find shelter.

I hooked a tow strap to the car, and we slowly began to move. It seemed to be working all right. The heater was going full blast in the truck, the windows were all iced up, and the power steering seemed sluggish, but poor Donna had no heat and no power steering. We couldn't do this for too long.

After a few miles, I noticed a glow of light on the horizon. Cresting a small hill, I saw the red maple leaf of a Petro Canada sign! Kluane Wilderness Village—a welcome outpost with a gas station, small motel, and café. I pulled in, towing the car. An old guy came out and said, "Froze up, eh? Pull her over here into the shop and we'll thaw it out."

It finally dawned on me: our diesel fuel had gelled! I had filled the tank in balmy Bellingham with normal diesel fuel. It never occurred to me that we needed winterized diesel up north. How could I have been so stupid?

The guy told us it was -50°F! No wonder we had "froze up." He pushed the car into the garage to thaw and told us he'd drain the tank and fill it up with arctic-grade fuel. Meanwhile, we got a room at the tiny motel, the only guests. The kids went inside to keep warm while Donna and I lugged in our belongings, including two milk crates of homemade huckleberry and strawberry jam we couldn't send with the movers. The jars would freeze and break if left outside for only a short time.

We were famished and went to the little café next door. Our burger order consisted of a meat patty between two slices of white bread with two pickle slices on the side—eight bucks each! Welcome to the far north. But we were glad to be safe and sound and gladly paid the price. We were snug and warm and together somewhere in the Yukon.

December 5, 1990—It got down to -50°F that night, dangerous cold. With a tank full of arctic-grade diesel and the car running smoothly, we set out for Fairbanks, Alaska, crossing at Beaver Creek customs. Driving north, the trees grew smaller; millions of acres of spindly black spruce that looked like bottle brushes dominated the landscape. A few birch, aspen, and cottonwoods grew along rivers and streams, all frozen, of course. It was a bleak but beautiful landscape, unlike anything we'd ever seen.

After a lunch at Fast Eddies Café, a local landmark in Tok (pronounced Toke), we continued on the Alcan toward Fairbanks. We got our first glimpse of the Alaska Pipeline where it crossed the frozen Tanana River at Delta Junction. It was exciting to actually see this famous icon that had been so controversial when it was built in the mid-1970s.

The short day turned into night, and we began to see signs of civilization—small cabins, a few small businesses, and even power poles. Nearing the town of North Pole in the darkness, there it was—the golden arches of McDonald's! The girls were excited—maybe this wouldn't be so bad after all. It was -40°F when we arrived in Fairbanks. The city was shrouded in ice fog—a phenomenon that occurs in extreme cold when water vapor from vehicles and heating sources is suspended in the air as a dense fog. Visibility was so poor that we could barely make out the traffic lights. Fairbanks, 125 miles and two and a half hours from Denali, would be "town" for us: groceries, doctors, haircuts, airport, and car repairs. Friends were amazed that we would go 250 miles round-trip for bread—we got used to it.

Driving south on the Parks Highway led us to our new home in Denali. Roads in Alaska have names: the Steese Highway, the Seward Highway, the Dalton Highway, and so on. There are fewer miles of roads in all of Alaska than in New York City and no U.S. highways or interstates.

By late afternoon, the light began to fade. Sunset was at 2:53 p.m. Kelly was confused and thought the sun was coming up in the wrong place—to the south. Near the winter solstice at this northern latitude, the sun makes a tiny arc across the sky, both rising and setting in the southern sky. In the pink glow of the setting sun, we arrived at the park entrance—we made it!

At the log headquarters building, chief ranger Ken Kehrer greeted us warmly. He introduced us to a few people, then showed us our quarters, an apartment in a six-unit building. We unloaded our few belongings and set up temporary housekeeping until our van arrived. In my diary, I wrote, "Beautiful mountains all around."

Alaska is a land of superlatives, especially evident in its national parks. At 6.1 million acres, Denali ranks third in size of Alaska's national parks. Established in 1917 as Mount McKinley National Park, the name was changed in 1980 to Denali National Park and Preserve as a result of the Alaska National Lands Conservation Act. The name "Denali" stems from the Koyukon Dene native word for "The High One," referring to 20,310-foot Denali, the highest mountain in North America. On a clear day, it is visible from 200 miles away.

Most of the park is located in interior Alaska, north of the Alaska Range. Park headquarters is 125 miles south of Fairbanks and about 250 miles north of Anchorage. The mountaineering program that oversees climbing and SAR on the mountain is administered from Talkeetna, about 140 miles south of headquarters. The mostly unmarked park boundary is 600 miles long. My North District was more than 4 million acres, twice the size of Yellowstone. It's hard for even me to comprehend.

The park has more than 12,000 lakes and ponds, 18,000 miles of streams and rivers, but only 35 miles of constructed trail. There are 40 named and hundreds of unnamed glaciers in the park.[1]

The narrow 90-mile, mostly gravel park road winds its way over tundra, mountain cliffs, and rivers to the remains of the old gold mining town of Kantishna. To access the park beyond the first 15 miles of road, visitors must ride a concession-operated tour bus or shuttle bus. It's a system that works well and may be the future of overcrowded parks such as Yosemite and Yellowstone. Denali is the most visited park in Alaska with more than 642,000 visits in 2017. Compare this to the 4,000 visitors in Wrangell-St. Elias and 4 million in Yellowstone.

One would think a park of this size requires a huge staff to operate, but that is not true. When I arrived in 1990, there were about 45 permanent staff, with five permanent park rangers for the 6-million-acre park. We all fit in one small room at staff meetings. Today, there are 113 permanent staff and 197 seasonals.

After settling into our quarters, we spent the next few days getting acquainted with people and exploring the nearby village of Healy, population 487, where the girls would attend school. There were a few businesses, including a small grocery/liquor store, gas station, and café. The Usibelli coal mine, Golden Valley power plant, and school are the main employers.

On Monday, I met my ranger division coworkers with whom I would form lasting friendships. Sandy Kogl, a longtime Alaskan, became my mentor in all things Alaska. Sandy and her husband came to Alaska in 1964 and homesteaded in the remote Yanert Valley south of the park where they ran a sled dog freighting operation.

Sandy's experience with dogs led her to a job in 1975 at Denali's kennels, where she revitalized the dog mushing program, established a formal breeding plan, and renovated the kennels facility. She became a law enforcement ranger at a time when few women were hired into that job. She was sort of a den mother to many young seasonals and permanents struggling to make sense of the job and living in Alaska, myself included.

Sandy was dedicated to protecting wild places and truly "walked the walk" of treading lightly on the land. Often the conscience of the park, she always advocated for protecting the resource. Sandy made sure I got to experience the "real Alaska," arranging backcountry trips and kidnapping me away from my paperwork. "Come on, you need to get out of here," and off we went, dog mushing or hiking for a few hours.

Clare Curtis came to Denali as a fee collector in 1982 and moved up the ranks to supervisor in the Interpretation Division. Clare was the consummate outdoorswoman, hunter, skier, accomplished snow machine operator, and general "fix-it" person. Beside these skills, Clare was a great backcountry cook and pathfinder, earning her the nickname "Sacajawea."

Most of the large Alaska parks have a plane and ranger pilot because flying is the most efficient, practical, and sometimes only way to get around these vast areas. Park pilot Jim Unruh arrived in Denali with more than 800 hours of quality flight experience. Meticulous in the care and maintenance of the park plane, Jim instilled a sense of confident professionalism whenever he flew. I always felt very safe flying with him. Flying with Jim helped me understand the immensity and complexity of Denali and of Alaska. Among my fondest memories is hearing Jim say on the radio, "McKinley park traffic, 33 Charlie Tango off McKinley park strip," or, on landing, "Well, we cheated death one more time!"

Park headquarters is a small collection of log and frame structures, most built in the late 1920s and early 1930s. Some were cobbled together out of necessity, others adaptively used. The four of us rangers were crammed together in what used to be a motor grader shed that once had a dirt floor. Sandy, Clare, and our division clerk shared one room. Jim had a small space he shared in summer. The back room belonged to the sub-district ranger and seasonal patrol rangers. I was fortunate to have my own space, complete with a window and a door that I could close for privacy. Except for the superintendent and division chiefs, who had private offices, people were packed together, working in cramped spaces with no privacy.

Crowded conditions were not unique to the Ranger Division. Donna worked with two or three other people in a converted generator shed with only a space heater. Clare and I later shared offices in a renovated public restroom. Eventually, funding was obtained for infrastructure including maintenance shops, a communications center and ranger office, a science and learning center, and visitor services facilities.

At first, I felt I had stepped back at least 10 years in terms of technology and equipment. We had first-generation Compaq portable computers or stand-alone word processors. There was no computer network. File sharing meant carrying a floppy disk to another office. There was no dedicated IT person. The phone system was unreliable, inadequate for expanding needs. Our radio system was pretty basic, and much of the park was without communications. Outlying areas such as Toklat and Wonder Lake relied on diesel generators that were turned off at night. People living south of headquarters didn't have commercial power until the late 1990s. Yes, Alaska was rough around the edges, and it would take some getting used to, but I was thrilled to be here.

It was -30°F when our moving van finally arrived. Donna enrolled the girls in school, Kelly in sixth grade, Katie in third. We learned that the Tri-Valley School was one of the top-rated schools in the state. The teachers were excellent, and our kids got a good education. Donna began setting up the house with a goal of having everything squared away for Christmas.

I jumped into my work full throttle. One of my first tasks was to purchase a new ambulance. Alaska Senator Ted Stevens's office wanted to buy an ambulance for the park and needed to know "right now" how much it would cost. Unfazed, chief ranger Ken Kehrer picked the number $75,000 out of thin air, which became a line item in the federal budget. That's how it's done when a powerful senator wants something.

Wheeled Coach, located in Florida, held the government contract for ambulances. After poring over specs of several models, I picked one out that met our needs and placed an order. It cost $60,000 and arrived a year later on a barge in Anchorage. I spent the remaining $15,000 on medical equipment and supplies, sharing the bounty with the South District mountaineering program.

Along with the ambulance, I was tasked with establishing a park-medic program with advanced life support capabilities. Many of Denali's visitors are "beyond middle age," and heart attacks, strokes, and respiratory emergencies are common. "My doctor said I could make the trip" was a common phrase. Fairbanks Memorial Hospital staff had never heard of a parkmedic and were skeptical at first. I presented the protocols to the emergency room docs and administration and gained their confidence. Once they understood the program, they were enthusiastic to have more advanced care available in the park. We got a physician sponsor and were in business.

ADJUSTING TO LIFE IN THE FAR NORTH

Christmas came quickly. It was strange, sitting around the tree, opening our gifts on Christmas morning, total darkness outside. Sunrise was 10:44 a.m., and it felt like the middle of the night. Sunset on that date was 3:26 p.m., a very short day!

> *December 31, 1990—Minus 25° this morning, clear. Jim and I went to inspect a moose carcass at the railroad crossing on Parks Highway. A wolf was waiting to feed on it. Full moon, beautiful.*

Collisions between moose and vehicles are a real problem in Alaska. The largest moose on the planet, *Alces alces gigas*, weigh up to 1,400 pounds with an average antler spread on bulls of 5.9 feet. With an estimated moose population of between 175,000 and 200,000 and few roads, it's likely that a driver will hit one at some point. Hundreds of moose are killed annually by vehicles on Alaskan highways, resulting in millions of dollars in property damage and personal injury. Injured and dead moose can be legally recovered with a permit from the state. Alaska State Troopers maintain a callout list, and folks must respond at any hour and any weather. Moose killed on the railroad are deposited at the next crossing for pickup. It's a good program that provides hundreds of pounds of edible meat for people and keeps other wildlife that may feed on the carcass from getting hit.

> *January 1, 1991—Put up the new TV antenna on a higher mast—at 22° below—and got a picture, finally! Skied up the road, the mountains are red in the late afternoon sunlight.*

TV reception was a challenge. We received only something called RATNET—Rural Alaska Television Network—operated by the State of Alaska for bush communities. It broadcast programs from the three major networks and a potpourri of bush-related programming. Sometimes, there were live broadcasts of native village council meetings, native dancing, or the Eskimo Olympics. Many programs were delayed for weeks—we got Christmas commercials in February.

The best part of RATNET was the *Alaska Weather* program. The state is so big that an entire half hour was devoted to weather. The forecast included marine conditions and the all-important aviation weather, pass conditions, icing, and winds. It was fascinating, made all the more enjoyable by meteorologist Mark Evangilista, the Soupy Sales of weathermen. Mark one time described weather in the Aleutians as "always shitty."

I mounted a "super-deep-fringe" antenna on a 20-foot iron pipe mast and attached a Vise-Grip tool for a handle to turn it while looking through the window into our living room, seeking the best reception—kind of Rube Goldberg, but it worked. When changing channels, I or one of the kids went outside to turn the antenna, even at –40°. Years later, the park installed successive generations of satellite TV equipment, and our community voted on what few channels we would watch for the next year on the shared dish. It was a huge improvement.

GONE TO THE DOGS

February 13, 1991—Gary and I left the kennels at 0935 for Sanctuary patrol cabin with two teams of dogs. Stopped at Savage patrol cabin. Arrived Sanctuary about 1245, got the cabin ready for an overnight stay. Broke new trail to Teklanika River and returned. Fed the dogs, shoveled the roof. A beautiful clear day with good views of the mountain. Temps in the 20's.

February 14, 1991—Up at 0745, watered the dogs, had breakfast, packed and harnessed our teams, off by 1035. Cloudy, windy but good traveling. Back to HQ by 1300.

This was my first overnight trip with a team of dogs. Denali rangers have used dogs since 1921 when ranger and first superintendent, Harry Karstens, used dogs to patrol the new park. As more rangers were hired, each was assigned a team of seven dogs. Skill in mushing dogs was a job requirement. Ranger Grant Pearson, hired by Karstens in 1926, recalls being told that he was lacking in experience but considered capable of learning. To test him, Karstens said, "I'll send you on a patrol trip alone. You will be gone a week. If you don't get back by then, I'll come looking for you, and you had better have plans made for a new job."[2] Now that's the way to do a job skills assessment!

A kennels building, constructed in 1929, still stands today. The kennels is home to 34 Alaskan huskies that are bred and trained for patrol and freight hauling. Dog mushing patrols average 3,000 miles annually. Why do we use dogs? Mechanized equipment is not permitted in winter in the original, or "old," park, which is managed as wilderness. Dogs can get into places that snowmobiles can't. Patrols look for wildlife conditions and poachers, enforce regulations, and haul freight to cabins or summer project sites. Tons of trash have been hauled out of the backcountry by dogsled. Old-time ranger John Rumohr once said that a "dog's carburetor doesn't ice up," and when you "cuss at a machine it just sits there but when you cuss at a dog, it at least perks up its ears."[3] The kennels is the most popular interpretive program in the park, with more than 65,000 visits in 2016. Interpreters educate visitors about the history of dog mushing in Denali and harness a team for a dramatic short trip on a dogsled equipped with wheels for summer use. Visitors may approach the dogs, all of which have been socialized for the thousands who greet them.

A litter of pups arrive annually and are named by theme. When I arrived, the "Candy Kids" had been born: Taffy, Gumdrop, Licorice, and Fudge. Pups begin the socialization process early. It was a sight to see kennels manager Gary Koy walking through headquarters followed by a passel of frisky pups. Sometimes, our office door opened, and four to six puppies tumbled in, tipping over waste cans, dragging boots, nosing into everything—and we loved it. I don't know any other Park Service area where this can happen.

In 1986, Gary Koy came to Denali for a five-day backpack trip from his home in Wisconsin and stayed for 13 years, working in a variety of concession and park jobs. He began volunteering at the kennels and in 1991 became the permanent kennels manager—the only such position in the entire Park Service.

The dogs recognized Gary as the "alpha male," their leader, and lived to please him. Gary is a big guy, six foot five, all muscle, and one of the strongest men I've ever known. He is soft spoken and never yelled at the dogs, and they loved him. I call Gary "the gentle giant"; he taught me about dogs and allowed me the unforgettable experience of seeing a piece of Alaska from the back of a dogsled.

Harnessing an 85-pound squirming dog that is barking in your ear and pulling you around is not easy. There is general chaos in the kennels when hitching up a team with 30 or more barking dogs pleading, "Take me, take me." We usually traveled with a team of six or seven dogs: experienced lead dog in front, then team dogs, and, finally, the powerful wheel dogs. Once in harness, they strain at the tug line, barking furiously. The sled is tied to a stout post. When you "pull the hook" and release the slipknot, all barking ceases, and the dogs take off like a rocket. They run vigorously for a few minutes but soon settle down into a nice "dog trot" pace. The only sound you hear is the swishing of the sled runners over the cold snow. It's a thrilling experience.

Standing on the runners of a dogsled is not like steering a horse using reins and a bridle. There is no direct physical control of a dog team. Instead, the dogs respond to verbal commands: "Gee" for right, "Haw" for left, and "Straight ahead." Hopefully, they stop at "Whoa." No one uses "Mush"; instead, a simple "Okay" or "Let's go" does the trick.

I soon learned that driving a dogsled is hard work. It's not like you see in the movies, standing on the runners, gliding gently over the snow. Sometimes, you have to get off the runners and jog, pushing the sled uphill to assist the dogs. When snow is deep, you may have to snowshoe a trail in front of the team so they can pull the sled. It's exhausting work dressed in bulky winter clothes and heavy boots, and you better be in shape.

The number one rule of dog mushing is *don't let go of the sled!* Most teams will just keep going until the sled turns over or they get tangled in brush. Woe to the dog driver who loses his sled, for he is in for a long, arduous slog to catch his team. And keep an eye out for moose because the dogs go nuts, and mushers and dogs have been severely injured by irate moose. It's a situation to avoid at all costs.

We stayed in the historic Sanctuary River patrol cabin, built by the Alaska Road Commission for its construction camp in 1926. It's a typical Denali roadside cabin, with one room, a woodstove and propane cookstove, two bunks, a table and chairs, and a chuck cabinet for food. It's quite comfortable in winter.

The dogs are staked to a stainless-steel cable spaced a few feet apart. They bed down, nose to tail, in the snow or sometimes with straw carried on the sled. Our cabins were stocked with dog food each fall for these trips. The first order of business is to get a fire going and start melting snow for dog water. As in backcountry travel with stock, care of the animals comes first. Once the dogs are fed and watered, it's time to make your own dinner.

I was not prepared for the intermittent lonesome howling in the middle of the night. A chorus of 12 dogs singing under dark starry skies is a haunting sound you never forget. Sometimes, they are answering a wolf howling in the distance, but no one really knows why they spontaneously do this. I thought of Jack London's tales of travel in the Yukon and couldn't believe I was out there too. Traveling with dogs is one of the best experiences I had in Alaska. No other park does this on a routine basis, and I felt honored to continue the tradition begun in 1921. I'm lucky to have been among the few rangers who have done it.

"Tom, You Need to See This Place"

March 2, 1991—Jim and I went flying all day, over five hours. Flew to the extreme southwest corner of the Preserve, saw the Cathedral Spires. Ate lunch and refueled in Talkeetna. Flew up the Ruth Glacier and into the amphitheater—it was magnificent. Crossed the range and flew up the Muldrow Glacier and north side river drainages. Home at 1700. Fed the dogs.

I was sitting at my desk one Saturday morning, a bluebird day, not a cloud in the sky. Jim Unruh and I were the only rangers on duty in this 6-million-acre park. Jim came into my office and said, "Tom, it's about time you saw this place. Let's go flying." And we did, 734 statute miles, for the remainder of the day.

Heading south, Jim flew up several of the 40 named glaciers: Eldridge, Buckskin, Tokositna, Kanikula, Dall, and others. I peered down to see tortuous frozen rivers of turquoise blue and white ice, miles wide and dozens of miles long, many with dark black stripes of ground-up rock, flowing sinuously down the centers. With deep, cavernous crevasses and blue ice, frozen ponds of meltwater, and jumbled blocks of ice the size of houses, it was like looking into the bottom of a frozen hell, a no-man's-land. The glaciers end in large terminal moraines, small mountains of millions of tons of pulverized rock chiseled from the mountains by immense forces of freeze-and-thaw cycles, pressure, and mass. A glacier is a conveyer belt moving rock and ice under the force of gravity relentlessly downhill, leaving a traumatized landscape.

In the far southwest corner of the park lie the remote and little-explored Kichatna Mountains. Within this range are the Cathedral Spires, a collection of sharp granite pinnacles, supposedly the densest collection of granite towers in North America. It looked like I could reach out and touch these steeples of stone as Jim banked and turned our tiny plane. A maneuver like this could be done only in perfect weather, and we had it. Extremely difficult to access, these peaks are seldom seen or climbed.

We landed in Talkeetna, the town where most flights to the mountain originate. A funky sort of place, it's rumored that Talkeetna was the inspiration for the hit TV show *Northern Exposure*. It's known as a "small drinking town with a climbing problem," and our South District office is located there.

After a quick lunch at the Roadhouse and refueling, 33 Charlie Tango took off, flying the standard mountaineering flight route into the 44-mile-long Kahiltna Glacier, site of the climbing base camp at 7,200 feet. I had never seen anything like it: hundreds of thousands of acres of ice and snow, towering granite peaks, a truly wild place. It felt almost spiritual, a heavenly place, high up on a mountain. We flew up the Great Gorge of the Ruth Glacier, with soaring walls 4,000 feet high and glacial ice deeper than the Grand Canyon; skirted the Moose's Tooth, an iconic granite monolith at 10,335 feet; and circled the Don Sheldon Amphitheater, an immense bowl of perpetual ice and snow with towering granite walls at the top of the gorge.

We flew west over the range on our return, skirting more glaciers: Peters, Foraker, Herron, Traleika, and Harper. Rising from the base of Peters Glacier, the sheer granite Wickersham Wall rises 9,000 feet, making it the second-highest sheer mountain face in the world, larger than anything on Mount Everest. With no real reference points, it's impossible to understand the enormous scale of such places. Distances and objects vanish into the immensity of the landscape.

Veering east, we crossed still-frozen Wonder Lake and turned south, flying up the Muldrow Glacier past Karsten's Ridge and angling toward the headwall and summit of Denali. Gaining altitude, I crouched down, looking *up* at soaring granite walls, ice, and snow, at least another 6,000 feet above us. What appeared to be a narrow gorge was actually miles wide. The shadow of our plane skimmed over the landscape below like a mosquito. It looked like the wingtips would scrape the walls, and I could clearly see details of the granite and ice wall. The Muldrow, a 34-mile-long river of ice, was in my district, and I liked to tell people to think of a place that was about 30 miles from their home and imagine a river of ice in that distance. It always boggled their minds, and I still have trouble with it myself.

We returned to headquarters, flying along the range, the Toklat, Teklanika, and Savage river drainages beneath our wings. It was a truly unforgettable day, and I began to comprehend the immensity of this place and understand how it all fit together. And we hadn't even touched the Outer Range and vast tundra expanses to the north. What a place!

Springtime in Alaska

With our home in order and the girls in school, Donna was looking for something to do. She applied for a position as administrative assistant to chief of maintenance and was immediately selected. Donna, with two college degrees, can do anything and managed the division's $9.5 million budget. She shared an office in a repurposed generator shed with the park engineer—they almost froze to death in winter. She loved it and became indispensable to her boss, Mike Shields.

It was March, and snowplows began clearing the 90 miles of road west to Kantishna. Ken and I made periodic trips to monitor their progress and see my new district. I saw my first Alaska grizzly and Dall sheep, and roads foreman Brad Ebel let me "drive" a D7 dozer on ice in Igloo Canyon. I was having a ball.

Seasonal staff began to arrive, and the pace quickened with orientation, firearms qualification, and moving to seasonal duty stations. Donna and I set up summer housekeeping at the ranger A-frame in Toklat road camp. Road camp is located 50 miles from headquarters and serves as the base of operations for the west end. The complex includes basic housing, maintenance shops, a shower house, and a rec hall, all powered by a generator. I spent two days per week out here covering the resident ranger's days off. It was great to get out of headquarters!

FATAL FALL ON CATHEDRAL MOUNTAIN

June 3, 1991—Began gathering information on an overdue hiker, Joe Scheerer, an employee at Lynx Creek Pizza. Started a planning session and acquiring resources for search.

Joe Scheerer, in his twenties, did not report for work as scheduled on June 3. His roommate said that Joe had gone backpacking alone somewhere in the park. He obtained the required backcountry permit and got off the camper bus at the Igloo Ranger Station, about Mile 30 on the park road.

It was early in the season and my first major incident in Denali. It was a pretty straightforward search: establish the point last seen, gather as much information as possible, develop a strategy, organize teams and resources, and search. There were numerous grizzlies in the vicinity, adding to the urgency and safety concerns.

On June 4, Sandy and I flew air recons in the park's Lama helicopter for much of the day in windy weather. This is rugged country with glacial rivers, steep mountains, and many hazards. As the search expanded, I established an incident command team and began detailed planning.

June 5, 1991—Flew to Igloo, briefed ground search teams, spent all day as IC (incident commander) on search matters. Joe was found dead at 1520 hours on the northeast slope of Cathedral. Tent located in dense forest. Flew the body to headquarters airstrip. Home by 2100.

After hours of unproductive searching from the air, ground teams deployed to conduct a grid search. A team led by ranger Gerry Reynolds discovered Joe's unoccupied tent in dense spruce near the base of Cathedral Mountain. There was no sign of anything unusual in the immediate area. A few hundred yards away, Gerry found Joe's body lying on a talus slope. He had apparently fallen, severed his femoral artery on sharp rocks, and bled to death. He had placed an improvised tourniquet on his leg to stem the bleeding, but it wasn't enough. In these types of circumstances, it's fortunate that he wasn't found by a bear.

I spent the next few days in the field on the investigation. On June 7, I flew to the scene accompanied by Joe's brothers, Larry and Phil. It was a sad thing but helpful to the family. A plaque dedicated to Joe hangs in the restaurant where he worked. As a result of this event, we doubled our efforts at concession and local employee safety orientation, using Joe's untimely death as an example of how things can quickly go wrong. Hiking solo is not recommended. Joe might have had a chance had he had a partner to go for help.

THE LONGEST DAY—SUMMER SOLSTICE

June 21, 1991—Drove to Toklat with the family, saw two bears swim across the river. We went to Wonder Lake to watch the sunset, stayed out there until twilight at 0215. It was beautiful, the sun's rays finally off the summit of the mountain at 0100. A beautiful, clear, quiet evening.

In the Lower 48, the summer solstice mostly goes unnoticed. In Alaska, however, it's a big deal. Sunrise in Denali was at 3:23 a.m. and sunset at 12:36 a.m. (the next day!) for a total of 21 hours and 12 minutes of direct sunlight. At this time of year in Alaska, it never really gets dark. The Midnight Sun Classic baseball game in Fairbanks begins around 10:30 p.m. with no lights.

Our family went to Wonder Lake to experience this special evening. The ranger station commands a direct view of Denali with picturesque Wonder Lake in the foreground. I can't think of a more scenic ranger station in the entire park system than Wonder Lake. The mountain virtually glowed in the setting sun, as if lit up from within, turning from deep orange to gold to pale pink. As the last rays of light faded off the summit, the mountain turned a ghostly gray, a shadow looming over the vast tundra plain. A few hours later, the process reversed itself as the first rays of the morning sun struck the summit. It was spectacular. We didn't know how lucky we were to have such a clear evening, this first of many Alaska solstices. It usually rains on that day!

It took some time to adjust to the long days. It was too easy to be outside at 11 p.m., unaware of the hour. We told our kids, jokingly, to "be home before dark." Gradually, our internal clocks adjusted, allowing us to sleep in the evening light.

I hired two sub-district rangers, Gerry Reynolds and Tom Chisdock, who immediately relieved my personal workload. Gerry worked a short season; Tom was full-time. He was responsible for the Wonder Lake Sub-District, and I appreciated his quiet, thoughtful demeanor. Tom fostered good relations with the private landowners and businesses in Kantishna. Tom left after a few years and went on to his first love, the U.S. Fish and Wildlife Service. He became a special agent, duty stationed in Asheville, North Carolina. Both agencies benefited from his dedication to the resource.

THE SUNSET GLACIER SEARCH

September 14, 1991—Drove to Toklat, the second day of road lottery. Received a report about a tent blown over on the Sunset Glacier.

Backpackers Eran Hood and John Campbell are overdue. Got a flight from 33 Charlie Tango (park plane) but very turbulent winds. Requested technical mountaineering team from Talkeetna. Search gearing up.

It seems I can't escape searches! This one was unique for me because it involved the hazards of glacier travel, requiring technical mountaineering expertise. Fortunately, the rangers in Talkeetna were some of the best in the world and took charge of glacier travel.

Local employees Eran Hood and John Campbell set out to climb Scott Peak a few miles from Eielson Visitor Center. The climb required ascending Sunset Glacier, always a hazardous proposition. They were reported overdue when they did not return to work as scheduled.

On September 15, after a late-night planning session, the Talkeetna mountaineering team and others were flown onto the glacier. They established a base camp under severe windy conditions and began a ground search.

September 16, 1991—High winds and low clouds all day, "snarky" weather. A search team arrived from Anchorage and was air-lifted onto the glacier. Flying very limited due to poor conditions. Eran's parents arrived from California, gave them a briefing. We're all very tired. Flew back to Toklat from Eielson, got to bed at 2300.

It's dangerous to put people out on an active glacier, and I was concerned for rescuer safety. Fifty-knot winds with gusts to 70 knots made flying impossible at times. The first ground team found the missing hiker's camp, but there were no other clues indicating direction of travel. They could have fallen into a crevasse, drowned in the river, or wandered off, totally lost in the fog and wind-driven snow. We deployed Alaska-based volunteer rescue teams, Alaska State Troopers, and the Alaska Fire Service.

Having the parents present added some stress, but they were very understanding and appreciative of all we were doing. It always takes some tact to deal with anxious parents and relatives. I tried to keep them all informed as to what was happening in the field.

With improving weather on September 17, more ground searchers explored nearby river bars for clues. Flying weather improved. On a hunch and with his knowledge of the area, park pilot Jim Unruh flew over the range to the south side to check drainages leading up to the crest from Scott Peak/Sunset Glacier. Jim spotted the pair walking slowly down the Chulitna River drainage and dropped them some food. Once we got that news, I flew in the Bell 212 helicopter, landed, and scooped them up. The reunion with parents at the search base was heartwarming, and I thought about how I would feel if my kids were missing.

On debriefing, we learned that Eran and John had summited Scott Peak, got disoriented in the fog, and descended on the wrong side of the mountain. Eran fell into a crevasse and was rescued by John. With minimal gear and no food, they spent eight miserable days either trying to cross back over the range or descending and making a camp. They stayed in the camp, eating soapberries, the only food they could find. With a map but no compass, they realized their error and committed to a long, arduous trek to civilization, 20 miles away. They were very lucky young men, and they knew it. Eran's parents wrote a very nice letter of thanks to me personally; it was copied to the secretary of interior and the White House!

An Expensive Moose Hunt

September 23, 1991—Flew into two hunting camps on the Swift Fork River. Landed at Amos Lakes to interview reporting party, George Palmer. Jim and I circled in 33CT while the others looked for the moose kill. I got very airsick in 40-knot winds. We seized meat, antlers, etc. Finished up 2030 hours. Saw one grizz.

What began as a simple poaching case quickly grew complicated with conflicting reports, multiple violations, a foreign national, and a plane wreck. Hunting guide George Palmer reported that a neighboring commercial guide's client had taken a moose illegally within the original "old" park, where hunting is not permitted. Hunting with a federal permit is legal in Denali Preserve lands, which lie adjacent to the original Mount

McKinley National Park and 1980 park additions. A team of rangers, along with a U.S. Fish and Wildlife Service agent, flew via fixed wing and helicopter to the remote camp on the Swift Fork River, about 100 miles west of park headquarters. It was a long day, flying a minimum of 300 miles in turbulent weather.

We interviewed the alleged offending guide and his client, "Gunther," a member of the Austrian parliament. Gunther had paid $10,000 for the guided hunt, not including airfare to the United States. He admitted to shooting the moose, a 72-inch-antler-spread trophy bull, under the direction of his guide. While rangers and the agent began looking for the kill site, Jim and I circled in the park plane to direct them from overhead. Bouncing around, getting beat up in the turbulent air and making increasingly tight circles, I began to experience symptoms of airsickness: sweating, lightheadedness, and queasy stomach. Out came the barf bag, and I filled it. I still had to do my job as spotter and keep my eyes on the team down below, but I was in no shape to do much else. I just wanted to die. I was so happy when we landed on the dirt strip, my legs wobbly as I got out of the plane, trying to look "professional."

After interviewing all persons involved and collecting evidence, including the trophy moose and Gunther's beautiful, expensive rifle, we returned to headquarters. Gunther was not happy—he lost the trophy of a lifetime and his rifle, neither of which were returned.

Weathered out on September 24, we returned on September 25 to gather more evidence. On approach, we were advised by Rescue Coordination Center Elmendorf AFB that an emergency locator transmitter (ELT) beacon was activated near our location. The source turned out to be an aircraft owned by George Palmer, who had attempted to land near a third, previously undisclosed hunting camp. He had cracked up his plane attempting to land on a gravel bar but wasn't injured. The case was getting more bizarre. Eventually, a total of two moose and one caribou, all illegal, were seized from the two guiding parties. The trophy moose antlers were so large that we flew them externally, strapped to the skids on the front of the helicopter. It made quite a sight.

A trial at federal court in Anchorage revealed that Gunther's guide had used a set of outdated maps with incorrect park boundary lines.

He tried to convince the judge that he thought he was doing right by staying out of the park, but the judge wasn't sympathetic, telling the defendant that he could have avoided all this by buying a current map for $5. As for Mr. Palmer, who thought he was doing good to turn in a bad guy, he too was charged with illegal hunting, lost his valuable guide's license, and crashed his plane. And Gunther went home empty-handed.

"WHATEVER YOU DO, DON'T LET GO"

March 9, 1992—Flew to Kantishna at 0900, windy but clear. Exchanged sled dog crews. Stopped at the Roadhouse to deliver their mail. Noah and Chaos got into a dog fight; Noah lost a tooth. Made it to Wonder Lake Ranger Station about 1230. Staked out the dogs, unpacked.

This was my first big trip with the dogs, and it remains one of the best experiences of my time in Alaska. I flew in the park plane to Kantishna,

Three modes of transportation: exchanging crews at Kantishna airstrip.

an old mining community at the terminus of the park road near Wonder Lake. After exchanging crews, we skied four miles to the ranger station towing our gear on sleds.

It was an enjoyable few days at the station. The weather was sunny, with temperatures in the forties and a clear, blue sky. I took advantage of the good skiing and explored places that are difficult to access on foot in summer. One afternoon, I sat on the front porch in the warm sun eating lunch, everything dead quiet except for the drip, drip, drip of icicles melting off the roof and the occasional cackling of a ptarmigan in the willows. The mountain, 23 miles away, looked like you could reach out and touch it. Spring was fast approaching.

March 12—All too soon, it was time to head back to "civilization." Gary Koy and I each would take a team of seven dogs the 90 miles back to headquarters. As we hitched up that frosty morning, dogs lunging and barking furiously, Gary reminded me, "Whatever you do, don't let go of the sled." The start was downhill, then across frozen Wonder Lake and into a large stand of trees called "Big Timber."

Acknowledging that I was ready, Gary pulled his hook and was off like a shot, the dogs straining at their harnesses. I bent down to release my snow hook and cut my right index finger on a sharp bolt protruding from the handlebar when the sled jolted forward. I was bleeding like a stuck pig, but there was no time to stop and take care of the wound. I stuffed my bleeding hand into my glove, and we were off, the dogs chasing after their buddies already down the bottom of the hill. I've never traveled so fast on a dogsled before or since. My finger stung like hell, but I concentrated on hanging on.

In the trees at Big Timber, we stopped to let the dogs settle and catch their breath. I quickly got out my handkerchief, tied it around my finger, and stuffed it back into the glove, the cold helping the clot to form.

Traveling up the McKinley River bar, hoarfrost glittered in the hazy sun, the Denali massif, the highest point in North America, off to our right, looming in the blue March sky. The dim sun felt good on my cheeks, but it was cold down on the river, frost forming on my fur ruff. I was so excited to be doing this. My dreams of Sargent Preston had come true! "On King, on you huskies!" If only my buddies in the Lower 48 could see me now—Tom Habecker, Alaska dog musher! It doesn't get any better than this.

Gliding on in near silence, the only sound was the panting of the dogs, the hiss of sled runners on the crystalline snow, an occasional "gee" or "haw" from Gary, or a raven squawking in the cold sky. We stopped for lunch at Thorofare patrol cabin, which is hidden in steep, rocky Gorge Creek. The dogs stretched out to snooze in the warm sun. I dug my first-aid kit out of my pack, cleaned my wound, and bandaged it properly. Gary was mortified that he had neglected to see the sharp bolt on the sled that had injured the district ranger, his boss, but I assured him I would survive.

After crossing the sweeping, braided Thorofare River bar, we climbed the open tundra to Stony Pass. By late afternoon, with Denali fading behind us, we gradually descended across the treeless, rolling tundra of Highway Pass toward Toklat and the end of a 36-mile day. Ephemeral sundogs framed the low, hazy sun, lighting up a rainbow of ice crystals in the gauzy air. Like an apparition, Gary and his team disappeared in and out of the fog, a ghost musher gliding across the open tundra. It felt like being in a snow globe of ice crystals and sunshine. Divide Mountain was clothed in the gold of the setting sun, the frozen Toklat River in the valley far below. It was so perfect and peaceful.

We got to the Toklat cabin and began melting snow on the oil-burning stove to water the dogs. It can take well over an hour and many buckets of snow to get enough water to reconstitute dry dog food. After feeding the dogs and bedding them down for the night, we ate our supper. I had stayed in this cabin many times, and it felt like home. The cabins, especially in winter, are welcome refuges for weary travelers and have even saved lives. Every cabin has a logbook where cabin users record their comings and goings, weather, trail conditions, and wildlife sightings. They are part of ranger lore, filled with tales of incredible trips and hardships along the trail. I loved to read the stories of my predecessors and hoped that I could measure up to their heroics. I wrote about our day in the log and hit the sack.

There is nothing so quiet as a cabin deep in the Alaska wilderness in winter. The only thing you hear is the crackle of the fire or the hiss of the

Coleman lantern. On this night, we heard the mournful wail of a lone wolf on Divide Mountain across the river. The dogs answered back with their ghostly howl, and then all was quiet again.

March 13—Stepping outside the cabin this morning, I heard a wolf howling in the distance. What a special way to start the day in this magnificent place. After a hearty pancake breakfast, we pulled the hook for the next leg of our journey. My first challenge this morning was "surviving" notorious Ice Cream ("I Scream!") Gulch. It's famous among mushers for its inclined river of blue-green ice. The dogs don't like traveling on ice, but it was the best route. Digging their toenails into the ice, I ran, slipping and sliding, pushing the sled uphill on the polished surface. The sled began to pendulum wildly on the glass-smooth ice, and I hung on for dear life as the runners hit an obstruction, almost turning me over, then pinballing me back in the opposite direction. A flock of white ptarmigan erupted from the willows; moose, caribou, and wolf tracks flew by as brush slapped me in the face. Gary was amused, but I made it without killing a dog or myself.

Slip sliding away on Ice Cream Gulch.

Sable Pass is the last high point of the trip. We "rough locked" the runners to get down the icy trail. Rough locking involves wrapping a short piece of chain around the runners to provide friction against the ice. It's kind of like automatic braking on a car. We eased our way down and made it to Igloo cabin for the night—a fine spaghetti dinner, cowboy coffee, and a friend to share it with. The aurora danced overhead as I dreamed of a ghost musher disappearing in the ice fog.

A sunny day greeted us on March 14 as we made our way east. We pushed and shoved our sleds up the dreaded "Teklanika Drop-Off," a steep embankment leading from the river bar that eats rookie dog drivers. We stopped at Sanctuary patrol cabin for a quick lunch and proceeded on up Hogan Creek and the Savage River to the park road where the plows were working. The kennels truck arrived to take us back to the kennels.

The trip had ended, but it will never be over for me. I'll never forget the sights, sounds, and smells of those days in the winter wilderness that is Denali. It's why I came here.

On August 29, I flew with Ron Purdum to Mystic Pass on the Tonzona River to pick up a backcountry ranger. We landed on the unimproved gravel airstrip bisected by Ripsnorter Creek and a large boulder at the end of the strip. There was a big splash of water when we hit the creek, the boulder looming larger by the second. Ron did a great job controlling the plane on the rough terrain, and we made it back safely. Ranger Ron Purdum assumed the park pilot position after Jim Unruh and his wife Joanne transferred to Great Basin National Park. We were sorry to see them go. Ron came to the Park Service after retiring as chief of detectives in Rockland County, New York, where he had a distinguished 20-year career in law enforcement. He learned to fly under a special education program for law enforcement officers, earning his commercial, instrument, and flight instructor rating.

THE ROAD LOTTERY FROM HELL

September 11, 1992—Road lottery began today. Snowing, road open to Giglioni bridge. I checked the road, snowing hard at Polychrome Pass. Moved road closure to Teklanika, then back to headquarters as snow worsened. Worked into the night to get folks out, hikers from backcountry, professional photographers ("pro-phos"). Overnight at Toklat.

Always a hectic four days, this year's road lottery event was one for the record books. The Denali Road Lottery began as a special event in the late 1980s when the park allowed visitors to drive their own private vehicles into the park after the bus system closed for the season. There were accidents and rollovers on the narrow, gravel road. Dogs chased caribou, and visitors fed wildlife and tried to camp overnight. It was a circus, and the rangers dreaded it.

It was so popular that, after a few years, a lottery was implemented to control the crowds. Up to 400 vehicles per day are permitted to drive into the park. Although it's a special treat for visitors to experience the park at their own pace, things can quickly go awry.

Weather in September in Denali is a crapshoot. Sometimes, the weather is beautiful with warm, sunny days. Just as often, it rains and snows. This large, early winter storm was a surprise to everyone. It began snowing a few hours after the lottery began, and there were hundreds of vehicles out on the road. Conditions quickly deteriorated as cars began to slide into ditches and get stuck. People were unprepared for cold, snowy weather. We worked until almost midnight that first day getting people unstuck and out. Many feared they were going to get stranded as we herded them out in convoys, accounting for every vehicle.

I shoveled through four-foot drifts on Polychrome Pass on September 12 to get home that night, picking up a few stranded hikers along the way. It snowed all day. There were 14 inches of new snow on September 13 with 27 inches on the park airstrip at headquarters.

September 15, 1992—Made a helicopter flight late in the day to video the entire road to Kantishna. Up to 15-foot drifts in places. Superintendent and chief ranger also on board to see the situation. Stopped at all the businesses in Kantishna to discuss evacuation plans.

The flight with the superintendent was a stroke of luck. He hadn't understood the gravity of the situation until seeing it with his own eyes.

When we returned to headquarters, he told me and my boss to do whatever was necessary to safely get the stranded visitors out. He then got on the phone with the regional office and secured emergency funds to lease a large D9 Caterpillar dozer and overtime compensation.

It snowed all day on September 16. Fifty-eight people and 10 horses remained stranded in Kantishna. I made several helicopter trips to rescue stranded hikers. Our road crew performed heroically, battling high winds, poor visibility, and massive snowdrifts. The plows arrived in Kantishna on September 18. We escorted everyone out in convoys, working into the night. I locked the gate for the winter, and the 1992 road lottery from hell was over.

LIFE IN THE DEEP FREEZE

February 1, 1993—No school today, -59° in Healy, -42° at our house.

February 2, 1993—Minus 42° again, "warmed up" to -20°, light snow.

A period of deep cold hit our region. Strange things happen at these extreme temperatures. Tires develop flat spots from sitting, car seats freeze into bricks, fan belts and hoses shatter, and windshields break. Exposed skin freezes in seconds. I "burned" my fingertips on the cold glass while changing an outdoor lightbulb. Our kids liked to throw boiling water into the air and watch it turn to ice crystals before it hit the ground. Frozen Jell-O shatters when hit with a hammer—don't ask me how I know. I have a friend who entered a backcountry patrol cabin at -30°F, found a bottle of vodka, took a big swig, and flash froze his esophagus.

We dressed in layers: long johns or thermal skins for a base, then polypro-, fleece-, or wool-insulated coveralls, a parka with hood and fur ruff, and sock liners under heavy wool socks. "Bunny boots," the white rubber boots worn in Antarctica, saved our feet. They have multiple insulating layers in the soles and an air bladder that can be inflated for flying. If your feet get wet, they still keep you warm. My feet never got

The Michelin Man all dressed up for cold weather.

cold in bunny boots. Gaiters keep snow and ice out of the boots. Mittens are warmer than gloves. A face mask protects your face from frostbite; a balaclava is also handy. Goggles protect your eyes while driving a snow machine. Donna sewed a fur ruff to my hood, creating a microclimate of warmer air around my face. Working outside on a snow machine or dogsled, covered from head to toe, I looked like the Michelin Man, only green!

Some people say that after −20°F, it's all the same, but that's not true. I could always tell when it was colder than −20°F because my nose hairs froze. At −30°F, frost building up on your eyelashes begins to freeze your eyes shut when you blink. At −40°F, the air becomes visibly dense and burns your lungs. Icicles begin to form under your nose. Deep cold stings exposed flesh and takes your breath away. Cold seeps into the tiniest opening. Fingers, no matter how well protected, begin to go numb and stiff. You have to learn to do everything with gloves on. Cocooned in your house, you pray that the heat stays on and the pipes don't freeze.

We didn't drive to town at −40°F unless absolutely necessary. Our truck carried a full complement of emergency gear: extra hats, mittens, socks, sleeping bags, shovel, food, extra flashlight, and batteries. There were no cell phones in those days. If you saw a car stopped along the road, you stopped and rendered assistance. It could be a life-or-death situation, and it might be you next time.

Driving in town became hazardous, cars sliding through ice-coated intersections on the red light. Dense ice fog hung over the city as most people left their vehicles running while in stores or restaurants, even while at the movie theater. Many businesses had outdoor electrical receptacles or "plug-ins" where you plugged in your car's block heater to keep the engine warm. I equipped our truck with a block heater, an oil pan heater, and a battery blanket. Every vehicle had a pigtail plug wire sticking out of the grill and carried a blue cold-weather extension cord. We used an ice chest equipped with hot packs to keep our produce from freezing on the long trip home. No one looked askance when we lugged a bag of lettuce and bananas into a restaurant to keep them from freezing while we had dinner. As I've said, Alaska is a strange place.

Flying back to Fairbanks from "Outside," which is what Alaskans call the rest of the world, you arrive into a world of darkness, stinging cold, and ice fog. I've never been to Neptune, but I bet it's much like Fairbanks in the dead of winter.

School was rarely canceled in winter, hardly ever for snow. But the deep cold made travel unsafe for those riding the bus. Kids were required to have coats, boots, a hat, and gloves, or they couldn't get on the bus. Outdoor recess was canceled only at -20°F or colder. It was often too cold to snow with little moisture in the atmosphere. Our kids never missed a day due to snow, but there were times when it was deemed too cold to run the school buses.

January 5, 1999: -54°, a new all-time record at HQ; warmed up to -36° by 1600; only a few made it into work.

January 19, 1999: -47° at Riley Creek at 2030; Sun hits the office today at 1145!

January 19 was a much-anticipated day in our office. It was the day the sun reappeared over the hill at noon at park headquarters. It may seem silly, but seeing the sun cast a shadow for the first time in two months was cause for celebration. We gathered around staring at the few weak sunbeams streaming through our office window. Often, the low sun was not visible, depending on your horizon. Winter sunlight in Alaska is glorious, peach-colored alpenglow most of the day. It's like living in an old hand-tinted photograph. It lifts your spirits knowing that the days are visibly getting longer.

The record of -54°F set on January 5 still stands. There were colder places, but the weather station at headquarters was "official." At these temperatures, the air is thick and dense, and you can actually see the cold as it settles to the ground. Only a few of us ventured forth to record the weather and check on the dogs. And then it "warms up" to -30°F, and you breathe a sigh of relief. After such cold, -20°F felt downright balmy, and we often opened the doors to our office to let the "warm air" in.

The River Wild

July 20, 1993—Flew in park plane to Lake Minchumina, very smoky from wildland fires. Rendezvous with George Wagner and

Sandy Kogl who made the trip by boat from Nenana. Spent the night with the Collins family at their homestead. Sandy flew back to headquarters.

This was an extraordinary experience for me. It was Sandy's idea to get me out of the office and experience true wilderness under the guise of posting boundary in this most isolated part of the park. For most of the time, we were at least 100 miles from the nearest paved road.

Lake Minchumina, near the geographic center of Alaska, is a 27-square-mile lake near the northwest corner of the park. There is a modern, paved runway maintained by the State of Alaska, a few cabins, and several abandoned homes built by the Federal Aviation Administration for the long-abandoned flight service station. The latest census records a population of 13, mostly summer residents. It's about as far from civilization as you can get.

We stayed with Dick and Florence Collins, true Alaska pioneers. Dick managed the flight service station for many years, and Florence was an early aviation pioneer. They raised twin daughters, Julie and Miki, who make a living hunting and trapping. George and I had supper with the family and bunked in a guest cabin. I was shocked when Dick turned on his TV to watch CNN via his satellite dish, quite a contrast to the wilderness setting they lived in.

The next morning, George and I departed on our 300-mile trip, navigating the river leading from the lake in his 16-foot flat-bottomed Jon boat with small outboard motor. The Muddy River, true to its name, was a serpentine maze of loops and sloughs, slowly winding its way to join the larger Kantishna River. It's truly wild country, but there are signs of former habitation: old trappers' and prospectors' cabins, slowly sinking into the ground; a long-abandoned Native village; and a Native cemetery with weathered, wooden Eastern Orthodox–style crosses hidden in the brush. We explored one of the timeworn cabins. There was an old-fashioned cast-iron cookstove still inside, and I thought, "If this stove could talk, what a tale it could tell. How did it get all the way here from Seattle? Who lived in this tiny hovel? How did they exist in this lonely place?" The long-forgotten village and trapper cabins were quiet, melancholy

Relics of long ago—a trapper's cabin on the Kantishna River.

places, ghosts of long ago when early explorers and settlers with hopes and dreams of striking it rich or making a new start made their way into this remote wilderness. I felt I was intruding on their memories and admired their ambitions and determination. It was a privilege to visit these lonesome places, which few people ever see.

Hordes of mosquitoes, no-see-ums, and blackflies attacked relentlessly every time we came ashore. There were black clouds of the devils trying to get to exposed skin, and without a head net, it was hard to breathe. They couldn't penetrate my life jacket but did get to my hands and through my trousers. Bug spray was a joke; it was as if they had been waiting all their lives to attack me. We hurried back to the river to escape the torment.

We camped on a large sandbar in the middle of the Kantishna River. In a clear stream that joined the river, I caught a northern pike, a prehistoric fish with large, sharp teeth. The creek erupted when it savagely attacked my fishing lure. I'd never seen a fish fight so ferociously before.

We cooked the fish on a driftwood fire, using a willow stick as a skewer. It doesn't get any fresher than this; we were living off the land. I'll never forget that evening, sitting by a small driftwood fire, sipping some whiskey, telling stories, and watching the sky turn to gold near midnight. It was so peaceful and quiet, the only sound the swish and gurgle of the river, so far from anything else. It felt like we were the only two people on Earth.

July 22, 1993—Up at 0700 and on the river by 0900. Traveled about 130 miles today, posted some boundary with signs. Stopped at old village site of Bearpaw, saw several abandoned cabins and native burial sites. Spent the night in Foresberg's cabin with permission. Great to get away from the bugs! Hot today, saw the mouth of the Toklat River where it enters the Kantishna River.

Wildlife was abundant: Moose, startled to see us, splashed out of the river and disappeared into the thick alder brush, and ducks and geese took flight. Momma merganser herded her raft of ducklings to safety in the rushes. Muskrats, dozing on their reed houses in the sun, stared as we quietly drifted by. Beaver, slapping their broad tails, insulted at our presence, disappeared into the water, peeking up to see what these strangers were. These critters may never have seen a human before.

You couldn't see your hand six inches below the surface of the silty river. We got stuck on some sandbars, the river "too thick to drink and too thin to plow." George changed the prop after hitting a submerged stump. There were other hazards: "sweepers," trees lying just under the surface, that could easily swamp a boat, and fallen trees, jutting out from the banks, rhythmically slapping the water. Undercut banks suddenly caved in, adding to the slurry, and I saw white melting permafrost ice dripping into the river. Swirling currents caught us, spinning us around and driving our underpowered craft into logjams. Watch for the boils: that's where the deep water is.

We managed to post a few boundary signs to make the trip "official." I doubt that anyone has seen them. Around noon on July 23, we entered the large Tanana River, which flows west into the Yukon. George said that we needed to be careful of barge traffic and hope that our motor didn't quit lest we float downstream into the mighty Yukon. Traveling 70 miles upriver, the Tanana brought us to the small town of Nenana on the highway system to Fairbanks and home. Those four days, like my whole career, sometimes seems like a dream.

CLEARWATER DAYS, CABIN NIGHTS

March 10, 1994—Left Stampede at 1130 with George, Clare, and Bill Perhach, en route to Wonder Lake via snow machines. Ate lunch at "the bus;" refueled at Stampede airstrip with gasoline cached there. Got to Lower Toklat patrol cabin, hauled our gear using skis and sleds. Had a fine chili dinner at 2000 hours.

I always looked forward to spring trips on the north boundary. While the route was the same, each trip differed in trail conditions and challenges. This was first of many winter north boundary trips I made over the years. It's about a 100-mile journey, requiring three days of arduous travel via snow machine. The original Mount McKinley, or "old park," is managed as wilderness in winter, precluding the use of snowmobiles. However, Wonder Lake can be accessed over state and new park addition lands located along the north boundary. We began the trip on the old Stampede Trail, a primitive "road" pioneered in 1903 by miners seeking access to the Kantishna Mining District. The road quickly deteriorates into a crude trail ending at the abandoned Stampede Mine. After that, the route is cross-country, using the frozen Clearwater River corridor to get over Myrtle Pass and into the Moose Creek drainage and Kantishna. The trip is never easy but is always fun.

Clare Curtis, aka "Sacajawea," guided us through the maze of creeks and rivers, hills, and natural obstacles. With 12 hours of daylight and daytime temperatures in the forties, it's a good time to travel before ice and snow deteriorate.

After crossing the frozen Teklanika River, we reached the notorious "magic bus," made famous by Jon Krakauer's book *Into the Wild*. It's the story of Christopher McCandless, an idealistic young man who, in 1992,

"Two old Swedes." Mark Motsko and author at Upper Toklat patrol cabin.

wanted to get away from civilization and live alone in the wilderness and died in this bus.

We stayed our first night at Lower Toklat patrol cabin, located deep in the wilds and difficult to reach in any season. Adhering to regulations, we parked our machines at the wilderness boundary and skied a short distance into the cabin, towing our gear on sleds. The cabin is a typical Denali boundary cabin, constructed of logs with a corrugated metal roof and overhanging porch roof. Built in 1931 by "two old Swedes," it was completed in two months. Later, 12 log doghouses and a raised food cache were added. The doghouses are still visible, but the cache is gone.

The 12- by 14-foot cabin is a welcome refuge after a hard day's travel. It's nestled in the spruce forest, the Toklat River a short distance out the front door. Like most Park Service cabins, it has a woodstove, a chuck box that folds down into a kitchen worktable, two sets of double bunks, a table, chairs, lanterns, tools, water buckets, candles, a deck of cards, and the cabin logbook.

The first order of business when entering a cabin is to remove the protective "bear door" studded with sharp nails to keep bears from trying to enter and then remove at least one window shutter to allow light inside. Next, make a fire to begin melting snow or bust a trail to the river and lug back the water buckets, then find a bunk, unload your gear, get supper started, and have a drink of whiskey if you have it. Finally, enjoy being with friends, snug and warm, deep in God's country. There's nothing like being in a rustic cabin deep in the Alaska wilderness with the "lights" swirling overhead at night.

The cabin was cold in the morning with an inch of ice in the water buckets. A quick fire in the woodstove and a hearty pancake breakfast with plenty of hot coffee got us going.

We continued up the Clearwater the next day. It's a beautiful trip, traveling on smooth turquoise blue ice for miles, nestled in a steep valley, forested with spruce, alder, and willow. Frozen rivers become "highways" in winter in Alaska. It's a bit unnerving traveling on a frozen river. In clear areas, you can see water flowing and air bubbles traveling under the ice. Pressure ridges form, and sometimes the ice booms as it expands and contracts, sending a crack between your feet and causing your heart to skip a beat. With experience, you learn to read the ice, looking for color changes, avoiding thin spots, and listening for sounds of live water. The trick is to not go through the ice in a bad spot and by all means, *stay out of overflow.*

Overflow, also known as "Aufeis," German for "ice on top," forms in cold weather when water wells up from ice dams on rivers or streams. It also occurs when streams freeze almost solid, forcing water under pressure to the surface, where it continues to build successive layers of slushy ice, sometimes creeping up embankments onto land. Overflow is like frozen quicksand and can easily snare anything that strays into it. Winter travelers need to keep a sharp eye for the telltale signs: slushy blue-gray ice, bubbling water, and ice on land where it shouldn't be. Experienced sled dogs can sense overflow and will jump up onto the sled to avoid it. George Wagner got into overflow on this day, his heavy snowmobile mired in frozen slush. It can take hours to get a heavy machine back onto solid ground. We always carried a come-along winch, shovels, and saws to extricate ourselves from this hazard. Sometimes, we had to build a fire to thaw out a frozen snow machine track. It was a rare trip to travel up the Clearwater and not get caught in this frozen mess.

Stuck in overflow—how fun!

Once again, we got into overflow that had migrated high up on land away from the river. You can be into it before you realize it. Slush and water flooded my gear-filled sled. I wasn't worried, knowing my sleeping bag and clothing were secure in a waterproof "dry bag" designed to keep contents perfectly dry.

Climbing out of the Clearwater drainage, the terrain opened to tundra with groves of aspen and willow. Gaining Myrtle Pass, we got our first view of Denali, always impressive, its magnificent hulk looming ghost-like over the flatlands below. We pioneered a trail down to Glen Creek, Moose Creek, and the Parker cabin through deep drifts and brush, at times having to snowshoe and pack a trail to get the heavy machines across the steep slopes. It's grueling work.

The Parker cabin sits on a bluff overlooking Moose Creek. It was built by miner Johnny Parker during the Kantishna gold mining days. It's roomy and comfy, with two rooms and a picture window with a stunning view of the mountain. At this time of year, the evening light is soft and peach colored with a hint of lavender at sunset. There's also a classic elevated food cache outside and the obligatory outhouse.

After dinner, I unpacked my gear and was shocked to find a soggy sleeping bag and wet clothes! Unbeknownst to me, a bolt on my sled had worn a hole into the dry bag, allowing water to soak all my belongings. My cabin mates thought it was hilarious. There I was, with a wet sleeping bag and mostly wet clothing. Being the resourceful ranger I was, I found an old caribou hide and a wool blanket and made my bed by the woodstove. After the raucous laughter and crude comments subsided, I created an impromptu clothesline and dried my stuff out, keeping the fire going all night.

March 11, 1994—Saw the moon set over the mountain. Off by 1100, and down Moose Creek, negotiated an overhanging ice shelf. Stopped at Kantishna Road House to visit the winter keeper. Parked our snow machines at the boundary and skied up to the ranger station. Dog teams hauled our gear later. A beautiful evening, a good meal. There are six dog teams here with a total of 60 dogs!

The next day, we made our way down tortuous, alder-choked Moose Creek to Kantishna, parking our machines at the wilderness boundary. From there, we snowshoed about a mile to the Wonder Lake Ranger Station, arriving in late afternoon. A team of rangers with sled dogs is stationed there most of the winter to patrol the area and have a presence on the west end of the park. They were glad to see us, and we enjoyed swapping stories into the night. Wonder Lake is always a great place to spend some time, and winter is no exception. The station has perhaps the most scenic view of any in the park system, overlooking the 649-acre lake with Denali looming 23 miles away. I spent the next day skiing under blue skies and temperatures in the forties, enjoying the deafening silence and magnificent landscape.

1995—A Year of Change

The year began with the presentation of my pin for 25 years of service by the regional director. Where did the time go? We moved into a Mission 66–style home just up the street and made a cozy bedroom for Katie in the basement. For the first time in their lives, each of the girls had her own room.

On May 11, my ace-in-the-hole Wonder Lake Sub-District ranger, Tom Chisdock, accepted an offer to become a special agent with the U.S. Fish and Wildlife Service. It was Tom's dream job, and I was glad for him. On Tom's departure, Sandy supervised west-end operations.

I began the long process of recruiting and selecting two permanent sub-district rangers. Alaska is a difficult place to work and live, and I wanted people who really desired a challenge. On July 18, after many weeks of research, phone calls, and meeting with park management, I offered Mark Motsko the position of Wonder Lake Sub-District ranger. Mark and his wife Phyllis were working at Theodore Roosevelt National Park in North Dakota after tours of duty at Great Smoky Mountains and Crater Lake. Mark had a reputation for working with people who might not be fond of the government—such as the private landowners in Kantishna. He came highly recommended and readily accepted my offer. It was a great choice, and I couldn't have been more pleased. Mark is one of the finest rangers I've ever worked with, and he and Phyllis remain our best friends to this day.

On August 3, I offered Chuck Passek the Savage River Sub-District ranger position. Chuck and his wife Jan were working at Everglades National Park. You can't get much farther from Alaska than Everglades. Chuck was a great addition to my staff. He never got rattled in desperate situations, quietly went about his work, had good ideas for improving operations, and was a competent medic. Both Phyllis and Jan became valued members of park staff, working in concessions and wildland fire, respectively. We were glad to have them all on board.

Things were going well. Then Sandy Kogl announced her retirement, effective October 14. We were all sad to see her go. A local legend, confidante, and friend, she taught me so much about Alaska and helped me appreciate this special place.

Some Dark Nights on the Parks Highway

November 22, 1995—Off today, my Thanksgiving holiday. Called out at 2100 to a multi-car accident on the Jonesville bridge, outside the park. There were two cars, four fatalities. MAST military helicopter on-scene along with state trooper special investigation unit. Snowing, home at 0400.

A bad evening, just before a family holiday. It was dark, windy, cold, and snowing. The cars hit head-on, probably driving too fast for conditions. Four people were dead in the mangled wreckage. Someone told me a dog had jumped off the high bridge and drowned in the frigid waters below. I worked with the Tri-Valley ambulance crew from Healy, all good folks who knew their business. We provided care to the survivors, who were evacuated by the military helicopter. The troopers were in charge, and we all worked as a team. I arrived home exhausted, mentally and physically.

The Passeks and Motskos arrived the next day and joined us for Thanksgiving dinner. I was still recovering from the previous night's experience but thankful that these fine folks had arrived safely from their long journey and were now a permanent part of our community.

December 6, 1995—Called out at 2000 to back up Trooper Ellis on a stolen vehicle stop north of Cantwell. He arrested one male. Windchill calculated at −79°!

We periodically got called to back up our local state troopers. Roger Ellis, based out of the village of Cantwell, was a local legend. Short in stature but tall in courage, Roger never hesitated to do his job despite being alone with only the Denali park rangers and another trooper 40 miles north for backup. He was responsible for public safety of more than 100 miles of primary highway, along with thousands of square miles of other territory. The truckers on the Parks Highway all appreciated Roger and stopped to assist him if he needed help—now that's respect.

On this night, Roger had stopped a vehicle reported stolen in Fairbanks. The driver had just been released from jail, stole a car, and headed for Anchorage. Roger pulled the guy over on a lonely stretch of road along the Nenana River, about 20 miles south of park headquarters. I was his closest backup.

When I arrived, Roger had the guy in handcuffs in the back of his patrol car. I got out of my car and was stunned by the intense cold. We didn't remain on scene very long as Roger took his prisoner to a holding cell at his post in Cantwell. I later calculated the windchill at -79°F. It was dangerously cold, but Roger did his job. There's a brotherhood in law enforcement, and we helped each other numerous times. Roger retired a few years later, and the whole community turned out to wish him well. I was sorry to see him go but happy for his new adventure.

THE PRINCESS HOTEL FIRE

March 20, 1996—At 0715 the fire brigade responded to a fire at the Denali Princess Hotel. This large fire burned 180 rooms, the restaurant, lobby, and gift shop. Six fire departments fought the blaze, along with helicopter water drops and a large loader from nearby Usibelli Coal mine. We were released at 1500 and returned to headquarters and prepared for the next call. Held a quick critique.

Coming down the hill from headquarters in Engine One, I saw flames and black smoke shooting into the sky from the Princess Hotel across the river. I said to my partner in the adjacent seat, "We're not going to save this one." It was the largest structural fire of my career—few rangers get to experience such a large inferno.

The Denali Princess is a 280-room hotel located just outside the park. It serves nearly 60,000 Princess Cruise Line passengers annually and pumps millions into the local economy. With first guests scheduled to arrive May 14, a fire of this magnitude was a devastating blow to all concerned.

We arrived on scene and took up a position near one of the guest room wings that was not on fire. I conferred with Rusty Laselle, fire captain of the local Tri-Valley Fire Department, and together we came up with a plan of action. Rusty's crew was attempting an interior attack in part of the building, trying to keep flames from spreading. My crew began applying water to the nearby wing to assist their efforts.

The fire grew, flames spreading unseen through the overhead, though the interior crews were unaware of this. The fire was advancing rapidly in multiple directions. Additional resources arrived from departments as far as 50 miles away. Water supply, always a problem in rural situations, was critical. Hydrant access was limited this early in the season, and we began to shuttle water via water tenders from hydrants in the park, six miles distant. Someone eventually cut a hole through the ice in the nearby Nenana River, allowing tankers to draft from that source, shuttling water to portable tanks near the fire.

The fire gained on us, flames shooting 80 feet into the air. Fortunately for the fire crews, the normally windy canyon was dead calm that day. Any small wind would have driven the fire into adjacent structures, with the possibility of the whole canyon business district being lost.

My crew continued their exterior attack as the fire advanced toward our position. Flames were gobbling the building before our eyes. As it grew hotter, I noticed that one of the plastic side marker lights on our engine was beginning to melt! It was time to move, and we repositioned our apparatus to a safer location.

I lost track of time until I saw that a food wagon, courtesy of the Fairbanks Chapter of the American Red Cross, arrived with sandwiches and beverages. Then I noticed a TV crew and reporters taking pictures. This was becoming a major news story.

A helicopter appeared and began water bucket drops on the fire, dipping from an open spot in the river. I conferred with Rusty. We were losing this thing and needed to do something drastic. I remembered hearing about the large fire at the Gardiner school outside of Yellowstone. Firefighters saved part of the school by plowing a fire break through the building with a large front-end loader. The fire stopped when it ran out of available fuel. Rusty worked at the local coal mine and immediately realized that they had a *huge* loader there that could do the same thing. He called the mine and requested a loader and water truck. The loader was so large that there was concern that it might collapse the Windy Creek highway bridge that spanned the canyon to the north. They took a chance, and about 45 minutes later, a monster loader appeared at the scene. We instructed the operator to plow a swath through an unburned wing of the building in advance of the fire. This tactic worked, and we were able to stop the flames and gain control of the blaze. We all breathed a sigh of relief that no one got hurt.

Battling the Princess Hotel fire.

The state fire marshal determined that the fire began near a floor furnace that had been brought online the evening before. Arson was ruled out.

Seattle-based Princess Tours was already planning to rebuild and refurbish the hotel even as it was burning. They had booked all available hotel rooms within 100 miles and were contracting with a major construction company to begin work as soon as possible. Orders for a complete line of kitchen supplies and furniture had already been issued. Hundreds of tourists had booked their vacations and were expected in less than three months. The goal was to rebuild within 60 days. No one thought it possible. By Friday, a temporary phone line ran to a construction office trailer already on-site. Princess threw hundreds of people at the job and was able to open most of the facility on time. The estimated loss was $25 million. Our crew received a letter of commendation from the director of the National Park Service.

Taking a Chinook to Base Camp

April 18, 1996—Flew to Talkeetna with Stan in 33CT. In late afternoon, we flew in U.S. Army Chinook helicopters to the climber's basecamp at 7200 feet. Off-loaded supplies and 800 gallons of jet fuel. I flew back to Talkeetna in the park's Lama helicopter. Slept on the floor in the office. Skeeters are out!

To support the climbing operation, a base camp consisting of WeatherPorts and a fuel depot are established each year on the Kahiltna Glacier. The Chinook helicopters based out of Fort Wainwright in Fairbanks do the work as a high-altitude training exercise. All equipment is removed by July each season.

My counterpart, South District ranger J. D. Swed, invited me to help put in this year's camp. It's a multiday operation, often delayed by poor weather or high-wind conditions. I came prepared and camped out on the floor of the ranger office.

I had been in many different types of helicopters, but the Chinook was a totally new experience. The Boeing-Vertol CH-47D Chinook is a twin-rotor, $35 million workhorse used by the military to transport heavy loads at high speed with excellent performance at high altitudes like those in Afghanistan. The aircraft can transport 33 fully equipped troops and carry up to 26,000 pounds via external sling-load. For this mission, the two aircraft were equipped with four large skis, costing $10,000 each. This was an impressive machine!

We lifted off from Talkeetna and flew toward the mountain. There were five rangers and about five crew members with room for plenty more. It was strange to be able to stand up and walk around inside the helicopter and look out of the Plexiglas bubble windows. I peeked out the cockpit windshield as we got into the mountains. It was like looking at an IMAX image, the peaks growing larger as we flew toward them.

We began to circle and lose altitude, and I didn't know what was happening. The crew chief partially lowered the large rear loading ramp door as hurricane-force rotor winds whipped up a blizzard of swirling snow. I felt a bump as we touched down, continued to move forward, and then

Taking a Chinook to base camp on Denali.

lifted back into the air to circle again. After repeating this maneuver four times, the pilot told us he was doing "skid landings" packing a "runway."

After landing and allowing the engines to wind down, the ramp fully extended onto the glacier, and we began unloading gear. We were instructed to use the onboard oxygen system between loads if needed. It was arduous work, carrying heavy loads in deep snow at an altitude of 7,200 feet. When the job was done, I took some time to marvel at the spectacular scenery and kept my camera busy. I knew I might never get back here again.

J. D. and I flew back to Talkeetna in the park's contract helicopter, an Aérospatiale Alouette Lama. Like its namesake pack animal, the Lama is capable of carrying heavy loads at extreme altitudes. A Lama still holds the helicopter world altitude record, set in 1972, of 40,820 feet. This aircraft can fly over Mount Everest and is perfectly suited for rescue work on Denali's summit altitude of 20,310 feet.

J. D. wanted me to see his unique, magnificent district and asked the pilot for the 50-cent tour. With oxygen available, we flew near the summit with ease and explored the tortured terrain of this ethereal realm. We were surrounded by a sea of sharp granite peaks and hundreds of thousands of acres of ice and snow, the birthplace of the large glaciers flowing to the valleys miles below. Flying in this tiny machine at 20,000 feet, I felt so insignificant surrounded by such astounding mountain scenery.

Tragedy on the Dall Glacier

On February 1, Brad Johnson, age 27; his wife Cheryl, 21; and their 21-month-old daughter left Port Allsworth, west of Anchorage, in a single-engine Piper Pacer bound for Anchorage. At about 4 p.m., Johnson radioed flight service that he was disoriented above low cloud cover and was low on fuel. Thirty minutes later, Rescue Coordination Center Anchorage picked up an ELT near the Yentna Glacier in Denali. The Rescue Coordination Center launched a 210th Alaska Air National Guard Pave Hawk helicopter and a C-130 fixed wing for communications cover. Both aircraft turned back due to poor weather after repeated attempts to get to the site. The park was notified and assumed command of the incident.

Mark Motsko, Dennis Knuckles, and I left for Talkeetna at 2000 hours shortly after receiving the call. We loaded two snow machines, extra fuel, skis, snowshoes, and our personal gear and made the 150-mile drive south to Talkeetna, the staging area for the search. It's a long drive in the dark on icy roads, dodging moose and fighting sleep. After a quick briefing at 3 a.m., we managed to "sleep" for about 90 minutes on the floor at the ranger station.

Denali State Park ranger Dave Porter, local guide Chad Valentine, and two EMTs escorted Dennis and me the 50 miles into a wilderness lodge located more than 30 miles from the crash site. There's a maze of recreational snow machine trails and thousands of acres of rough terrain in the area, and Dennis and I would never have found our way without the local experts.

We arrived at Angel Haven Lodge in the late afternoon, guided by owners Tom and Larry Angel, who met us midway. After unpacking and grabbing some food and hot coffee, six of us began breaking trail toward the Dall Glacier. Travel conditions were poor with deep snow, high winds, and blowing snow. Deep in the wilderness, there was no trail, forcing us to bushwhack. In fading light, we pioneered a route along the river through dense tangles of willow and alder and over rocks and fallen trees, the unconsolidated snow up to our waists. We didn't really know where we were but followed the river corridor toward the glacier. With only eight hours of daylight at this time of year, after 17 miles, we decided to return to the lodge in the dark. We later learned that the 210th made several attempts to reach the crash site during the day but were turned back due to snow and high winds. The pilot reported that it was "the most sporting flying I've ever done." Still in rescue mode, our ground assault became even more critical.

The Angel family spent years building this lodge on the banks of the Yentna River, hauling materials with snow machines in winter or flying into the gravel airstrip in summer. It was very plush by backcountry standards, and we enjoyed a hot shower and a wonderful meal prepared by Mrs. Angel. I had never eaten so well on a rescue! The Angels were true angels and treated us like royalty over the next few days and couldn't have been more gracious.

The next morning well before dawn, eight of us continued to break trail to the toe of the glacier. We struggled all day to get there, 36 miles in deep snow and whiteout conditions. Reaching the glacier, we found a place to establish a base camp with a possible landing zone for a helicopter. A short break in the weather allowed a Black Hawk helicopter to insert a team of Park Service volunteer mountaineering rangers onto the glacier. Ranger Roger Robinson, team leader, reported that teams would have to be roped up in order to probe a route into the crash site. Plans were made to transport additional mountaineering personnel into the area by snow machine if flying conditions worsened. With darkness and intense snow falling, we returned to the lodge at 2000 hours for food and some rest. The search was really ramping up—at its peak, more than 60 persons were assigned to the incident.

Early the next morning, the support team returned to Talkeetna while Dennis and I made our way back toward the glacier. Nearing the landing site under clearing skies, we heard the periodic loud *thrum* of a large helicopter in the basin and local radio traffic between the pilot and the ground team. The Air National Guard helicopter had located the plane at the 2,900-foot level on the Dall Glacier, almost two miles from the plotted ELT location. The crew was able to determine there were no survivors. Later that day, a team of four mountaineering rangers were airlifted into the site to extricate the bodies.

Returning to the lodge near dark and unfamiliar with the route out, we decided to spend one more night and travel in full daylight the next day. We returned to Talkeetna and made the 150-mile trip back to park headquarters, driving in a snowstorm, exhausted and psychologically drained.

The plane was well off course, almost 100 miles north of Anchorage, when it crashed. We learned that air traffic control had made repeated attempts to vector it back to Anchorage, but the pilot, who was not instrument rated, evidently became disoriented in the clouds. Investigators determined that the plane apparently blindly flew full speed into the glacier and disintegrated, killing everyone instantly on impact. Later, the Alaska National Park Service regional director presented the Angel family an engraved plaque and letter of appreciation for going out of their way to support our rescue operation. I'm told the plaque hangs in the lobby of the lodge.

"Can You See My Husband?"—Life with the Emergency Phone

For after-hours emergencies, four ranger residences were equipped with a party-line emergency phone. When a call came in, the phones rang in all four homes until someone answered. Only the Fairbanks Emergency Dispatch Center and the State Trooper Dispatch had the number. It was for *emergency calls only.*

One night in May, at about 3 a.m., the phone rang, and I jumped out of bed, heart racing, to answer it. A lady calling from Chicago said that her husband was climbing "Mount McKinley" and wanted to know if I could see him. He was wearing a red coat. After a short pause to collect my thoughts, I told her that it was 3 a.m. and dark; the mountain was 90 miles away, and I could not see it; and even if I could, there was no way I could see a person, even if he was wearing a red coat! Another time the phone rang in the middle of the night, and the guy wanted to know how the fishing was this time of year. Another "emergency" call was from a guy who was planning a trip to the park and wanted to know if he should bring a gun. No!

How did people get this number? We later learned that new dispatchers at the Emergency Center hadn't been told that the Denali number was for emergencies only. All they knew was that when they dialed the number, someone always answered! We got it straightened out, and the information calls stopped—another "perk" of living in a park.

In late April, Donna and I spent an evening in the Toklat patrol cabin. It was just the two of us out there, the road still closed to traffic. We saw 25 Dall sheep on "Sheep Mountain" across the river and five caribou on the river bar in front of the cabin. Lying in bed, the light fading at 10 p.m., all you hear is the low rush of the river in its rocky bed, the flute-like trill of the varied thrush, or the cackle of a ptarmigan in the alder. It was so good to be back out here, feeling like we were the only people left on Earth.

In May, Kelly graduated from high school with honors, receiving nearly $50,000 in scholarships. In September, we flew to Spokane, Washington, where Kelly began classes at Whitworth College. I cried like a baby when we had to leave her.

DEATH ON THE RIVER BAR

July 23, 1997—Cloudy, catching up on paperwork. Called out at 1315, report of a person in trouble on the McKinley River bar, CPR in progress. Flew to the scene with medic Janie Laselle, two rangers on scene. A 39-year-old Russian climber drowned. Flew the body back to headquarters.

Russian mountaineers Fedor Lounev and Dimitri Oborotov had successfully summited Denali after several weeks of climbing and were ending their expedition by doing a traverse, exiting on the north side near Wonder Lake. Their last obstacle, within sight of the park road, was crossing the McKinley River south of Big Timber. At this time of year, the river was about 42°F and running high with glacial runoff. While crossing the third braid of the river bar, the two men, both carrying heavy packs, were swept off their feet and separated. Oborotov was able to swim to the next gravel bar, but Lounev was carried downstream. Oborotov dropped his pack and ran downstream, where he found Lounev and dragged him out of the water. Lounev was unconscious, not breathing as his partner started CPR. After 30 minutes with no success, Oborotov covered Lounev with clothing, ran three miles to the trailhead, and flagged down a bus driver to report the incident.

Wonder Lake rangers Brian Johnson and Greg Russell overheard the radio traffic, commandeered a nearby helicopter assigned to a resource management crew, and flew to the scene. They called park dispatch for help and restarted CPR.

Medic Janie Lasalle and I flew to the scene in a chartered commercial tour helicopter, about a 40-minute flight from park headquarters. Landing on the small gravel river bar, I saw Greg and Brian still doing CPR, the river rushing just a few feet away. I told them to cease CPR, placed the heart monitor on Lounev, and observed asystole—no electrical activity. I established a phone patch with Fairbanks Memorial Hospital through our communications center and told the responding physician our situation. I explained that CPR had been in progress for well over an hour with some interruption, there was no pulse or electrical activity, pupils were fixed and dilated, and we were in the middle of a river bar. The doc immediately called it and told us to cease resuscitation efforts. We put Lounev's body into a body bag and flew back to headquarters.

An incident like this leaves everyone involved emotionally drained. The images of that day still are with me. But the story doesn't end there. We had the body of a Russian national and all his belongings to deal with. I arranged for a mortuary to transport the body to Fairbanks until we could make further arrangements. I interviewed Oborotov, who told me that Lounev's parents lived in a remote part of Russia and spoke no English. This was not going to be easy. I inventoried and packaged up Lounev's belongings. Talkeetna rangers, who deal with foreign national fatalities frequently, advised me to contact the nearest Russian consulate, located in San Francisco.

On Saturday, I called the Russian consulate's office and identified myself as a U.S. park ranger in Denali National Park, Alaska, and explained that a citizen of his country had died in an accident. Before I could explain further, the man said in a thick Russian accent, "Is weekend, call back Monday." Click. I was dumbfounded.

A few days later, we made the necessary arrangements to return Lounev to his homeland. I spoke to his parents through a translation service and gave them the details of their son's untimely death. I'm not sure how much they understood, but they seemed grateful for the call. It was such a sad situation, and I can only imagine what the emotions were on the other end of that call. How ironic that these two men successfully climbed the highest mountain in North America and did a challenging traverse only for one of them to drown in a river within sight of the park road.

DESPITE YOUR BEST EFFORTS

June 6, 1998—Called out at 0600 for ambulance response to Grizzly Bear Campground, five miles south of the park. An 18-year-old girl coded with an asthma attack. We did CPR, intubation, full ACLS protocols. She did not survive. Back from the Healy Clinic 0930.

An early start to a bad day. This young lady and her friends had just graduated from high school and were on an outing to celebrate. Their whole lives were ahead of them. The girl had an asthma attack; her medications were ineffective. We arrived moments after the Tri-Valley ambulance crew, who were doing CPR. Working as a team, we performed advanced cardiac life support (ACLS) procedures: heart monitor, IV access, intubation, and bagging the airway. The girl remained unresponsive as resuscitation efforts continued on the 20-plus-minute trip to the local clinic.

At the clinic, the physician's assistant and nurse took charge. There were about six of us working on this girl in the tiny emergency room. Additional drugs were administered, CPR continued, and the airway was maintained. We worked for nearly an hour trying to get this girl back to life. Finally, with concurrence from a physician at Fairbanks Memorial, resuscitation efforts ended. It was over, the finality of death staring us in the face. We were all emotionally drained and physically exhausted. What began as a beautiful Saturday morning with a group of friends celebrating their recent achievement and looking forward to their next adventure in life ended in tragedy.

June 13, 1998—Day off. Called out at 1600 for a cardiac arrest of a 71-year-old man on a tour bus at Mile 16. Attempted defibrillation, unsuccessful. Tri-Valley crew and helicopter on scene. He didn't make it.

When I became a medic, I knew I would experience death up close and personal. It never got easy. It seems that I was continuously dealing with tragedy in many forms: medical situations, vehicle accidents, plane crashes, drownings, bear maulings—the list goes on. Sometimes, I got lucky and saved someone's life or helped them out. It made me feel good. But you can't win 'em all, and sometimes people die despite your best efforts. It's something you must understand if you are to succeed in this business. Sometimes, on days like this, I just went home and hugged my kids.

Fall is my favorite time of year. Warm days and cool nights, cobalt blue skies, and flocks of thousands of sandhill cranes heading south. The tundra becomes a riot of color, and aspen leaves glow in the golden sunlight. Bull moose congregate for the rut, grunting and panting, their ivory colored antlers flashing in the sunlight. Caribou sport magnificent velvet-covered racks; Dall sheep laze on hillsides, soaking up the sun's last bit of warmth. Grizzlies vacuum up all the blueberries they can while spring cubs tumble and play nearby. Winter is coming all too soon.

In late September, with the road closed for the season, I spent a quiet afternoon out west. Sitting at Stony Dome, the incredible mountain that is Denali looming in the distance, I thought about my family back in Pennsylvania, wishing they could be here to share this with me. I saw my family only about every two years and missed them, the years fleeting by. God, it's so quiet here. What a privileged life I've led.

Donna began her new job as the school counselor for the Denali Borough School District. Education and working with kids have always been her first love, and I was glad she finally got the opportunity to do what she does best. The school district is the size of Massachusetts with only three schools, and she drove about 500 miles per week between the schools. She also commuted the 125 miles to Fairbanks each week for six semesters to earn her school counselor license. She loved her work.

Together, we made the decision to stay in Denali until my mandatory law enforcement retirement in 2005. She had sacrificed her career for mine all these 30 years, and now it was her turn to thrive. We were very proud of her.

MOOSE CREEK AND THE "ALASKA STATE BIRD"

July 5, 1999—Kelly, Katie and I drove to Moose Creek pit to begin our hike into Moose Creek cabin, about five miles distant. Started at 1515, the bugs terrible. Arrived at the cabin 1745; glad to be inside, rain shower in the evening. After supper, we read, played Scrabble and killed mosquitoes. Saw six bears on the trip in.

July 6, 1999—Up at 0715, oatmeal and bagels for breakfast. Closed up the cabin and began hike out in wet grass; got drenched immediately, a slog through willow thickets and soggy tundra. Had cold drinks at Toklat, then home, tired but happy.

We tried to have a family outing at least once per season. This occasion was a father–daughter trip, made special with Kelly home from college. It was a hot, muggy day as we followed the faint trail across open tundra, then down into the dense spruce forest to the Moose Creek patrol cabin. Katie wasn't into hiking that day, and I kept telling her it was "just a bit farther," convincing her that the five-mile trip was only three miles.

When we got down into the spruce forest, we heard a low humming sound, like a power transmission line. There was no electricity here—just billions of hungry mosquitos! In Alaska, mosquitoes are sometimes known as the "Alaska state bird." I've never experienced so many bugs concentrated in one place. We instantly became their prey. Insect repellant was worthless. We sprinted toward the cabin hidden in the dense forest and made a beeline for the door. Unlocking the door, we dove inside. Being a good dad and brave ranger, I reemerged to remove the window shutters and get a bucket of water from the creek. Everyone was on their own to use the outhouse!

Inside, I showed the girls the miracle of Buhach, a powder made from pyrethrum flowers. When burned, the nontoxic smoke kills any bug known to man. We watched in amazement as hundreds of mosquitoes dropped from the air. I've seen Buhach only in Alaska, and, sadly, it's no longer being made—a loss to mankind!

What a treat to spend time with my girls in a small rustic cabin in the wilderness. We joked and talked, played cards, and ate well. We still talk about that memorable trip. You can't replace these moments, and I'm thankful to have had the opportunity to do this type of thing with my family.

The turn of the millennium found me sitting in my office at midnight, tasked with making sure all of our computers would work. This was a result of the Y2K scare that digital equipment would cease to function properly. After calling in the okay to the regional office, it was time to cut loose. As acting chief, I decided to bend the rules on this historic occasion. We had accumulated a large cache of confiscated fireworks over the past few years, and I decided it was time to celebrate. Donna, Mark, Phyllis, and I met in the street in front of my house shortly after midnight. It was -36°F, with about three feet of snow on the ground, perfect launch conditions. We ran for cover as star shells, cherry bombs, bottle rockets, and assorted explosives lit up the night sky. A highlight was the bottle rocket that landed on the superintendent's house. My glove caught on fire; we laughed hysterically. And yes, alcohol was involved.

When Life Isn't Fair—Cale Shaffer

June 20, 2000—Awoke to a terrible day—learned that Cale Shaffer, two volunteers, and pilot are missing and presumed down somewhere near Kahiltna Glacier; many phone calls; at 1630 heard that the plane was located with no survivors. We all feel so bad.

There is some truth in the saying "Only the good die young." Cale Shaffer, an Eagle Scout who grew up in a small town in central Pennsylvania, dreamed of becoming a park ranger. During summers as an outdoor recreation student, Cale worked as a camp counselor at several youth camps and later as a juvenile probation officer in Arizona before getting a seasonal ranger job at Grand Canyon. In 1999, at the age of 24, Cale realized his dream to come to Alaska when he was hired as the Wonder Lake seasonal ranger.

Cale loved his job and threw himself wholeheartedly into his work. A personable fellow, Cale made friends with the local business owners who didn't always trust the government. Cale was constantly ready to respond to any situation and pitched in wherever he could to help others. He was a model ranger, every supervisor's dream, the kind of young man you want your daughter to marry.

Living at Wonder Lake, Cale could see Denali from his front door. He longed to become a mountaineering ranger and climb the mountain. He once told Mark Motsko, his supervisor, "Someday I'm going to be on that mountain." In 2000, Cale accepted a job as a mountaineering ranger based out of the Talkeetna Ranger Station. Climbing the mountain was compelling, but, true to Cale's personality, he wanted to help others. He was looking forward to this second patrol—perhaps he would get a chance to get on the summit.

On June 19, Cale, mountaineering volunteers Brian Reagan and Adam Kolff (both 27), and commercial bush pilot Don Bowers took off from Talkeetna en route to the Kahiltna Base Camp to swap out crews. They never made it.

The weather at base camp had been "skunky" all day, with low clouds and intermittent snow. Bowers had checked the weather on an earlier flight, but the route to base camp was obscured by clouds. The weather had improved when the Cessna 185 departed Talkeetna shortly after 5 p.m. On the trip in, Bowers communicated with other pilots who told him that base camp was weathered in again and inaccessible. The return route closed in behind them. At about 6 p.m., Bowers radioed he could see sunlight on the Lacuna Glacier to the west and would return by that route. That was the last radio transmission he ever made.

No one really knows what happened that day. There was no ELT transmission or "Mayday" call. The plane was reported overdue shortly before 8 p.m.

An air search began in adverse weather—poor flying conditions with low clouds and high winds. An Alaska State Trooper helicopter located the wreckage on a brushy hillside near the confluence of the Yentna and Lacuna glaciers at about 4 p.m. on June 20. The plane had broken up in flight, both wings entirely sheared off, the aircraft in pieces, and the fuselage burned. The occupants apparently died instantly. The bodies were retrieved and returned to Talkeetna.

Investigators surmised that the plane encountered severe turbulence and was forced to the earth by a sudden, violent downdraft. Heavy rain and four inches of hail were reported at a wilderness lodge a few miles away. Small planes like this are not equipped with radar or terrain-avoidance equipment. They flew unknowingly into the storm. There wasn't even time to call for help.

On the morning of June 20, I awoke to the news of the missing plane. The entire park was bewildered. Three employees had been killed in the line of duty. People were visibly upset, spoke in low tones, and went about their work in a subdued way. The close-knit work group on the west end, where two of the three young men had worked, was devastated. I went about my duties in a fog, overcome with personal grief. Cale was a friend and a good ranger, young and full of potential. Cale's former supervisor, Mark Motsko, drove the 80 miles to Wonder Lake to personally break the news to employees along the route. Mark solemnly lowered the flags at each ranger station as he went.

As the acting chief ranger, it was my responsibility to make notifications to the Federal Aviation Administration, Washington Office, and other agencies. I met with the superintendent about a memorial service. I arranged for a Park Service critical incident stress debriefing team to come to Denali for employee support and counseling. It's a service that is used all too frequently these days, but it shows how far we've come in the profession.

On June 25, the superintendent, Mark, and I, along with more than 500 people, attended a memorial service in Talkeetna. Chief ranger Ken Kehrer flew back from his detail at Capitol Reef. Don Bowers was a beloved member of the community, a very experienced mountain pilot with more than 9,000 hours of flight time. That town was hurting badly, as was the Denali Park community.

I was asked to host the park memorial service, held at the McKinley Village Community Center. The place was packed, and emotions ran high as friends and coworkers expressed their grief. The program celebrated Cale's life, a moving tribute to an outstanding young man. I managed to get through that evening, a lump in my throat the whole time. After it was over and folks departed, I went outside, crumbled to my knees, and cried uncontrollably, a week's worth of pent-up emotions spilling out. I didn't cry that hard at my father's funeral. Emotionally drained, physically weak, I had to get it out of my system, and that moment helped me get back to a better place.

The end of this sad story is this: Mark volunteered to accompany Cale back to his parents' farm home in Pennsylvania. He traveled with Cale's cremains in a small backpack, always by his side—Cale would have wanted it that way. Cale was never alone, always with someone who loved him. It's Mark's story, a tribute to two fine men.

LOST AND FOUND

August 20, 2000—Up early, plans for SAR; Jeff Caulfield and I flew four hours on Stoney-Thorofare; located lost female hiker at 1215; flew her back to HQ, then I flew back to Toklat.; then transported 40 y/o female with urinary tract infection by vehicle to east side; back to Toklat by 1800—another long day.

A short entry for a long day, but things went well for the two people who needed help. Twenty-five-year-old Rachel Stanton from Grand Canyon, Arizona, began her three-day backcountry hike in good weather. A skilled hiker in good physical condition, she was appropriately equipped for the bad weather that overtook her.

On her second day, low clouds and fog rolled in, obscuring the landscape. In the open tundra, there are few landmarks, and everything looks the same. There are only 34 miles of trail in Denali, and hikers must rely on their experience and skills when they encounter trouble. Rachel lost her way in pea soup fog and walked 13 hours in the wrong river drainage. Realizing she was off her intended route, Rachel made the wise decision to stay in one location rather than wander around, which would make it more difficult for rescuers to find her. She set up her tent on an open ridge, waiting for the weather to clear or for help to arrive. Her friends reported her overdue, and we began an aerial and ground search.

A wilderness permit is always a helpful tool to get a search under way. It shows dates of travel, intended route, and equipment. Backcountry users in Denali are required to view a 30-minute video highlighting the dangers of river crossings, route finding, low-impact camping, and bears. The Denali backcountry is divided into management units that are sometimes hundreds of thousands of acres with only five people allowed at a time. Fortunately for all of us, the terrain Rachel was in was mostly open tundra.

Flying low, down a sweeping drainage, I spotted someone waving frantically from the ridge. We landed nearby, and I walked up to the tent. Rachel was overjoyed to see me in my pumpkin orange flight suit. She said she felt "like an idiot" for getting lost, but I told her she had done the right thing by staying put and not wandering aimlessly around. When we got her back to park headquarters, she gave me a quick kiss—I'd never had anyone do that before, and it was kind of sweet!

Rachel sent me a kind note, which reads in part,

Dear Tom

Thank you for making my day, week, year, life. It was such a joy to see your bright smiling face as you jumped out of that helicopter. Your kind words and humor made me feel like much less of an idiot through the whole thing. I will think of Denali and all the wonderful people there often.

It's nice to get such a letter, and I've gotten my fair share. It makes all the hard work you do worthwhile. It's one of the many reasons why I wanted to be a ranger.

August was a busy month for the Habecker family. Kelly returned to Whitworth College for her senior year—where had the time gone? Now it was Katie's turn. She graduated from high school as valedictorian in May and was also attending Whitworth in the fall. I'm not sure Spokane was ready for both of the Habecker girls, but there they went!

Katie and I flew to Spokane on August 30 to get her settled at school. It was a busy week, and I fulfilled my role as dad, carrying luggage and buying computer supplies. What an experience to see both your kids at school, growing into young women right before your eyes. Back home, we were now empty nesters, getting used to the quiet and less crowded bathroom.

2001—A MOMENTOUS YEAR

April 12–13, 2001—AR15 semi-auto rifle training at the range; will be carrying in vehicles.

A short diary entry but a big change in our law enforcement profile. We transitioned from revolvers to semiautomatic pistols in 1994. Responding to the times, rangers had to adapt. We were issued AR-15 semiautomatic rifles to help equalize the threat of increased firepower from adversaries—a necessary but sad comment on our times.

We had a week of intense shooting drills and "Simmunitions" training using weapons modified to shoot correct-caliber paint slugs. Getting shot was painful, even with all the protective gear we had to wear. These realistic exercises are designed to induce stress and make you think and react accordingly. They are as close to the real thing as you can get—I guess.

In May, we traveled to Spokane for Kelly's graduation. With a triple major in English, French, and education, she was on her way to becoming a first-rate teacher. I had the pleasure of driving back to Alaska with Kelly, just the two of us enjoying the scenery and getting to know each other again. She was a young adult now, and I saw her in a new light. It was a great five days together, a father–daughter trip I'll long remember.

In late summer 2001, Donna and I traveled to Bozeman, Montana, where we had purchased a plot of land to build our retirement home. We were preparing for a life after the Park Service. And then it happened.

September 11, 2001

September 11, 2001—An ugly but historic day: terrorists struck the World Trade Center and Pentagon—a nightmare; was called out at 0630 by dispatch to turn on the TV; a quiet day, employees sent home; called out at 2200 to Denali Park Resort for a drunk employee; put him to bed; home 2330.

There are specific dates in history when everyone remembers where they were and what they were doing. For our parents and grandparents, it was December 7, 1941, the attack on Pearl Harbor. Those of us of a certain age remember November 22, 1963, when President John F. Kennedy was assassinated in Dallas. A few remember the space shuttle *Challenger* disaster on January 28, 1986. Now there was a new date marking a change in our lives.

Alaska is four time zones apart from the East Coast. I was still in bed, thinking about getting ready for work, when my phone rang. It wasn't unusual for my phone to ring at odd hours, and it was seldom good news. Dispatch supervisor Diane Brown seemed upset when she said, "Tom, turn on your TV." I asked why, and she replied, "Just turn it on." Donna had already left for school; Kelly was teaching in Kake, Alaska, and Katie was at school in Spokane.

Like everyone else, I was shocked at what I saw. It took a while to sink in, didn't seem real. New York was far away. Was this really happening?

I dressed quickly and went to the office. Were we now at war? What were we, as federal law enforcement officers, supposed to do? Park staff, except for rangers and a few essential employees, were sent home. We met with the chief ranger to discuss what we should do. No one knew how widespread this attack was or what to expect next. For lack of a better idea, we decided to check the highway bridges and railroad crossing for anything suspicious. Public spaces such as the visitor center and post office were checked for bombs or anything unusual. Patrols were extended to midnight.

I felt helpless, not knowing what might come next. I spoke with Donna on the phone. She and her coworkers were trying to explain to students what was happening in New York and offering emotional support. Kelly was safe on the small island of Kake. Katie called later in the day and asked what was going to happen. I told her that I didn't know and that I was glad she was safe.

There was great concern about the security of the Alaska Pipeline, running from Prudhoe Bay to Valdez. Exposed for much of its 800-mile length, it could be easily sabotaged. There was a rumor that some of us would be sent to guard it. This proved false, as we learned the pipeline was being patrolled by aircraft, Alaska State Troopers, and private security.

We received word that our park plane was grounded until further notice. No aircraft were flying; the skies, which usually hummed with small aircraft and commercial jets, were eerily silent. Hunters in remote bush locations, without radio or phones, had no way of knowing what had happened. No planes were flying despite good weather. Days went by, and hunting camps were running out of supplies. When the ban was lifted, people were stunned when pilots brought them newspapers and they learned of the tragedy. In Denali, we settled in for whatever might be coming. I hugged my kids extra tight when they came home for Christmas.

"KEEP THE WATER BEHIND THE DAM"

April 23, 2002—At Fairbanks International 0600 for flight to Redding, California, arrived 1930. It's green down here! Checked in to the hotel, got gear ready. Tired and glad to be done traveling.

After 9/11, there was high anxiety about another attack. Critical infrastructure, such as large dams and power plants, were possible targets. There was a concern that America's icons and historic sites were at risk.

The Statue of Liberty, Independence Hall, the Gateway Arch, Mount Rushmore, the Pearl Harbor Memorial, and Washington, D.C., monuments—all symbols of America's history and greatness—were being protected. As federal officers, U.S. park rangers were assigned to guard these and other federal installations.

Alaska rangers were told that most of us would be rotated for three-week details in the Lower 48. We were to be ready to leave on short notice, having our law enforcement credentials in order and weapons prepared for air travel.

On April 17, I received a call from the regional office informing me I would be going to Redding, California, to guard Shasta Dam. Lake Shasta provides irrigation water for much of California's Central Valley agriculture, vital food supply for the nation. The irrigation water behind that dam and the power-generating plant are critical infrastructure. And they wanted me to protect it!

April 24, 2002—Our first day at Shasta Dam. Got a full orientation of the dam and surrounding infrastructure. There are over five miles of corridors inside the dam! We're told our mission is to "keep the water behind the dam." It's 83 degrees, hot for me! I'll be working day shift for the next three weeks.

Twelve rangers met at the dam the next day. We got an orientation of the mission and the dam and prepared to relieve the crew that had been there for the previous three weeks. Our two crews of six each would be working 12 hours on and 12 hours off, seven days per week, for three weeks with no days off.

Shasta Dam, 600 feet high and seven-eighths of a mile long, was completed in 1945 and was the second-highest dam in the United States at the time. The impounded Shasta Lake is nearly 30,000 acres, the largest man-made lake in California. While it's unlikely a terrorist could blow up the dam, there was a fear that the water intakes could be damaged, rendering the impounded water unusable. We were told to "keep the water behind the dam." We even made up some T-shirts that said "Shasta Dam Counter Terrorism Deployment—Keeping Water Behind the Dam Since 9-11-2001."

I was fortunate to be assigned day shift. We relieved the night shift at 7 a.m., and they took over by 8 p.m. The dam was closed to all vehicular and foot traffic, all tours canceled. A line of protective buoys kept watercraft from getting near the structure. The far side of the dam was protected by hidden intrusion sensors that sent a signal to our command post if someone walked past them. The sensors were checked daily and batteries changed when needed. It was all so surreal, dressed in black utility pants and "boonie hat," carrying an AR-15—not your traditional park ranger image.

We were told to be highly visible and carry our sidearm and rifle wherever we went. We were given keys to access all parts of the dam. I never realized how complex a dam this size was. There are more than five miles of interior corridors, accessed by an elevator and elaborate system of catwalks. It was a bit unnerving to see water squirting from multiple places *inside* the dam but learned this was perfectly normal, that all dams leaked. Permanent gutters carried the water away.

One day, my partner and I decided to go all the way to the very bottom of the dam to bedrock. We took the elevator to its lowest level, then made our way down a maze of steel catwalks to the base of the dam, standing on granite rock more than 600 feet from the surface of the lake. It was cool, about 50°F. I struggled to imagine the amount of water and pressure being held back by the thick concrete. I could feel the vibration of the water cascading through the penstocks to the hydro plant below. We found a light switch and turned off the lights. I'd never experienced such total darkness and had to place my hand on the wall to keep oriented. It was an unnerving sensation.

Patrolling inside the hydro plant, its giant turbines spinning loudly, required hearing protection. Everyone wanted to go "under the river" at least once. We were shown the entrance to a small tunnel that went under the river and exited on the other side. I did it, popping out of a manhole at the base of the dam like in a Roadrunner cartoon. You might say I really got to know Shasta "dammed" well!

Our days were repetitive, like an endless loop in a movie: get up, have breakfast at the hotel, drive to the dam, get a briefing from the night shift, patrol all day, brief the night shift, return to the hotel, have dinner, and fall asleep. Repeat for three weeks—*Groundhog Day.*

The dam ranger.

We had a small command trailer with a sun awning and mist system to help us stay cool. It was hot, in the eighties and nineties, and I was not used to the heat, as it had been in the forties when I left Alaska. There was a grill, and we often chipped in and sent someone into town to pick up food for our evening meal. Grilled salmon and fresh local veggies were a real treat. I went into town to pick up our groceries one day dressed in my black "Ninja pants" and boonie hat. When I checked out, the little old lady clerk said, "How are you boys doing up at the dam? We feel safe knowing that you're there." It made me feel good, knowing that we might actually be making a difference in people's confidence.

After three weeks, it was time to leave. Our day shift crew had bonded, and we were hesitant to say good-bye. This had been an emotional experience for us too, validating that things had changed in our daily lives. We met at a Mexican restaurant, drank our share of margaritas, said farewell, and wished each other well.

"The Lights Are Out!"

October 28, 2003—One of the best auroral displays ever! Spectacular dancing curtains of light. A solar storm is hitting the Earth. Beautiful!

We never tired of seeing the northern lights, visible nearly every winter night. I always looked up to the sky when walking to work in the morning to see the fading light of an earlier display. When a particularly good display was occurring, we called around the neighborhood to alert folks to the show. Everyone stood in the street, oohing and aahing.

Many have tried to describe the aurora borealis. I've never seen an adequate description in print. It's something you have to see with your own eyes. Some say you can actually hear the lights, and I think there's some truth to that. It's part of the mystique of northern latitudes, rich in native lore. All I can say is that a good display on a quiet, cold night is perhaps the most beautiful thing I've ever seen in nature: dancing painted lights, shades of red, green, violet, and white; serpentine waves of color writhing overhead; rhythmic pulsing or strobe-like flashes lighting the sky; and crowns of rays shooting spears of light toward Earth. Displays fade, then magically reappear in another quadrant.

Man will never create a better light show. I tried to grasp the science behind it—charged particles from the sun exciting electrons of gases in the thermosphere that give off energy in the form of light—but it seemed more than that. For me, viewing the lights was an almost mystical spiritual experience that reinforced my own insignificance.

HAPPY NEW YEAR—YOU'RE GOING TO WASHINGTON

January 14, 2004—Got a call this morning that I will be going to Washington D.C. next week on another Homeland Security detail.

With the constant threat of terrorist activities in our country, federal officers continued to be assigned to special details. I was detailed to a three-week assignment at the Department of Interior (DOI) Annex Watch Desk in Washington, D.C. Just like my tour at Shasta dam, it would be 12 on and 12 off with no days off. We were to carry our firearms.

I reported for duty the day after the long flight from Alaska. My partner and I worked the night shift from 2000 to 0800. Our job was to answer the phone! The Watch Desk serves as the hub for taking law enforcement and critical incident calls from all DOI lands. We were also supposed to surf the Web, looking for terrorist "chatter" against DOI assets. I didn't find bin Laden but did manage to shop for light fixtures for my new home. In the three weeks we were there, the phone rang once—a minor incident in a park in New Mexico. I thought it a waste of a GS-12's time, but at least it got me out of the cold, dark Alaska winter for a while.

After a fine hotel breakfast and a nap, I took in the sights, riding the Metro to the Smithsonian and other cool places. One day, I walked the hallowed halls of the Main Interior Building and peeked in the door of the secretary's office. This is the fountain of all wisdom passed down to park rangers driving dogsleds. I now understood it all.

THE LAST BEST SUMMER

Our family continued to prosper. In May, Donna and I proudly watched Katie graduate from Whitworth College with a degree in kinesiology and athletic training. Better still, she was accepted into graduate school at Utah State, beginning in the fall. Our girls were off to a good start.

Faced with severe budget cuts, we weren't able to hire the usual complement of seasonal staff. As a result, at a staff meeting in April, chief ranger Pete Armington informed me that I would be the Wonder Lake Sub-District ranger for the summer. I would be living in the Toklat patrol cabin, 55 miles from headquarters. It was my last summer before retirement. I would get to be a "real ranger" in the field for one last time. Pete told me he probably wouldn't see me all summer, that I knew what I was doing and didn't need any coaching from him. I told him I'd see him in September. Happiness is headquarters in the rearview mirror.

I moved into the Toklat cabin on May 19. The single-room 14- by 16-foot log cabin was one of five similar cabins built in 1930 by the Alaska Road Commission for road crews building the park road. There

The last best summer at the Toklat patrol cabin.

is a small attached storage shed that serves as a rescue cache and an out-house 50 feet up the hill with a nice view of the Toklat River. The cabin is equipped with a pot burner oil stove, a four-burner propane range, and a refrigerator. A small sink drains into a slop bucket underneath. The only running water was out in the river, so I hauled water in five-gallon containers from the nearby Toklat Road Camp. The cabin was sparsely furnished with a table and three chairs, a bed and folding bunk, a chest of drawers, and a drying rack over the stove. A large window looked out on the Toklat River bar and the Divide and Sheep mountains. I could watch Dall sheep, caribou, bears, and even wolves as I ate my dinner. The flagpole outside announced I was open for business. It was cozy, and I loved it.

I was the "lone ranger" in this part of the park. My nearest backup was at Wonder Lake, about 30 miles west. Typically, there were two additional rangers in cabins to the east. I had about 50 miles of gravel road to patrol each day, along with the busy Eielson Visitor Center and Toklat bus/visitor/maintenance complex. I was going to be a busy boy but was thrilled to be here.

The first order of business, after tidying up the cabin, was to muck out the tiny Toklat ranger office, located at road camp a mile down the road. Did I mention there was no electricity in my cabin? Road camp had it all—running water, hot showers, a rec hall/community building, an auto shop, a car wash facility, even sporadic internet access. There was a base radio and phone system that (usually) worked by way of a crude repeater system. The phone was a party line, the reception poor. Some-times I had to commandeer it by saying, "Get off the phone. I really need to use it right now." I took everything out of the office, sorted through the junk, wiped the incessant dust off of everything, and organized my files. I didn't spend much time here, but it was the place for conducting business when needed.

May 24, 2004—Went to Wonder Lake, a bald eagle perched in a tree, loons laughing on lake, beaver swam by my feet, ice slushing up on shore—real special experience; in afternoon washed fire truck and

*ambulance; began cutting brush in front of my cabin, looks better; sow
and triplets at Eielson Visitor Center (EVC).*

Just like my early days in Gettysburg, I was eager to call "in service"
each morning. It was so much better than sitting at a desk answering
email. Every day was different, filled with surprises. I was in the heart of
the park, with dozens of tour buses filled with visitors from all over the
world. Wildlife was everywhere; it was like living in a zoo without bars. It
was rare not to see several bears each day. I enjoyed stopping to chat with
visitors at Stony Overlook and hear about their experiences. Everyone
wanted a picture of the ranger, and I took theirs as well. I answered their
questions, told a corny joke or two, and made some friends for the Park
Service. I tried to spend some time each day at Eielson Visitor Center,
kibitzing with visitors, answering their questions, and enjoying the scene.
It's what we're supposed to do, but many times, it gets lost in the daily
chaos. I always told my staff not to forget why we're here: to get out and
talk to people and learn something from them.

*June 6, 2004—Beautiful day; 70s; got to Toklat after stops at HQ
and Teklanika; scrubbed the outhouse, hadn't been done in a while;
lots of bears, spring cubs near the road; film crew getting footage;
trimmed more brush; made a new toilet seat.*

I was doing real ranger work. Even cleaning the old outhouse was
fun! In these parts, a toilet seat made of two-inch blue foam insulation
makes for a more "comfortable experience" on a cold day. I felt like an
old-time ranger, taking care of his cabin, hauling water, cooking breakfast, and raising the flag. I was having a blast.

*June 16, 2004—The girls rode with me to Toklat; nice supper, spa-
ghetti, bread, fruit, wine; good talks of old times in Alaska. It's good
to be with your kids!*

*June 17, 2004—Made breakfast for the girls and took them to Tho-
rofare Pass for a hike up Gravel Mountain. Said good-bye to Katie*

Katie (left) and Kelly ready for a tundra hike.

who is returning to Spokane—I'm sad; saw them off at Toklat rest
stop after their hike.

I enjoyed every minute I could with my girls. They were young ladies
now, going out on their own. They did solo hikes and backpacking trips.
I must admit I was a nervous wreck until I saw them get off the camper
bus after a night out in grizzly country. They grew up to be accomplished
outdoorswomen, and I'm proud of them. Getting to spend time with
them at Toklat was special.

June 20—Called to Friday Creek to assist a 30-year-old female who
fell off her bike and dislocated her hip. To make matters worse, it was the
couple's honeymoon. I stabilized her and arranged for an air taxi flight to
Fairbanks. I felt bad for both of them.

At 11:30 p.m. on this beautiful summer solstice, I went out to Highway Pass, just a few miles west of my cabin, to enjoy the lingering sunset
and alpenglow on Denali. Seeing a black wolf a mile from my cabin was
a bonus. I knew my time was getting short, less than a year to retirement,
and I wanted to savor every minute of this special place.

June 21, 2004—Called out at 2330 to EVC, campers had a bear in
their camp on Moose Creek; put them up for the night at the visitor
center; home 0030; potluck in the evening (22nd) Very dusty and very
smoky—big fires up north, can't see the mountains; even the river is
obscured in the morning, terrible air quality, endlessly washing my
vehicle due to dust.

Large fires were burning in Alaska this summer. At that time, it was
the worst fire season in Alaska on record; 701 fires burned more than 6
million acres. It never made the news in the Lower 48. We had a 6,000-
acre fire in the park that had been burning for three weeks before it was
accidentally discovered. By the end of June, blue skies were a rare sight.
In the mornings at Toklat, smoke lay low on the river, with perhaps a
few hundred yards of visibility. We all breathed smoke for the next six
weeks. Sometimes, I felt nauseous; my eyes watered and throat burned. I
felt sorry for visitors on their once-in-a-lifetime trip. Denali was all but

invisible, and it became difficult to see wildlife from the busses. I talked to a pilot who told me that when he got above 10,000 feet, the air was clear, the sky blue. There was a collective feeling of living in hell.

There was a wolf den up the road within walking distance of my cabin. I watched them all summer, the adults bringing home ground squirrels, even a caribou leg. As the six pups matured, they ventured farther from the den, exploring the world around them. Like bear cubs, they rolled and tussled, biting ears, chasing tails. One quiet evening, they paid me a visit. I looked out my window and saw a ball of fur tumbling around in my dooryard. Mom was nearby, hunting for a meal. My dream had come true. Here I was, living in a cabin in Alaska with wolves in my front yard and getting paid to boot.

Evenings at the cabin were idyllic. After supper and a quick shower at road camp and a few minutes hanging out with folks at the rec hall, I returned to my retreat a mile down the road. The long Alaska twilight was exceptional. Sitting at my table, the low murmur of the river always present, looking out the window at sheep grazing on the hillside, a few caribou milling around on the river bar, a thrush singing its sweet melodic song, and the periodic clucking of a ptarmigan in the willows, reminded me of the famous Edward Hicks painting *Peaceable Kingdom*. I lay in my bed after a busy day, feeling at peace with the world.

One morning, still half asleep, I walked up to the outhouse and almost into a grizzly that was probably still half asleep himself, walking down the same path. Both our heads were down when we suddenly each realized the other's presence. The bear stopped, snorted, and wheeled around. I uttered an expletive, wheeled around, and dashed back to the cabin. I was definitely awake now. It's a thrilling way to begin your day.

August 2, 2004—At EVC due to bears, then to HQ; took a report from a hiker who said he was injured by a bear—said he drove an ice axe into the bear's shoulder!

There isn't much to say about hitting a grizzly bear with an ice axe except it was stupid. I don't recall all the details, but I do know that the bear was being more than generous in not mauling this guy. He got off lucky and lived to tell the tale. Bear spray is the recommended tool for warding off problem bears.

August 26, 2004—Termination dust! Distant peaks are white; light rain here.

"Termination dust" is a euphemism for the first snow of the season. It signals the end of summer when seasonal staff are "terminated." That's the official lingo for "your job is over." It remained very smoky, but there was a chill in the air, foliage beginning to change colors. Autumn comes early in the north and lasts only a few days.

September 21, 2004—4" of new snow and snowing, drove to EVC, blowing, can't see the road, clearing by afternoon—beautiful; began packing up, pulled wildlife closure signs. MY LAST NIGHT AS THE TOKLAT RANGER—it's been a great experience, and I'll never forget this summer.

It was a sorrowful time for me. I realized that my last full summer as a ranger was coming to an end. I began to see things in a new light. It became a time of "lasts": my last road lottery, the last seasonal potluck, and the last hikes to some favorite spots. I visited places I knew I would never see again and began saying good-bye to people who I wouldn't see before my departure the next June. It was a strange feeling, and I had some sad evenings alone in the cabin. I reflected on all the things I had seen and done since that first day in the chief ranger's office in Gettysburg. The time had flown with enough experiences for two lifetimes. How I loved this job and this place.

I spent the next day doing final cleaning, getting things ready for winter. Dog food was already stored in mouse-proof cans, the fuel tank was full, buckets were turned upside down, bedding was secured overhead, food rations were plentiful, and candles were ready to light. I fastened the window shutters, locked the door, and put up the bear-proof outer door. I took down the flag one last time, folded it, and decided I deserved to keep it as a memento. I didn't want it to end, but it was time to leave. I would return in spring to get things ready for the new ranger, even spend a night or two. But it would never be the same for me. The Last Best Summer had come to an end.

A Season of Lasts

January 1, 2005—Our last year in Alaska began with a New Year celebration with our good friends the Motskos, champagne, and fireworks. The "season of lasts" had begun.

On March 11, 2005, I made my last snow machine patrol up the Clearwater. The five-day trip was more of a fond farewell for me with good friends Clare, Sandy, and George. We never made it to Wonder Lake because of severe overflow conditions. But it's all about the journey, and seeing Denali from Moonlight Creek and cabin nights with old friends was my good fortune.

The last few weeks of spring flew by. I signed my final retirement documents, an exciting, sobering experience. I completed a fancy Power-Point slideshow to show at my retirement party and finished the "how-to-do-it" manuals I wished I'd had when I arrived. The new Toklat ranger would have an immense jump start by not repeating the same mistakes I and others had made over the years.

I gave my last bus driver orientation and was very moved when they gave me a standing ovation. Pete, my boss, said he had never seen anything like it—concessions folks loving a ranger. I guess I had done something right throughout the years.

I'm Too Short for This

May 11, 2005—With only a little more than a month to retirement, I was getting "short" as they say in the coast guard. I just wanted to do my time peacefully and get out of this alive. When the phone rang at midnight, I knew it wasn't good—it never is. The dispatcher said there was an intoxicated person at the concession employee dorm. Everyone was at law enforcement training in Anchorage, except chief ranger Pete Armington and me. It was "send a ranger" time, and Pete and I were on deck.

I scrambled to get dressed, got my gear, and picked Pete up at his house. At the dorm, we found a kid out on the balcony, yelling and screaming obscenities, drunk out of his mind. We asked him to come with us peacefully, but he resisted, forcing us to dump him on the ground and apply the handcuffs. He was going to jail in Fairbanks, 130 miles away. I had four weeks to go, and I didn't need this crap!

All went well until the kid puked in the car. Then he went to sleep, and we rolled the windows down. We got to town and booked him into jail. By now, it was about 3 a.m. We had to take this guy for his initial appearance before the magistrate in a few hours. It made no sense to drive all the way back to the park. We decided to get a motel room and catch a few hours of sleep.

Pete and I walked into the lobby of the Comfort Inn, dressed in our uniforms, body armor, and firearms. I said to the young clerk at the desk, "Hello, we need a room for a few hours." He looked at us kind of warily and said he had plenty of space. It wasn't until we both reached for our wallets that we realized that, in our haste, we had left them at home. We didn't have a cent on us. I said to the clerk, "Oh, by the way, we don't have any money." Now he was really getting leery. Here were these two guys with guns, in the middle of the night, wanting to share a room for a few hours with no money. I explained our situation, that we were Denali rangers transporting a prisoner and had to be in court in a few hours. We would call our office assistant first thing in the morning and get our government credit card information and pay for the room. With a dubious look, the kid gave us keys to a room. Looking back on it, it was really hilarious.

We crashed and got a few hours of sleep. At 8 a.m., we called our office, got our card numbers, and paid for the room. The day clerk didn't really know what was going on, and we got out of there fast. We needed to get some food but still didn't have any money. At the federal building, we met with Assistant U.S. Attorney Stephen Cooper to sign a complaint, filling him in on the details. Steve told us to be back at 10 a.m. and loaned us 20 bucks for breakfast. At Denny's, I chided Pete because I qualified for the senior discount.

Arriving at court, we learned that a federal judge wasn't available, so a state judge was called for the arraignment. When it was time for the initial appearance, the kid was still drunk and not in any condition to appear. After waiting several hours, things got sorted out, all the players were present, and the kid pleaded guilty to public intoxication. Pete and I got back home at 5:30 p.m., both exhausted.

Donna has a part in this story. I wasn't there when she got up to go to school that morning. Nothing unusual, I got called out repeatedly. When Donna returned in the afternoon and I still wasn't there, she grew concerned. She called dispatch and learned that I had "had a long day" and was on my way home. It was a good story at my retirement party, and Donna got the last word about "sleeping with the boss."

LAST DAYS

With my retirement date fast approaching, things began to happen fast. We were invited to dinners with friends, and people dropped by to say good-bye. It began to sink in that this life we had was coming to a close.

I tried to get out into the park as much as possible, seeing the mountain, visiting old haunts. On May 31, I spent my last night alone in the Toklat cabin. Almost in tears, I wrote my feelings down in the logbook—the job, this place, myself. It's still there for all to read, part of the history of the cabin.

My girls were able to attend my retirement party, Katie from Utah, Kelly working for the Park Service and living in seasonal housing. I took them to the range one last time to shoot the AR-15 with some of that "free" government ammunition.

My retirement party on June 3 at the Healy Community Center was packed with friends, coworkers, Donna's teacher community, and even some bus drivers. There was the traditional ranger roast, and I had given them plenty to work with. We received special gifts from the Alaska Region, a beautiful quilt from our friend Phyllis Motsko and others. We were honored and overwhelmed.

I showed the PowerPoint presentation I worked so hard to produce. It was a synopsis of our lives: we as high school sweethearts, the parks, our kids, and many fond memories. When the music stopped and the lights came up, there was dead silence. Some people were silently weeping, and tears flowed from my eyes. I couldn't speak. I had attended many retirement parties over the years, but this one was mine. I didn't expect it to be so emotional.

After the party, we returned home with a few close friends, drank some good whiskey, talked about old times, and just enjoyed the moment. It was the perfect end to the perfect evening and the perfect career.

GOING 10-7, OUT OF SERVICE

June 10, 2005—My last day at Toklat, packed personal things; drove to Stony for the last time and chatted with visitors, said good-byes to folks at Toklat; had a flat tire on the trip in—it never stops!

After all the hoopla, potlucks, good-byes, and last times, I was ready to leave. I made one final trip to Toklat to get my personal belongings and see the mountain one last time. True to form, I had a flat tire on the trip in, one of dozens over the years. I dreaded saying farewell to folks and didn't want to prolong the agony. It was a very emotional period for me with the realization that my lengthy career was coming to an end. In contrast, Donna and I were excited to begin a new chapter in our lives.

My last official day of work was June 15, 36 years to the day I'd walked into the chief ranger's office at Gettysburg reporting for duty. At least by now, I had learned how to wear that T-shirt. So much had happened in the intervening years! I witnessed a lot of change, saw and did things most people only dream about, worked with some great folks, and got to raise my family in national parks. It doesn't get any better than that.

The moving van arrived, and things were in total disarray. I wanted to escape the chaos and went for a drive to Sable Pass with my brother-in-law Bob, who, with his wife Connie, had come to drive one of our three vehicles to Montana.

I signed off the radio for the last time: "700, this is 201, out of service forever." That's when it started. Folks from all over the park began responding with "Bye Tom," "Good luck, Tom," and "Thanks, Tom." I was truly moved, in tears, emotionally drained.

I went to the office and turned in my badge, defensive equipment, radio, and other gear. It's difficult to explain to a civilian the symbolism of turning in your badge and gun. It's what makes a ranger a ranger. Suddenly, I was a civilian. I felt naked without that badge on my shirt. I went to personnel, turned in my keys and government credit card, signed a property receipt, and walked to my house one last time. I was officially "retired." It had been quite a ride.

Epilogue

We drove out of the park into a new life. There would be no more late-night phone calls bringing tragic news, no fire sirens blasting me out of bed. I hadn't got shot or, worse, shot anyone. I hadn't died in a plane crash or drowned in a river. Life was good.

Now that I've been retired a few years, I've had the chance to reflect back on my Park Service experience. It often seems unreal, a fantasy. Did I really do all those things? And how?

People ask if I miss it. The answer is yes, at least most of it. I don't miss all the bureaucracy, politics, endless meetings, and reams of paperwork. I *do* miss the wonderful people I worked with, talented people who cared about their work. I miss the opportunity to share the wonder of the parks with people from all over the world. And, of course, I miss skiing in a full moon across an alpine meadow, swapping stories with old friends in a tiny cabin deep in the Alaska wilderness, seeing the aurora dancing overhead, and riding a horse down a lonely trail. To me, being a ranger is one of the best jobs in the world.

As I said at the beginning of this book, parks are special places that must be valued and protected. Now more than ever, the parks need your help. Woefully understaffed, they are experiencing record-breaking visitation; infrastructure is outdated and overworked. Parks are under duress by local encroachment, urban sprawl, and potential resource exploitation. And climate change is having a dramatic impact that we are just beginning to comprehend. People who love the parks must promote their continued well-being. Advocate for adequate funding. Get involved in local "friends of" groups. Educate yourself about the issues facing the parks. Volunteer and get your hands dirty—you won't regret it.

The next time you visit a park, please consider all that goes on behind the scenes to make it work. Always remember that these are *your* parks. Love them, respect them, and treat them well.

Acknowledgments

ONE OF THE MOST IMPORTANT THINGS I'VE LEARNED IN THIS ENDEAVOR is that it takes many people to write a book. Research, editing, proofreading, fact-checking, advice, and words of wisdom and encouragement are all part of this effort. I could not have completed this book without the help of the following people.

First, I would like to thank the good folks at Globe Pequot Press/ Falcon for making this book a reality. Acquisitions editor Katherine "Katie" O'Dell took the chance on an unknown author and convinced her boss it might make a good read. Mason Gadd offered valuable advice on structure and content. Bruce Owens caught my *numerous* punctuation mistakes and trouble with compound words. Production editor Nicole Carty and unknown others guided the final manuscript into production. Thanks to all of you.

Tom "Smitty" Smith was the impetus for getting started. After telling me many times that "you need to write a book," I finally took his advice. Thanks for kicking me in the ass to do it.

Good neighbor Judy Farrin spent countless hours reading, editing photos, and offering words of encouragement. She kept me on course and helped me believe I could do this.

Thanks to Michael Ober, ranger friend and professional librarian, for introducing me to the world of publishing and giving me advice. You kept me honest.

Ranger-pilot Jim Unruh for his detailed information on flying in Alaska and giving me insight into the world of bush aviation.

Charles "Butch" Farrabee for his advice on publishing and for the information in his wonderful book.

John Dill for shepherding my Freedom of Information Act requests in Yosemite and answering my questions about several SAR events.

Sarah Brown for taking time out of her outlandish schedule to review and advise on some of the Yosemite material.

Jane Bryant for her insight on historical matters in Denali and sharing her publishing experience.

Best friend and fellow ranger Mark Motsko for setting me straight on details long forgotten and for having my back when things went south.

Childhood chum Harvey Westley for reading this thing with fresh eyes and offering invaluable advice. Yes, Harvey, I'm still alive.

The following persons, all Park Service colleagues, helped refresh old memories, provided important details and personal information, and helped make this book as accurate as possible. I couldn't have done this without their help: Ron Bryan, Valerie Cohen, Clare Curtis, Roger Dittberner, Jack Fry, Bob Johnson, Fred Koegler, Gary Koy, Ron Mackie, Cindy Mernin, Bill Michaels, Eric Morey, Dan O'Brien, David Olsen, Ron Purdum, and Mike and Elaine Shields.

And finally, a huge thank-you to my English teacher and daughter Kelly for her detailed examination of the original manuscript, checking grammar, punctuation, and sentence structure. I was striving for an "A," and she made me earn it.

To daughter Katie, who kept asking, "How's the book coming, Dad?," you give me joy.

Throughout this book, you've seen my wife Donna's name, always in the background: taking care of me and the kids, working hard to keep our home a safe haven from the everyday world. We were high school sweethearts and married just out of college. She knew I was going to be a park ranger and eagerly jumped in with both feet. I'm not sure she knew what she was getting into, but I'm glad she did. She stuck by me during some hard times, always there when I was down.

We had our share of adventures, almost drowning in an overturned canoe on a river in Maine, surviving near hypothermia in the Grand Canyon, sliding a mule down a snowfield in the Yosemite backcountry, and coming way too close to a grizzly bear in Glacier. She washed and ironed thousands of uniforms, making me look presentable. She endured substandard housing, drying diapers over a woodstove, and splitting countless cords of wood to keep us warm.

There was always a hot meal waiting when I was late and a good breakfast at zero dark thirty when I had an early departure. A miracle in the kitchen, she always came up with a good meal when I brought someone home unexpectedly, and the coffeepot was always on for drop-ins.

Donna never complained when I missed birthdays, anniversaries, or holidays—it was all part of the job. When the fire siren went off in the middle of the night, she'd jump out of bed, saying, "What do you need me to do?"

She sacrificed her own career aspirations to follow me around the country. Somehow, she managed to earn two graduate degrees and a professional license, driving thousands of miles in the dark, mostly in the dead of winter. She always managed to find a job and was good at whatever she did. I'm glad she finally got to experience her dream job as a school counselor in the local school district a few years before I retired, all this while raising two of the finest daughters a man could ask for.

They say that behind every good man is a better woman, and that is certainly true in my case. So, here's to Donna and all the Park Service couples who persevere. Thank you for enduring the isolation, the boredom, the loneliness, the countless moves and saying good-bye to friends, the long days, and the nights of worry. Thank you for raising children under difficult conditions, for seeing they got the best education available, for living in places many wouldn't tolerate. Thanks for who you are and for all you do.

Notes

Part II

1. D. Johnston, "Keeping the Peace in the Parks," *Police Magazine* 4, issue 5, 44–49, https://www.ojp.gov/ncjrs/virtual-library/abstracts/keeping-peace-parks.
2. Charles R. Farabee, *Big Walls, Swift Waters: Epic Stories from Yosemite Search and Rescue* (San Francisco: Yosemite Conservancy, 2017).
3. Ibid.
4. Dale R. Harms, "Black Bear Management in Yosemite National Park," in *Bears: Their Biology and Management*, vol. 4 (Medina, TX: International Association for Bear Research and Management, 1980), 205–12.
5. Ibid.
6. Ibid.
7. National Park Service, "Bear Management," https://www.nps.gov/yose/learn/nature/bear-management.htm.
8. Brian Palmer, "The C-Free Diet," *Slate*, July 10, 2013, https://slate.com/technology/2013/07/california-grows-all-of-our-fruits-and-vegetables-what-would-we-eat-without-the-state.html.
9. Randall Osterhuber, *Snow Survey Procedure Manual*, October 2014, https://cawaterlibrary.net/wp-content/uploads/2017/12/SnowSurveyProcedureManualv20141027.pdf.

Part IV

1. National Park Service, *Denali 2017 Fact Sheet*, 2017, https://www.google.com/url?sa=t&rct=j&q=&esrc=s&source=web&cd=1&ved=2ahUKEwjMv4TqibTgAhVqpIMKHRoMDdEQFjAAegQIChAC&url=https%3A%2F%2Fwww.nps.gov%2Fdena%2Flearn%2Fmanagement%2Fupload%2FRevised-DENA-2017-Fact-Sheet.pdf&usg=AOvVaw3O4RbtiAnjNTdKkaLXDyla.
2. National Park Service, "Kennels History," https://www.nps.gov/dena/planyourvisit/kennels-history.htm.
3. National Park Service, "Superintendent's Monthly Reports, Mount McKinley National Park," December 1946, Denali National Park and Preserve Museum Collection.

About the Author

Tom Habecker, during his 32-year career with the National Park Service, saw some of America's most beloved scenic and historical sites as he took on the iconic role of a national park ranger. He began learning the ropes as an intern at Gettysburg National Military Park and after earning his degree in park administration worked as an urban ranger at National Capitol Parks.

After a four-year stint in the U.S. Coast Guard, he moved with his wife Donna to Yosemite National Park, California. His experiences there, from rowdy campers to mischievous bears to providing emergency medical care for sick and injured persons, formed the foundation for the rest of his career.

He also had the unique experience of raising a family in the national parks. After 11 years in Yosemite, he moved with his wife and young daughters to Glacier National Park, Montana, where he served as the Lake McDonald Sub-District ranger.

In 1990, Tom realized a lifelong dream when he and his family moved to Denali National Park and Preserve, Alaska. For the next 15 years, Tom oversaw protection operations in the 4-million-acre North District. After a lifetime of adventure and unforgettable experiences, he retired in 2005.

Tom has written short stories for *Backpacker* magazine and a feature story for the National Park Service Centennial book *The Wonder of It All*.

He and Donna live in their dream home near Bozeman, Montana.